Dynamics of a Trusted Platform

David Grawrock

Intel
PRESS

ISBN 1-934053-08-2

Publisher: Richard Bowles
Editor: David J. Clark
Program Manager: Stuart Douglas
Text Design & Composition: STI
Graphic Art: Matt Statton and Wasser Studios (illustrations), Ted Cyrek (cover)

Library of Congress Cataloging in Publication Data:

Printed in China

10 9 8 7 6 5 4 3 2 1

First printing, February 2009

IMPORTANT

You can access the companion Web site for this book on the Internet at:

www.intel.com/intelpress/secc2

Use the serial number located in the upper-right hand corner of the last page to register your book and access additional material, including the Digital Edition of the book.

To my wife, Sherrill, who has put up with my travels and long work hours. To my children, Matthew, Jared, Steven, Evan, Christopher, Braden, and Alina, who have loved their father through thick and thin— even though he does work on computers. And finally, to my parents who are very surprised that their son is an author.

With my second book the dedication to my family remains, they are always in my heart. My family has grown from when I wrote the first book and I can now add my grandchildren, Landon, Cael, and Rhys. A Christmas dinner table with children, spouses, and grandchildren is where my joy in life is full.

Contents

**Chapter 11   Trusted Execution Technology
Design Principles   151**

Chapter 14 Intel Trusted Execution Technology Architecture 227

Chapter 15 Late Launch 247

Chapter 16   **Configuration Concerns   277**

Foreword

Thirteen years ago, my life was so much simpler: I used only one device with an IP address, and its operating system was simple enough that I could tell you what each of the running processes did. I needed just one password on a day-to-day basis, and the number of people actively scanning my system for vulnerabilities was close to nil.

Fast forward to today, where I've lost count of how many network-connected devices I have (I recently had to adjust my home DHCP server, because it was running out of addresses). I've lost track of how many operating systems I use on a daily basis (and I probably use some devices which have an operating system I'm not even aware of). I have passwords with service providers I've forgotten about (too often I remember the pass-word but not the Web- site!). I know that if I make just one false move, one or more of those systems, devices, or accounts will effectively fall into the hands of someone who wants to steal from me, or my employer, or someone else I come into contact with. As we have built more and more elaborate online communities, we have created entirely new kinds of asset—and entirely new kinds of criminal.

Networked computers are allowing distinctive new kinds of endeavor to take place. For example, there has been an explosion of projects under the banner of "e-Science." This stems from a realization that massive quantities of computational power and data storage allow us to undertake scientific experiments in ways never before possible. In Oxford, one of the projects we have created is *climateprediction.net*. The aim was to recruit hundreds of thousands of PC users around the globe, and have them run a detailed climate model, with the objective of determining likely outcomes for fifty years hence. Whereas previously, a PhD in climate physics might rest on five such model runs, now we could offer 100,000. This potentially gives an enormous scale-up in the fidelity of the results, as well as a way to explore improved models.

Or does it? Without having to think for too long, it is obvious that, short of giving identical tasks to several well-scattered PCs, and comparing the results (with a consequent loss in the scale-up we can achieve), there is no real way to know whether the results received really represent the outcome of the climate model. And in such a politically-charged environment, it is not inconceivable that someone would attempt to subvert those results for their own ends. Even worse, by distributing this software to the world, we are putting the university's reputation on the line, and could be inviting people to download software that will harm their systems in unimagined ways. The same kind of concerns applies to just about every e-Science application, and indeed, to a great deal of life in the online distributed systems we now use daily. Trying to resolve some of the resulting problems is what got me interested in trusted computing.

Because, happily, in the intervening years between my blissfully simple state and today, people like David Grawrock have been anticipating this complex networked world we now inhabit, and the broad range of hackers, thieves, organized criminals, hobbyists, and foreign powers who have an interest in disrupting it. Part of the result is the book now before you. Another part is a range of incremental changes to personal computers, to peripherals, and to networks, with the aim of tipping the technological balance in favor of the system's defender.

That such technological change is starting to appear in hundreds of millions of devices is testimony to the hard work that David and his colleagues have invested in their design. This book will tell you the why and the how. That is no small thing: the description here is born of years of reflection on the theory and practice of security. Some things seem ideal in theory, but fail in the field; sometimes the smallest thing turns out to have immense practical benefit. To grasp such subtleties, you need an expert guide who has experienced them for himself: that is just what you have here.

The book's subtitle talks of a "building-block approach". That is good, because no one can understand all of these things at once. As the succession of chapters unfolds, you will become aware of just how many diverse building blocks are needed. Let the reader beware though: if we could visualize these building blocks, they would certainly not have smooth, rectilinear sides. Rather, they depend on one another in all manner of surprising ways, and intertwine when you least expect it. Nevertheless, if you want to build a trusted platform today or tomorrow—or make use of one to build trusted applications—these are the blocks you need.

The opportunity is now available to start building many such applications, making this book very timely. For detailed implementation work, you will need other reference manuals and programmer's guides, but it would be foolhardy to start without a thorough understanding of the concepts; and this is what **Dynamics of a Trusted Platform** gives you. It may not be possible to return to my former world of simplistic bliss, but the building blocks described here are certainly able to imbue the infrastructure with a fresh level of trustworthiness, and we may all look forward to the many benefits flowing from that.

Andrew Martin
Kellogg College, Oxford
September 2008

Preface

Why write a second book about trusted platforms and Intel® Trusted Execution Technology (Intel® TXT). Well one major reason is that the first book used the codename LaGrande Technology (LT) and this book uses the term Intel TXT, why the change? The reason is very simple, marketing did not like the codename LaGrande Technology referring to a feature and they wanted to have a more descriptive term, hence Intel Trusted Execution Technology.

The change from LT to Intel TXT has been very difficult for me. LT falls off the tongue, Intel TXT seems to stick and make me stutter. Oh well, when dealing with external messaging marketing always wins.

The other reason to write a second book is that I am *still* adding many miles to the frequent flyer account. Truthfully, that will never change, but the book does answer many of the foundational questions. Over the past few years, I have used the first book in classes to security students many times. Some of the students even said the book helped.

The book came from a presentation known amongst Intel security wonks as the "6-hour LT presentation." The author never really gave it in 6 hours: it took anywhere from 1 hour to 3 days. Certainly, the days spent on the 3-day seminar were long and the conversations very deep. Over time, there were many questions regarding the entire trusted platform and how some of the platform features fit together. Voila, the need for a second book arises.

Geographic Primer

One of my favorite slides in the LT presentation is the slide explaining where the name LaGrande comes from. Intel picks code names from geographical features. One of the early members of the LT team, Richard Trinh, picked LaGrande as the code name from the next names on the list. As the project was working on a "technology" instead of a product, the full name of LaGrande Technology quickly became LT. LaGrande is a lovely place that I enjoy visiting. It has fly-fishing in the area and, at least to me, it has some lovely scenery.

> **The Intel Safer Computing Initiative Book Comments**
>
> In trying to keep some of the first book sections intact, instead of rewriting a section, I will sometimes add these boxes. The boxes will leave the previous sections without major modification and then explain why there are differences between the first and second books.
>
> In reference to LaGrande, the comments are still true; it is just that now with the new name of Intel TXT the LaGrande conversation does not always make sense. While that is a true statement to allow for a discussion of fly-fishing, the slides describing the naming of LT remain in many of my Intel TXT presentations.

Sabbatical

A funny thing happened on the way to finishing the second book, I got to take a sabbatical. At Intel, employees get a 8-week sabbatical every 7 years. In fact, you can make it even longer by using vacation time. As I was nearing the start of the sabbatical, I promised my editor and publisher that I would complete the book prior to the sabbatical. It did not happen. I have to finish this book upon my return from sabbatical. In the end, this is a good thing as the sabbatical did recharge my batteries and I have the energy to finish the book.

Remember those frequent flyer miles? Well they came in very handy, as part of the sabbatical was a vacation through Europe. The family saw many of the places that I have visited over the years. It was a very good trip.

I can also report that all fish that met me in various streams and rivers around Oregon swam back to their positions after removal of the hook in their mouth.

Book Structure

I would like to give the reader a roadmap to the subsequent chapters in this book. Before I do I would like to explain a "guilty pleasure" that I had in writing the book. The chapter template shows a quote that illustrates some theme about the chapter. I found it fun to search the Internet using phrases from the chapter and finding various quotes that matched, or somewhat matched, the theme. I ended up with more quotes than I could rationally use, but here in the preface, and especially here in the book structure section, I am going to use a few more of them. Enjoy the quotes and play the game of trying to see how the quote matches the section under discussion.

Background Information

The first two chapters cover the background of trusted computing. Intel Trusted Execution Technology is not the first use of the security concepts; rather it is the next product in a long line of research and products. The chapters provide you with an understanding of what research came before and how some products used the research. The quote for the background information chapters is:

> One's mind has a way of making itself up in the background,
> and it suddenly becomes clear what one means to do.
>
> —A.C. Benson

Chapter 1: Trusted Computing

One always needs to define terms. Especially when one deals with security and trust issues, a precise definition of terms is critical. Chapter 1 starts with basic definitions that are in use throughout the book. Understanding the definition of a trusted platform is mandatory before reading any additional chapters. The chapter also covers some basic cryptography terms and if the reader is familiar with those terms, the reader can skip the cryptography sections.

> This chapter remains relatively unchanged from the first book

Chapter 2: History of Trusted Computing

Chapter 2 is a history lesson. Many of the design features of Trusted Execution Technology are not new but designs that have been in use for years. The chapter covers some of the early research in trusted computing and the application of the research. The history lesson is important as with the knowledge of history the reader will understand that Intel Trusted Execution Technology builds on previous research and applications.

Another part of the history lesson is to understand the personal computer platform. An understanding of the basic parts of the personal computer is mandatory for understanding what Intel Trusted Execution Technology provides.

The first components under discussion are the Central Processing Unit (CPU), Memory Controller Hub (MCH) and Input Output Controller Hub (ICH). The history lesson shows you how the CPU changed over time.

The inner workings of the CPU with a special emphasis on page tables and ring structures provide a basis for understanding the Trusted Execution Technology enhancements.

A description of major platform busses explains how information moves between the various components.

> As history does not change much this chapter remains relatively unchanged from the first book

What Is Happening Today

> The problems that exist in the world today, cannot be solved
> by the level of thinking that created them
>
> —Albert Einstein

Moving from the past to the present, the next two chapters discuss what platforms look like today and what vulnerabilities are present in the current platforms.

Chapter 3: The Current Environment

Many users and program designers are unfamiliar with the width and breadth of attacks that are in the "wild." The wild is where attacks are roaming not just in a lab, but they are actual attacks that land on an individual's platform.

Understanding that changes to a platform, where change relates to manipulating software, can cause problems to applications. Manipulating software would include installing new software, applying patches or changing the configuration options of executing software.

One should understand what a "bad" platform is. How does one find a bad platform and what does one do with a bad platform.

> While most of the chapter is unchanged, there are some discussions on new attacks.

Chapter 4: Anatomy of an Attack

The best way to understand what to protect is to attack it. Chapter 4 defines an application and then attacks the application. To understand an attack, you need a definition of who the attacker is and what resources the attacker has available. Since Intel Trusted Execution Technology provides protection from software attacks, the attacks described in Chapter 4 use software mechanisms. Tying all of the attack mechanisms together reveals a common underlying vulnerability.

> This chapter is pretty much the same as in the first book.

Trusted Platform Elements

> Dust as we are, the immortal spirit grows
> Like harmony in music; there is a dark
> Inscrutable workmanship that reconciles
> Discordant elements.

William Wordsworth (1770 - 1850)

All of the chapters in this section are brand new. The idea behind this section is to describe the elements of a trusted platform. With 14 elements, it makes some sense to group the elements into functional groups, and the chapters of this section do just that. There are five groups and only four chapters in this section; the reason for the difference is that two of the groups only contain a single element and a full chapter is just not necessary so one chapter contains two groups.

Chapter 5: Elements and Their Groups

Chapter 5 identifies the elements and puts the elements into their groups. The identification of the elements and groups is just at a very high level here with the individual group chapters going into the details. The groups are:

- System Protection
- Physical Hardware
- Between Partitions
- Outside
- Inside

Chapter 6: System Protection

The system protection group deals with elements that protect the entire platform and are visible to the outside world. These elements form what many would perceive to be the major attributes of the trusted platform. The elements in this group are:

- PII Handling
- Evidence/Measurement
- Reporting/Attestation
- TCB Management
- Policy Engine

Chapter 7: Internal Protection

The internal protection group is a set of elements that the trusted platform uses internally to protect the platform itself. These elements are certainly useful in the system protection group also, but the idea is to separate into groups and this separation provides a rational grouping. The elements in the group are:

- Randomness
- Sequencing
- Protected Storage
- Detection and Inspection
- Architectural Performance

Chapter 8: Between Partitions

The between partition group is a set of elements that deal with how to separate trust domains, or domain isolation, and how to connect the domains when you have some form of isolation.

- Isolation
- Trusted Channel – This section contains much of the first edition Chapter 10 on protected input and output.

Chapter 9: Outside and Inside

Chapter 9 is our chapter that combines two groups, the outside group and the inside group. The names imply a connection, but the connection is not what one immediately thinks of. Read the chapter to get the real connection. The elements of the two groups are:

- Outside
  - External Access
- Inside
  - Protected Execution

Design and Objectives

> When you travel, remember that a foreign country is not designed to make you comfortable. It is designed to make its own people comfortable.
>
> —Clifton Fadiman

Chapter 10: Trusted Execution Technology Objectives

You get a description of what Intel TXT does, and what Intel TXT does not do. Intel TXT does not provide 100-percent security, nothing does. The trick is to understand what has protection and where no protection is available. You have no way to understand what has protection unless you understand the attacker and the resources of the attacker.

> The basic objectives of Intel TXT did not change with a name change; they remain, as they were when LT first started. Hence, this chapter remains very close to Chapter 5 of the first book.

Chapter 11: Trusted Execution Technology Design Principles

Chapter 11 describes the design principles that led the Intel TXT design team. The principles have been around for many years and have guided many security products.

> Just as the objectives did not change, the design principles do not change. This chapter is very close to Chapter 6 of the first book.

Chapter 12: Launched Environment

A basic component of Intel TXT is the use of Intel® Virtualization Technology (Intel® VT). VT provides the foundation for protected execution. This chapter provides a basic understanding of VT.

> My first review of the old Chapter 7 said that it would only need minor editing. I was wrong. There are some major differences between the old Chapter 7 and the new Chapter 12. The gist of the changes is that Intel TXT now refers to the Measured Launched Environment (MLE) not just a Virtual Machine Monitor (VMM). For this reason there have been some major changes in this chapter.

Intel Trusted Execution Technology Architecture

The secret temple of the Piranha women. Their architecture is surprisingly advanced.

—Dr. Margo Hunt. *Cannibal Women in the Avocado Jungle of Death* (1989)[1]

Chapter 13: Attestation

A critical building block for a Intel TXT system is the use of the Trusted Platform Module (TPM). The TPM provides the ability to store, report, and use measurement values, and a Intel TXT system provides the critical measurement of the MLE controlling the system. One needs a basic understanding of the TPM to understand the architecture of the Intel TXT platform.

---

1 I've never seen the movie and have no clue what it is about, but one has to admit it is a great architecture quote. The movie title alone makes it worth including.

> The principles of attestation do not change with different versions of the TPM. With no changes in the principles and no change in the version of the TPM supported by Intel TXT, Chapter 13 looks very much like Chapter 8 of the first book.

Chapter 14: Trusted Execution Technology Architecture

Chapter 14 is a real rubber hitting the road chapter. How software uses Intel Trusted Execution Technology dominates the explanations. Chapter 14 introduces the standard partition, the protected partition, and the domain manager. The three components together provide the framework for applications that use Intel TXT features.

How the components communicate provides some insight into the mechanisms that each component must provide to make the architecture work. An interesting discussion is what entities can provide the components. Who provides what gives some interesting results.

> There are some major differences between the first book's Chapter 10 and the second book's Chapter 14. While some of the concepts do not change, the change from discussing a VMM to an MLE, do make for some major changes in the chapter.

Chapter 15: Late Launch

Chapter 15 is one of the author's favorite Intel TXT features. Late launch is one of the cruxes of the entire Intel TXT architecture. If one does not understand late launch, one does not understand what Intel TXT does.

The idea is that a platform user wants to start and stop the Intel Trusted Execution Technology protections. Starting and stopping Intel TXT is very exciting as the protections are deep in the CPU and other motherboard components. Ensuring that only the authorized operations enable these protections drives many of the hardware changes required by a Intel Trusted Execution Technology platform.

How late launch works does not change. This chapter does not change much to accommodate the MLE versus VMM. The fact that this chapter does not differ that much from the previous Chapter 11, illustrates why the change from VMM to MLE is a more accurate representation of the features provided by Intel TXT.

Chapter 16: Configuration Concerns

Chapter 16 describes how certain hardware configurations can allow software to breach the Intel TXT protections. The configurations that cause the problems are detectable so the architecture must provide the detection and mitigation mechanisms.

The major issue is how the platform handles system memory. Ensuring an evaluation of the memory configuration during the Intel TXT launch mitigates the configuration concern.

Our issues revolve around the loss of the memory configuration when the actual memory location could still contain some Intel TXT protected information.

Configuration concerns remain in the trusted platform. How TXT interacts with those issues does not drastically change. For this reason Chapter 16 is very close to the first book's Chapter 12.

Chapter 17: Hardware Attacks

The Intel Trusted Execution Technology design principle is to protect from software attack. Most of the features provide protection solely from software and do not contemplate hardware attacks. Hardware attacks can occur and the Intel TXT system can defend against some of them. Chapter 17 describes the hardware attacks where current system provides protection.

Not much changes in this chapter. The hardware attacks previously identified are still identified and the potential mitigations are still part of the trusted platform. This chapter looks very much like the first book's Chapter 13.

Policy and Services

> Policies are many, Principles are few, Policies will change, Principles never do."
>
> - John C Maxwell

This is another brand new section for the second book. The idea here is that when we discuss elements and groups of the trusted platform, it brings up the fact that there are additional features of the trusted platform not contained in the elements. Policy and services are those additional platform features that are not core elements but features created by combining the platform elements.

Chapter 18: Launch Control Policy

This chapter looks at two aspects of policy on the trusted platform: the first aspect is the need for generalized policy engines, and the second is a specific form of policy that enables a fundamental shift in the use of the trusted platform.

Chapter 19: Services

When using my book at various conferences, the subject of this chapter came up many times, "how do I combine these elements to make the trusted platform useful to me?" This chapter is an attempt to answer the question with some real life examples. The list of services is not even close to complete but is a helpful starter set.

The Bottom Line

> I do not participate in a sport with ambulances at the bottom of the hill.
>
> —Erma Bombeck (1927 -1996)

The last couple of chapters are the bottom of the hill for this book. I hope that if you arrive here, you do not need an ambulance. By now, an understanding of Intel Trusted Execution Technology should lead one to anticipate the types of attacks that Intel TXT mitigates.

Chapter 20: Defending Against Attacks

Chapter 4 was all about describing an application and the attacks on the application. Chapter 20 describes how Intel Trusted Execution Technology mitigates those attacks. From accessing memory to manipulating input and output, Chapter 20 uses the Intel TXT features and shows how the attackers do not gain access to protected information.

Chapter 21: The Future

Chapter 21 is for gazing into the future. A product that provides security is never complete. Attackers learn new techniques; users require new protections. Intel Trusted Execution Technology must respond to these events and change over time. One obvious change would be for the Intel TXT objectives to change regarding hardware attacks.

Acknowledgements

Some might believe that this entire book is the sole responsibility of a single author. They would be wrong. Jim Sutton created the original 6-hour presentation. Jim is the author's silent partner. As much as I travel, Jim stays home. Jim is a great friend, a security architect without peer, and he comes up with as many crazy ideas as I do. One of the great pleasures of working with Jim is having either him or me say "What about this attack?" and realize that the whole architecture under creation just fell down[2]. If either of us got a penny for each invocation of that phrase over the past few years, we both would be retired. Luckily for me Jim is not retired and continues to provide ideas that further the work in Trusted Computing.

> In the years between the first book and the second, Jim did retire. For me it was an extremely sad day to see such a wonderful person leave the company. I knew why Jim was retiring, and in his shoes, I would have too, but still his retirement was a great loss to the security community, even though so few had ever met him. At his retirement, I presented Jim with the first of hopefully many flies he will use on the Deschutes river. I tied the flies myself.

I would like to thank those members of the Trusted Computing Group[3] Technical Committee and the Trusted Platform Module Workgroup. These two groups of people have influenced me in so many ways. The many discussions over the years have focused my thoughts on what is and is not possible. To the TPM WG I make the comment that you can never have any ambiguities, just context-sensitive interpretations.

---

2 One crazy history lesson is that when one of the two of us uses an attack to invalidate a mechanism, when the person who successfully attacked the previous design creates a new design, it will not mitigate the previous attack, and the other person will point that out.

3 URL is http://www.trustedcomputinggroup.org

> As I write this preface, which strangely for both books tends to be the last major writing that I do, I have just announced my retirement from the TCG WG. For close to a decade I worked closely with those in the WG and cannot say strongly enough how much the members of the WG have been so much fun to work with. That is not to say there have been no disagreements, there have, but always with a desire to get things right. I will sincerely miss the Thursday morning calls.

Inside of Intel I would like to thank Monty Wiseman, Ned Smith, Ernie Brickell, Baiju Patel, David Doughty, Kirk Brannock, Kerry Johns-Vanos, amongst others.

A specific thanks to those who made comments on early versions of this book including Graeme Proudler, Greg Kazmierczak, Simon Johnson, Dave Challener, Ken Goldman, and Paul England.

The last thank you I would like to give is to Gene Spafford who wrote the foreword to the first book. Spaf has a wonderful way of looking at a technology and really getting to the heart of it. I thank him for his thoughts on this book and Intel TXT.

> One of the joys of working in this industry is meeting new people. One person that I have truly enjoyed meeting is Andrew Martin from Oxford. I have enjoyed the conversations with Andrew and he has made me think on many occasions. In addition, I have had the opportunity to teach at some seminars at Oxford, so in addition to Andrew, I can say with a straight face, I have taught at Oxford. With the joke aside, I was very happy that Andrew said yes to write the forward for this second book.

Thanks for Reading

Well, before you launch into the book. I would like to thank you for giving me the opportunity to explain the Intel safer computing initiative. Hopefully, you will gain an understanding of why Intel TXT is built the way it is, what attacks Intel TXT can mitigate, what attacks Intel TXT cannot mitigate, and why Intel TXT will change in the future.

Intel® TXT represents a change in the basic nature of the PC platform. With the ability to measure and protect the MLE, what protections are possible and how outside entities can rely on the PC platform, fundamentally changes everyone's view of the PC platform.

As you know, I like to go fly-fishing. If you are interested in talking about security while watching an Orange Bomber float down the Trask River, drop me an e-mail and we will see what happens.

> Nobody ever took me up on the offer for the Trask river, so I now make the offer for the Fall River. The Trask is all about steelhead and some sea-run cutthroats. Fall river is a spring fed river that empties into the Deschutes; it is home to some very large rainbow trout. Fishing is harder in the clear cold water of Fall river, but the trout are very fun when they come out to play.

Trusted Computing

So in war, the way is to avoid what is strong and to strike at what is weak.
—Sun Tzu

Well here we are again. Oh wait—did I say that aloud? I certainly thought that upon completion of the first edition, my career as a writer was complete. How wrong that feeling was.

For a complete listing of where the meaty changes in the second edition are, read the preface. If you are like me and never read prefaces but you do start in the first chapter, then note that many of the chapters have only minor changes and others are brand new. The focus of the book remains the same, describe Trusted Computing. There are no change bars or blinking lights to inform readers of the first edition where the exact changes are, but I hope that the changes lead to a better understanding of trusted computing.

What is trusted computing? What is trust? Don't users trust their platforms today? If the user encounters any problems, can the current platform architecture support the improvements to alleviate those problems? In this book, you should find the answers to these questions. To start the learning process by making the first set of questions personal, consider the following two questions:

◼ Do you trust your computer to properly protect an online purchase of a book?

◼ Do you trust your computer to protect an online purchase of a million dollar home properly?

The answers to these two questions are likely to vary according to the individual. Some say yes to one but not the other; some say yes to both, and finally, some say no to both.[1] Creating a system that provides the flexibility and trustworthiness to allow the various answers is the purpose of trusted computing.

The Basic Problem of Trust

Why do rational individuals and companies trust a platform to perform one job, but they do not trust that same platform to perform another task? Underlying the difference is an inability to trust or understand how the platform works. People assume that software does not work correctly or that viruses change how applications work. The difference in their level of comfort with a simple transaction, like a book purchase, and a complex transaction, like the mortgage signing, highlights the uneasiness that the lack of understanding creates. Platform users should feel more at ease with the following pieces of information:

◼ The hardware nature of the platform provides protections.

◼ The currently executing software is taking advantage of the protections.

◼ When something does go wrong, the system has ways to provide protections from the "badness."

◼ Mechanisms are in place to allow the verification of information reported from the platform.

---

1   The author trusts the computer for book purchases but not for signing mortgages.

The design of a trusted computer should attempt to provide the information that a user needs in order to trust a platform.

One important piece of information to remember is that trusted computing is not about creating a 100-percent secure platform. As Gene Spafford has said:

> *The only truly secure system is one that is powered off, cast in a block of concrete and sealed in a lead-lined room with armed guards—and even then I have my doubts.*

In other words, there is no such thing as a completely secure platform. Attackers, with sufficient time and money, are expected to succeed. What trusted computing provides is a way to understand the current state of a platform, have some entity evaluate the state, and then make a decision whether the platform is appropriate for the current job.

A trusted computer assumes that attackers will continue to attempt to subvert the protections on the platform. The trusted computer assumes that some of the attacks will succeed. The trusted computer assumes that successful attacks could have no effect on other uses of the platform. All of these assumptions point back to the need for an outside observer to understand the current state of the platform.

Future versions of a trusted platform might provide additional protections from attacks that current platforms do not. Being able to differentiate between old versions and new versions is a critical component of a trusted platform.

Basic Definitions

The computer security industry, like any other industry, produces a language that often trips up newcomers. To spare you these problems, the next couple of pages provide the basic definitions of very important terms.

These terms mean different things to different people, depending on the context in which the words are used. Our first order of business is providing definitions for these terms so that you and I are thinking along the same lines. Ambiguity leads to incorrect decisions, and incorrect decisions in a security setting normally lead to bad things happening.

Our Definition of Trust

When discussing trusted computing, you first need to agree on the definition of trust. In general usage, trust has many meanings. Many meanings for the same term could lead to confusion and disaster that provokes mistrust. To avoid the resulting mistrust, let's establish one and only one definition of trust in use for this entire book. The definition of trust is:

> An entity can be trusted if it always behaves in the expected manner for the intended purpose. (TCG 2004)

The entity in the definition is a computing process or a human or something else. It doesn't matter. The definition makes no reference to the "goodness" of what of what is being trusted, as you can see when we work through some examples of this definition of trust.

First example: a standard doorknob. Normal individuals trust that if one walks up and turns the doorknob that the doorknob will work properly and allow the door to open. This action should occur each and every time, unless someone breaks the doorknob. Individuals trust the doorknob to work the same way every time. In fact, dogs and cats who open doors are trusting the doorknob to work correctly, too.

Second example: a program on a personal computer. Many users trust the platform to work the same each and every day. If one makes no changes on the platform that trust is not misplaced. However, making no changes is usually impossible, so each and every day the platform changes, perhaps with additional applications installed from the Internet, occasionally with inadvertent user changes to files. The user wants to trust the platform, but having the same entity each and every day is difficult.

Third example: a platform infected with a virus. The virus causes the platform to do bad things, like sending the virus to all members of the user's address book. Everyone who can determine that the virus is present on the platform comes to trust the platform to perform the bad operations. This last example exposes a critical point. Relying entities do trust the infected platform to perform bad operations. As a result, trust does not equal goodness. Just because the relying party is going to trust the platform does not mean that the relying party trusts the platform to do a good job. The opposite is true; the relying party may trust the platform to do a bad job.

The Trust Decision

Critical to trusted computing is the use of our definition of trust. If one can determine that the same entity is operating, and if one can know the properties of that entity, the relying party has the ability to make a trust decision regarding the platform.

The crux of the matter here is the ability to know exactly what entity is operating. The information cannot be merely close or an approximation, it must be exact. Approximations leave doubt as to the exact entity and do not allow the relying party the opportunity to differentiate between entities.

The relying party can make a trust decision once they know the identity of the entity on which they wish to rely. The trust decision is based on the premise that, with the knowledge of the entity's identity, the relying party determines whether the platform can be trusted to provide the services for the intended task.

The relying party can query a trusted platform and obtain the current status of that platform. The relying party then makes a decision to trust the platform or not. The relying party can trust the platform to perform operation A but not operation B. That is, just because a relying party trusts the platform to perform one operation does not obligate that relying party to trust the platform for all operations. In fact, the relying party can trust the platform to perform operation A at one instance of time and then decide at some other point in time to not rely on the platform. The role of the trusted platform hardware is to always work the same way and to report the current status of the platform accurately.

Trust Decision Direction

There is a critical issue that must be understood as we discuss the trust decision. This critical issue is *who* makes the trust decision. Notice that the discussion above uses the term "relying party" to indicate the *who* of the trust decision. For many years the manufacturer of a platform made the trust decision and published their findings. This is the way that most certification schemes work today[2]. The trusted platform wants to move the trust decision from the manufacturer to those wishing to rely on the platform. What becomes vital now is that the evidence provided to the relying party to enable the trust decision is

---

2   Chapter 2 contains a nice history of certification.

not what the manufacturer feels is sufficient to make the platform trusted, rather it is the relying party who determines what is sufficient.

Grandma's Permission

We will highlight this issue of sufficient evidence by talking about a slightly contrived use case. Consider a family group that wants to share photos and other information across a widely dispersed extended family. Few of the family members are computer literate and this family depends on Grandma to make decisions regarding the family network[3]. Now using all of the facilities of the trusted platform new family members join the network. But they can only join if Grandma says okay. It does not matter what the manufacturer or any other third party says, if Grandma says okay, you are in, if Grandma says no, you are out. Note that it does not matter if Grandma's grandson buys the most "trusted" platform in existence, as measured by all the experts in the world, the grandson cannot use his trusted platform in the family group unless Grandma says so.

This change in who makes the trust decision is critical in understanding why the elements of the trusted platform all revolve around protections and evidence. The issue is that Grandma has to have sufficient evidence, in a form that she understands, to be able to make the trust decision. Note that our grandson who has a wonderful trusted platform would provide the evidence of that special platform to Grandma. Grandma will evaluate and, if she is satisfied, allow the grandson access to the family network.

The last tidbit in the Grandma saga is that Grandma decides what evidence she needs. If she wants a digital photo of the motherboard before she allows access, then the grandson must provide that photo, even though all of the world's experts state that a photo adds nothing to Grandma's ability to evaluate the platform, if Grandma wants it, she has to have it. And to make it even sillier, Grandma could state that the motherboard picture must have her latest great grandson sitting next to the motherboard. While most of us would think that very silly, that is what she wants.

Let us turn from our family saga and look how this applies in the real world. An IT department could state that when adding a new trusted platform to the network, the user of the platform must go to an internal Web site and

---

3 Hey, this could be true, especially if the Grandma was someone like Grace Hopper. If you do not know who she was, look her up.

fill out a form indicating the purchase of a new trusted platform. Included in the web form is a field that states that attached to the web application the division admin must submit an e-mail with the number of trusted platforms in the division. From the outside we can see no reason for this requirement and it appears to be very silly. But that does not matter, to gain trust in this machine IT requires the admin e-mail. It is not for us to judge why that is appropriate, it is merely a matter for those involved with that IT department to supply the requested evidence.

The Platform

With a complete definition of "trusted," the next word to define is platform. Intel normally focuses on the platform as an Intel® Architecture desktop or mobile personal computer, but in the trusted computing paradigm, a platform can be any computing device. It could be an IA-32 device, or it could be a cell phone, router, PDA or another such unit that uses Intel Architecture components. Intel® Trusted Execution Technology (Intel® TXT) is one security mechanism available on Intel Architecture platforms that provides a building block to be able to create a trusted platform.

The Client

Just so that the problem has a boundary, a client platform has two characteristics:

- A human user can put his or her hands on the keyboard to control it.
- The platform provides services for the individual.

This definition eliminates infrastructure platforms like routers and switches.

Please do not get too wrapped up in this definition at this point. Certainly, individual client platforms provide server functions and servers act like individual clients. Client platforms may even act like routers; the point is to highlight the user-centered nature of the client and differentiate it from servers or other infrastructure components.

Owner, User, and Operator

Those persons using the platform could have different roles and responsibilities. The trusted platform makes a distinction between three different roles: owner, user, and operator. The roles differ according to their interaction with the platform.

Owner. The owner controls the platform. The owner sets the policies that determine what features of the platform are in use and what features are unavailable. The owner may be remotely located, not required to be present in front of the platform.

User. The user is an entity using the capabilities of the platform. The user could be either a human or a computing process. The user can only use the capabilities of the platform granted by the owner. The user may be remotely located; not required to be present in front of the platform.

Operator. The operator is a human, who has physical possession of the platform. The operator also can be an owner or user. The distinction is that, by definition, the operator must be physically present and manipulating the platform.

In a corporate setting, the owner would be the IT department, and the employee is both the user and the operator, normally. IT could perform maintenance or other operations, and thereby become the operator. In this setting, the IT department decides what capabilities of the platform are active. If the IT department decides that the platform needs to perform a special operation, the IT department can set up the platform to perform the operation. The user could disable the special operation but would experience some loss of services as a result.

In a home setting, the owner and user tend to merge into one combined role. In a home where only one individual uses the machine, that individual performs all of the roles; owner, user, and operator. In a house with multiple machines and multiple individuals, it's more than likely that one individual is the owner and the rest are users. In my house, for example, we have multiple machines and multiple children using those machines, so the author is the owner and the children are the users. Depending on who is actually operating the platform, either the author or one of the children would be the operator.

Building Blocks

Does the trusted platform provide one single function that magically makes the platform trusted? The obvious answer is no, there are going to be multiple functions that combine to form the trusted platform. We do however find ways to define those functions and group them. The following three definitions provide monikers for the various functions.

Element. An element is the base functional unit of the trusted platform. An example element is randomness: all trusted platforms have one, or more, devices that provide a source of entropy.

Technology. A technology is a specific implementation that provides one or more elements. An example of a technology is the Trusted Platform Module (TPM) that provides randomness amongst other elements.

Capability. A capability combines one or more technologies to enable a specific use model. An example would be a key generation application that uses the TPM to generate keys.

This book is going to focus on elements, some technologies, and few capabilities. The rationale for this is that elements are discrete units that lend themselves to discussions without diving into implementation details, technologies require platform decisions and are not very generic, and capabilities are, by their very nature, very implementation and platform specific.

By focusing on the elements, with only limited handling of capabilities, the book has more value over time. As platforms change and implement new capabilities, the platform will take advantage of new technologies. The underlying elements that the technologies are relying on do not change. If the reader has an understanding of the elements, then the reader is armed with a deep knowledge of the *why*[4].

Trusted versus Trustable

Hindsight is a wonderful thing. As events have unfolded, it certainly appears that the word trusted was not the best choice. Closer to what actually happens is that the platform is a trustable platform. The difference in the words is actually very important, trusted implies that the platform as it sits is trusted at all times, while trustable implies that those wishing to use the platform must

---

4   A secondary aspect of the focus on elements is that the author may avoid having to write a 3rd edition of this book.

perform some trust decision. The trust decision discussion in the previous paragraphs nicely described the actions a relying party is going through showing that the platform really is a trustable platform and not always trusted.

It is too late to close the barn door[5] and so the term trusted will remain as the moniker for the platforms that provide these services. However, the author would really like those reading to turn the word trusted into trustable, especially when in use with trusted platform. If the reader thinks trusted platform implies trustable platform and recognizes that some action is occurring by an entity to rely on the platform, then trusted platform correctly defines the situation.

The Weakest Link

Attackers always look for the weakest link. Sun Tzu asks us, why would anyone attack the strong point when an easier path is available? In the early twenty-first century's computing environments, most of the protections are available on the servers. Server owners have made tremendous efforts to provide servers with protection from various attacks. Some of the protections extend to the client; most of those protections do not.

A comparison of the level of protection against the amount of attacks, as in Figure 1.1, shows that while attacks on servers and the infrastructure are

---

5   This is a reference to the American idiom that says once the horse has run out of the barn, that it is too late to close the barn door.

mostly covered, client attacks are out of control. Remembering what Sun Tzu tells us, what device is an attacker going to focus on?

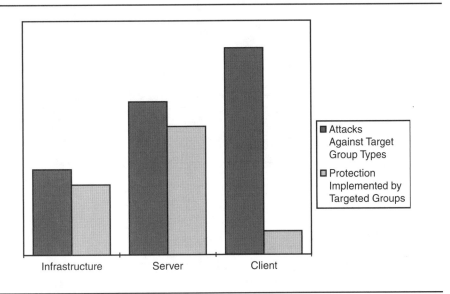

Figure 1.1   Protection Coverage versus Attack Incidents

The goal of a trusted platform is to increase the protections on the platform such that the protections on a platform come close to mitigating the software attacks mounted against the platform.

Another way to look at the protection issues between the server, infrastructure, and client is to take a view of the enterprise as an enclave. As illustrated by Figure 1.2, the enclave model's architecture uses a common view of the world: things outside are bad; things inside are good.

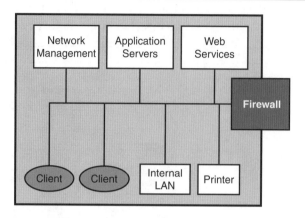

Figure 1.2   The Enclave Model of the Enterprise

The enclave combines platforms and services into a group and provides a wall around the group. The wall represents the protections provided to the group. The protections are both computational, like firewalls, and physical, like locked rooms. The wall treats entities very differently, depending on whether the entity is inside or outside the wall. The wall does not imply that all of the entities reside in the same physical location. The connections are quite likely to be logical ones that extend across physical boundaries. The best example is a mobile PC that connects to the enclave from a hotel room. After setting up the appropriate channels, like a virtual private network (VPN), the mobile platform is a member of the enclave.

Outside entities are thought to be very bad, and a considerable expenditure of effort keeps those entities out. Firewalls, user authorization, special connections, and other mechanisms all provide the same underlying feature, keep the bad guys out of the enclave.

Inside entities should behave properly; hence, they can use the services of the enclave at will. In some environments, the inside entities might have some restrictions placed on them, but once inside the enclave, the entity normally is trusted.

The attitude towards inside and outside of an enterprise leads to a problem exemplified by a Far Side cartoon. In the cartoon, two polar bears are standing next to an igloo. The igloo has a hole in the top. One of the bears is saying to the other bear "Just as I like them, hard on the outside, soft and chewy on the inside."[6] The same is true for computing enclaves, if the attacker can get inside, the enclave is very soft and chewy, and attacks can succeed in all sorts of places.

Protection in the Enclave

By combining the concepts shown in Figure 1.1 and Figure 1.2, you can see why inside the interior of the enclave is soft and chewy; the protection levels do not match the attacks. The outside edge of the enclave is the firewall, the servers, and other infrastructure components. The inside is the client. If the attacker can bypass the enclave protections and directly attack the client, the attacker's chances of success are much greater. Therefore, the first entity to protect within the enclave is the client.

Effect of Providing More Protections

If Sun Tzu is right, and he is, then providing protections on one type of platform sends the attackers looking for some other avenue of attack. The other avenue could be on the client or it could be on the server.

Looking at the problem from an enclave point of view shows that focusing on one type of platform creates the "igloo effect" again. The would-be intruder bypasses one type of platform that has sufficient protections to attack the vulnerable platform.

The result of the enclave view is the realization that all platforms in the enclave are going to need the protections of trusted computing. As the capabilities of the trusted platform grow, the soft and chewy nature of the client, and other platforms, will move more towards a hard piece of candy with no soft center.

Joining an Enclave

If one is going to consider each trusted platform as a specific entity, then knowing the identity of the trusted platform and the identity of the policies the platform is supporting is a necessary and mandatory first step to enabling

---

6   One of the author's biggest disappointments in writing this book was the information that Far Side cartoons are only useable in text books. If any professor is going to use this book as a textbook, please let the author know and maybe we can get permission to use the actual cartoon.

the inclusion of the platform in the enclave. To make this point as forcefully as possible:

> Without the knowledge of the policies in force on the trusted platform, there is no way to include reliably a platform in an enclave. (David Grawrock 2008)

Obtaining the identity of and reporting on the policies of the trusted platform should be a basic design goal of trusted platform designers.

The Basic Trusted Computer

Okay, we have a problem[7] and we need solutions. The previous paragraphs suggested that the trusted computer helps to solve these problems. What are the basic properties of the trusted computer? Subsequent chapters cover these points in detail[8], but for a quick teaser, here are the attributes of a trusted computer:

- *Isolation of programs.* It keeps program A from accessing information of program B.

- *Separation of user processes from supervisor processes.* As an example, the system provides a way to ensure that user applications do not interfere with the operating system.

- *Long-term protected storage.* It can store a value that has protections in some place that lasts across power cycles and other events.

- *Identification of current configuration.* It can provide the identity of the platform and the identity of the software executing on the platform.

- *A verifiable report of the platform identity and current configuration.* An outside observer has a mechanism that allows her to query the platform and obtain an answer that the observer can validate.

- *Provide a hardware basis for the protections.* Simply changing the software does not provide the protections necessary for a trusted computer.

---

7 Everyone has some sort of problem, but please just limit yourself here to just computing problems

8 Otherwise this book turns into a 20-page white paper.

When reading over the list, you might not see that it contains many changes from today's platform. That perception is only partially correct. While some applications require no changes to take advantage of a trusted platform, other applications might need an entire rewrite. One area that must change is the operating system (OS). While the interfaces that the OS presents to an application might not change, the way that the OS handles the interface and provides the actual operations of the interface is sure to change.

The crux of the requirements is the ability to change the hardware. Changing the hardware changes the game for software attacks—the attacker has to have physical possession of the platform to mount the attack. There is a perception that Intel is only a Central Processing Unit (CPU) developer; the reality is that Intel is a platform provider and the hardware changes to enable the trusted platform occur across platform devices.

Basic Cryptography

When many people first hear about trusted computing, their first reaction is that it all revolves around cryptography. While cryptography provides many of the building blocks for trusted computing, cryptography is not the main focus. For a reader of this book, a simple understanding of cryptography is all you need to cope with the security properties of Intel TXT.

If you really want to dive deep into cryptography, try these two outstanding books, both listed in "References" for your convenience: *Applied Cryptography* by Bruce Schneier (Schneier 1995) and the *Handbook of Applied Cryptography* by Menzes, van Oorschot, and Vanstone (Menzes 1996).

Symmetric Encryption

Symmetric encryption protects information using the same key for encryption and decryption. That is, both the message sender and the message recipient need to have the same key. Symmetric algorithms are fast, and they normally add little or no extra information to the message. The issue is how both sides get the same key. Simply sending the key without any protections, or in the clear, does not work, and encrypting the key with a symmetric algorithm would still require the transmission of a key. One way to handle the transportation of these keys is to use a trusted courier. Embassies used to send keys in the brief-cases of consular officials. The method works, but in the world of computing, sending briefcases with keys to all of the members of your address book is not practical. Another problem is that one needs a different key for each potential recipient. Having a key for each member of your address book and keeping track of the keys is an impossible task.

Some common symmetric algorithms are; DES, AES, RC4, and Blowfish. The mathematics behind these algorithms might differ, but they all have the same feature: that is, the same key that encrypts information decrypts the information.

Asymmetric Encryption

Asymmetric encryption uses a different key for encryption and decryption. The encryption portion is public and available to everyone; the decryption portion is private and available only to the key owner. The public and private nature of the key portions leads to their normal names: the public key and the private key.

Asymmetric encryption solves the problem of key distribution inherent in symmetric cryptography. The encryption key is public and the key owner can distribute the key to all who want to communicate with the key owner. No security is lost with multiple entities holding the public key.

The problems with asymmetric cryptography revolve around the circumstances of its use, in terms of both speed and size. Performing the mathematical operations necessary to perform asymmetric cryptography is orders of magnitude slower than the operations necessary for symmetric cryptography. The cipher text that results from an asymmetric encryption is larger than the plain text. The expansion can be quite large, depending on the actual algorithm.

Combination

A best known practice is to combine the two types of cryptography when creating systems. The result is known as *enveloping*, the bulk encryption of data uses a symmetric algorithm and the key for the symmetric algorithm is encrypted using an asymmetric algorithm. The bulk of the file uses symmetric encryption for speed and size considerations. The key for the symmetric algorithm uses asymmetric, where the speed is not a consideration and the expansion is not an issue because the key size is only 20 to 30 bytes.

Cryptographic Hash

A cryptographic hash takes some input and creates a fixed-size output. Cryptographic hashes have some important properties:

- Given the hash output, you have no way to determine the input to the hash.
- Changing one bit of the input causes at least 50 percent of the output bits to change.
- Input to the hash is order-dependent. Hashing A then B does not produce the same value as hashing B then A.

One way to think about cryptographic hashes is that the hash provides the "identity" of an entity. Normally, the entity is some piece of software, like a document or program code. Knowing the entity's identity is an important requirement for many of the trusted platform operations.

Trusted Channel and Trusted Path

Moving information from one location to another requires some sort of channel or path. In trusted computing, the terms have unique meanings and actually are not interchangeable.

Trusted Channel

A trusted channel moves information between two computing entities. A connection between two computers is a channel; a trusted channel adds the properties of integrity and confidentiality of the information.

The integrity of the trusted channel guarantees that the information arrives at the receiver exactly as it was transmitted by the sender. The confidentiality provides assurance that any entity who can observe the channel gains no knowledge of what the data on the channel looks like.

Trusted Path

The trusted path moves information between a computing entity and a human. The path requires some activity on the human's part to recognize that the path is present. Quite often, the trusted path indicates the presence of a trusted channel to the human.

Combination

Combining a trusted channel and trusted path gives the human using the trusted platform assurance that the platform is properly communicating with the human. On the Internet, for example, the SSL protocol provides a trusted channel between two computing entities, the server and the client. The SSL connection provides the integrity and confidentiality for the messages. The little lock icon on the bottom right of the browser window is the trusted path that indicates to the user the presence of the trusted channel. In a perfect world, before the user sends confidential information across the Web, the user would look to the bottom right to verify the presence of the trusted channel.

The Data Life Cycle

If the trusted platform sat around and looked pretty[9], it would not be very valuable. The trusted platform needs to deal with data, the platform owner's data and other entities data. The life cycle of that data would be create, use, store, move, and delete. Create, use and delete are actually all facets of the same operation, executing on the data. To make things easier to understand the life cycle compresses create, use, and delete into an execute phase, making the three phases of the data life cycle, execute, move, and store.

The three phases of the life cycle have a set of mechanisms that enable the tasks to be completed. Some of the mechanisms are unique for a phase and some of the mechanisms share across the phases. Some platforms may participate in all phases of the life cycle. Other platforms may only participate in a subset of the phases. Each phase has some interesting properties and takes advantage of specific trusted platform properties.

---

9   However there are people who really do believe they can make "pretty" platforms. I would suggest an Internet search on "computer case mod" and you will see some truly outstanding cases for ones computer.

Execute Phase

The execute phase is where the data is created, used, and deleted. Use of the data requires that the trusted platform protect that data according to the wishes of the data and platform owner. The wishes of the data and platform owner come in the form of policies that the trusted platform must enforce. In the execute phase the trusted platform must provide the policy enforcement mechanisms that protects the integrity of the data, protects the process operating on the data, and ensures that the data is only disclosed when appropriate.

The platform must be able to accurately and verifiably measure the policy engine and policy the platform is enforcing. It is possible for trusted platforms to be enforcing multiple policies at the same time; see Chapter 20 for a complete discussion of multiple policies. When queried, the trusted platform must be able to report which policy the policy engine is enforcing. Providing an accurate report on the currently in force policy allows outside observers to properly evaluate the current trust properties of the platform.

Move Phase

The move phase is moving data from one platform to another. A further refinement of move is that move actually moves data from one enclave to another; see Chapter 20 for details on the enclave.

The first part of move is the ability to identify, authenticate, and authorize the two endpoints of the transaction. The two parties agree on certain aspects of the communication and establish a trusted channel between the two computing entities. The channel properties can include confidentiality, integrity, and delivery guarantees. Channel establishment is not a difficult task and there are established standards for channel communication.

From the trusted platform standpoint, the hard work is in evaluating the trust policy of the other computing entity. There are really three cases:

- Same policies – When both sides have the same policy all the move phase needs to do is establish the channel and move the data.

- Different policy – Both sides need to evaluate the policy, and depending on the policy requirements, transform the data in some way. See Chapter 20 for a discussion of policy evaluation and data transformations.

■ Unknown policy – In this case the platform is unable to evaluate the policy and must treat the other side as having *no* policy. The implication is that with no understanding of the policy the platform must transform the data based on there being no protections at all in the new environment. Even if the new platform and policy provides better protections than the current platform and environment, the current platform will treat the destination as if no protections are present. Again, Chapter 20 covers this in detail.

Some move policies may require additional features on the actual move transaction. These requirements can include anti-replay protections, repudiation protections, and guarantees of delivery and acceptance of the data.

Store Phase

Store moves the data from the platform to some persistent storage device. The device provides the availability of the data across power events. The easiest example of a store device is a disk drive.

The store device may be very simple; again think of a client disk drive, or very complex; here think of a network storage farm. The device may provide inherent protection capabilities like confidentiality or the device may require the trusted platform to provide confidentiality of the data prior to using the storage device.

The use of the storage device requires a policy that the trusted platform will enforce.

Chapter 2

History of Trusted Computing

Although this report contains no information not available in a well stocked technical library or not known to computer experts, and although there is little or nothing in it directly attributable to classified sources, the participation of representatives from government agencies it its preparation makes the information assume an official character. It will tend to be viewed as an authoritative Department of Defense product, and suggestive of the policies and guidelines that will eventually have to be established. As a prudent step to control dissemination, it is classified CONFIDENTIAL overall.

—Willis Ware, 1970 Task Force on Computer Security

The concept of trusted computing is not new. Very early on, security researchers were looking at trusted computing. The first computers did mostly government work of a sensitive nature. From the "bombes" that helped decrypt the German Enigma traffic to the mainframes that helped with Venona,[1] the computer was dealing with very sensitive information.

1　The bombes were special purpose computers that automated the task of looking for the day key in use by the German military. The bombes were huge but they did a fantastic job of finding the day's key. Venona was the code name for a project that read messages from various Soviet embassies to Moscow. The task was to search through thousands of messages looking for patterns. Many of the messages were read. Doing Internet searches on these two terms could yield a wealth of information.

When a platform performs a single task, never changes from that task, and never shares information, dealing with sensitive information is a much simpler chore. Platforms that can share information and operate on multiple programs provide many opportunities to leak data to unauthorized entities. Multiple programs also provide an opportunity to disrupt concurrently running programs.

Early Papers

In the early 1970s, a series of papers funded by the U. S. government focused on computer security. These papers form the basic building blocks for trusted computing. The following discussion is by no means exhaustive; rather the list highlights some of the major findings of those early researchers.[2]

1970 Task Force

In 1970, long before personal computers, a computer task force made a seminal report on computer security (Ware 1970). The task force, lead by the Rand Corporation, was attempting to define the security requirements for computer systems that had a mixed of users and systems. While the thoughts of the group were concentrated on time-shared mainframes, the actual results hold true for client and server platforms of today.

The task force had some specific recommendations for both hardware and software. The hardware recommendations were:

- *User isolation.* The isolation requirement stated that each user program must be isolated from every other user program.

- *Supervisor protection.* The supervisor, or the entity managing the user programs, must have protection from every user program. One distinct recommendation was to create a user mode and a supervisor mode.

---

2   The author is a great lover of history and reading historical documents and findings. You can provide the impetus for solutions to today's problems by rereading these papers and coming to the understanding that many of the issues we face today are not new, that they are variations on an old theme.

The user mode would be restricted and the supervisor mode would have complete control of the system.

■ *Assurance against unanticipated conditions, including an interrupt system.* With programs not always operating correctly, something unexpected could always happen. The system must have the ability to handle the unexpected events in a set manner.

The software recommendations were:

■ *Language processors and utility routines.* For code in assembly language, the recommendation was to make the code particularly difficult to secure. High level languages—think FORTRAN[3] at the time this document was produced—should use libraries of evaluated utility routines.

■ *Supervisor program.* The key to the hardware's supervisor protection lay in these characteristics:

– Run as much of the supervisor as you can in user mode. This recommendation seems to have fallen on deaf ears. Many operating systems of today require user applications to have access to supervisor mode, and the size of the operating system is growing exponentially. The use of virtualization is an attempt to separate supervisor modules from user mode.

– *Clean up after sensitive data is in use.* After a user program uses sensitive data, the supervisor must ensure that all sensitive data is not available to any other process. While user mode should perform the cleanup, the supervisor must enforce the protection of sensitive data.

– *Orderly startup and shutdown.* This point is very important. The requirement is for a controlled startup that puts the machine in a known state. The shutdown must occur in a way that properly validates all sensitive information. Remember, this requirement in the design of Intel TXT.

– *Certified ability to control access to files.* The recommendation was to ensure that all file accesses were validated, and that they went through a known control point.

---

3   While the author hates to admit it, he actually coded FORTRAN on punch cards

One point to remember with this paper is the date, 1970. The requirements for a secure system are being defined before personal computers, before the Internet, before computers on every desk. The requirements come out of trying to share a computer that does more than one job at a time.

Bell-LaPadula

By 1976, research was taking some of the task force recommendations and diving deeper. The Bell-LaPadula paper (Bell 1973) presents a mathematical model of a secure system. The paper contains descriptions of all of the "actors" in a secure system and of the operations that are necessary to enforce the security. The basic building blocks are:

- *Domain separation.* Separate processes make sure that the resources of one process are not available to any other process. This recommendation matches the user isolation and supervisor requirements of the 1970 task force.

- *Identification.* The identity of the user is very important. The identity allows the system to make decisions about use that are based on the user's identity. For example, a user might be granted access to a process only during regular business hours. Without properly identifying the user, the system owner would have no way to enforce the use restriction.

- *Authorization.* Using the user identity, the system owner gives the user permission to perform various operations. As in the previous example, the authorization might allow the identified user access to the process during regular business hours or during weekend hours, depending on the job function of that user.

The Rainbow Series

In 1985, the U.S. Department of Defense released the "Rainbow Series." The individual volume that people most often remember is the "Orange Book" (Department of Defense 1985), which describes a trusted computer system, the evaluation criteria for a trusted system, and how to use the trusted system. Other colored volumes in the rainbow of this series describe the nitty-gritty details of the trusted system and its use.

Security System Evaluation

The Rainbow Series begat the European ITSEC evaluations, and the combination of the Rainbow Series and the ITSEC begat Common Criteria, an international agreement on how to evaluate security systems. Evaluation is way beyond the scope of this book. If you are interested in looking at evaluations, the Common Criteria Web site is listed in "References."

The Rainbow Series is a wonderful source of the requirements for a trusted system in the 1980s. It defines how to build, distribute, and use the trusted system. What it does not contemplate is how to work with a personal computer. The whole thought process behind the Rainbow Series, and the Orange Book in particular, takes place in the context of a mainframe computer sitting in a computer room. The idea that the user would be able to load programs, or change the operating system, is just not possible with the Rainbow Series. It turns out that getting an Orange Book evaluation of a PC is very difficult and depends on the system being "locked down." The Common Criteria begins to solve many of those issues, but creates other issues when attempting to apply those concepts to commercial products.

Industry Response

The U.S. Department of Defense was both a definer of trusted systems requirements and a purchaser of trusted systems. Industry provided to the government both the hardware and software to meet the Department of Defense requirements.

On the hardware side, industry leaders like IBM, Control Data, Digital, and others, defined and developed mainframe computers that provided the underlying features that enable trusted systems. From the ability to create user modes and supervisor modes, to the ability to separate applications, to the ability to handle unexpected operations, mainframe hardware supported trusted system development and deployment.

On the software side, mainframe operating systems used the hardware and provided the separation recommended by the various research papers. Some operating systems and applications implemented the mathematical models of Bell-LaPadula. A rich history of operating system research attempts to implement the necessary controls. A Google search of topics like "Trusted MACH," "Fluke," "Flask," and "SELinux" would show you the ongoing research to define and implement trusted operating systems.

The Future through the Past

Combining all of the original research leads to a list of requirements that contains the following main points:

■ Domain separation

■ Handling of events not anticipated

■ Separation between user and supervisor modes

■ Platform capabilities in the hardware to support the other requirements

The idea now is to combine the research requirements with the list of requirements from Chapter 1 to form the new requirements for a trusted computer. Table 2.1 provides that combination.

Table 2.1 Trusted Computer Research Requirements

Requirement	Research Requirement	Comments
Isolation of programs	Domain separation	Isolation is the same as domain separation.
	Handling unanticipated events	Isolation can provide a mechanism to handle unanticipated events.
Separation of user from supervisor	Separation of user from supervisor	The trusted platform requirement matches the research requirement
Long-term protected storage		Original research does not call out need for long-term protected storage.
Identification of current configuration		Original research assumes that platform identity is not an issue.
Verifiable report of current configuration		With no identity issues and an assumption of secure software delivery, no reporting of platform configuration takes place.
Hardware basis for protections	Hardware basis for protections	The trusted platform requirement matches the research requirement

A very interesting turn of events: the table has three requirements from the original research and three brand new ones. To discover the reasons for the three new requirements, you need some more history, moving ahead in time to the personal computer era.

Personal Computers

One way to compare today's personal computers and the trusted computing research of the past is to consider the environment on which the research was focusing. The researchers were moving from dedicated machines performing a single task to generic machines capable of performing tasks simultaneously. One major concern was that when the machine switched from one task to the other, the possibility of leaking information was present. For those old enough to remember, these machines' one common architecture was the central mainframe and user's timesharing of the mainframes resources. Compare that to a network today and you should see many of the same issues still remain. Also be aware that many differences exist and those differences drive our new requirements. To understand the security needs of a personal computer, one must understand the internal workings of the platform.

About Common Terminology...

A brief personal digression: As you can see in the biography on the back cover, I came with a background in software and learned hardware through working at Intel Corporation. In the very first few days, terms like, front-side bus, North Bridge, and ICH just seemed like a foreign language.

As most engineers know, each discipline has a language all its own. In the early days of Intel TXT, it was really fun to attempt to combine the languages of hardware engineers, software engineers, and the security architects. I would love to have back some of the time we spent trying to merge all of the terms and get the team reading from the same page. It reminded me of a comment made about the social dynamics during the filming of *Grand Prix,* the movie about auto racing. The real race car drivers started talking about camera angles and film speed, and the actors started talking about corner speeds and brake points.

To understand Intel TXT, a basic understanding of the platform components is critical. In addition to understanding the terms, knowing the history of the changes to the Intel® architecture will help you to understand the security initiative's direction.

Figure 2.1 illustrates the basic components and includes some of the synonyms in use on the platform.

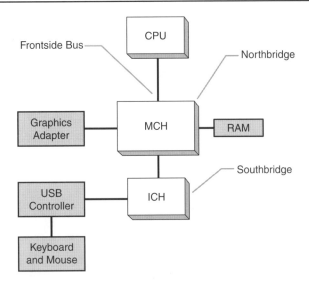

Figure 2.1   Basic Components

The definitions for each component are:

■ CPU. A central processing unit is the main processor for the system.[4]

■ MCH. The memory controller hub is the component that connects the CPU to random access memory (RAM). Newer platforms contain a graphics MCH (GMCH). Common aliases for the MCH include the North Bridge.

■ ICH. The input/output controller hub is the component that connects system devices, such as network cards, disk drives, audio components, and others to the system. The ICH can assume aliases like the South Bridge.

---

4   One would hope, dear reader, that your system is running an Intel® processor using Intel® vPro™ Technology.

- Chipset. The specific combination of a processor, MCH, and ICH into a coordinated unit is called a chipset.

- Front-side bus (FSB). As the connection between the CPU and MCH, the FSB allows for multiple CPUs to communicate with a single MCH.

  In the near future (after 2007) the connection between CPU packages and the chipset will not be a bus like the FSB, but a point to point connector.

About that FSB

As one would expect the author has access to internal Intel information. During the writing of the first version of this book, I was well aware of the development of Intel® QuickPath architecture. I certainly hinted at the fact that a point to point bus was possible and coming, but the date was only slightly off.

In Chapter 1 I made a reference to focusing on elements rather than technologies and capabilities. The change from FSB to Intel QuickPath architecture is a perfect example. While the underlying functionality is very different between FSB and Intel QuickPath architecture, the elements that these two busses provide is the same.

CPU Internals

The CPU, or processor, has some internal state and packing issues that influence the trusted platform.

Protected Mode

Protected mode provides the "rings" in a processor. When you see a reference to ring 0 or ring 3, that's a reference to the protection mode in the processor. The protection modes actually provide four rings: 0, 1, 2, and 3. Figure 2.2 depicts the layers of protection mode rings.

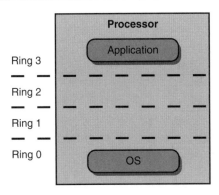

Figure 2.2 Protection Mode Rings

The intent of the ring architecture is to provide separation of the operating system (OS) and the applications that the OS manages. The ring structure also gives the OS a way to separate[5] and layer functions in the OS to improve the ability of the OS to protect itself. Chapter 3 explains how a current OS uses the ring structures.

Memory Management

The processor supports management of physical memory through segmentation and paging. In this simple introduction, I cannot possibly explain all of the options, permutations, and usages for managing memory. The canonical reference is the *IA-32 Intel® Architecture Software Developers Manual, Volume 3: System Programming Guide* (Intel 2003c). Chapter 3 of that document gives a much deeper overview of how to manage memory.

Figure 2.3 shows a simplified view of the memory management system.[6] Additional controls and tables provide the complete range of memory management.

---

5 Consider Table 2.1 and the requirement for user and supervisor separation

6 The author knows that the definition of "simple" here does not seem to fit, but trust me, this explanation only scratches the surface of the mechanisms in use here. Do not miss the main point: to go from an address in a program to the real physical page, you pass through control points that system entities can manage.

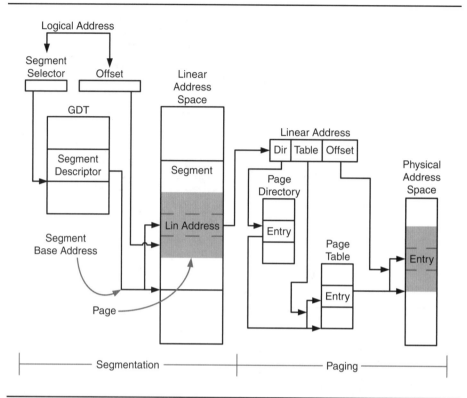

Figure 2.3   Memory Management

When an application requests access to a memory location, the system follows this map to convert the address that the application needs to a physical memory page and location.

1. The logical address breaks down into two components, the segment and offset.

2. The segment indicates a selector that provides a base page address and adding the offset produces a linear address.

    ■ If paging is not in use, the linear address would point to a physical address location.

    ■ Converting the logical address into the linear address is the segmentation task of memory management.

3. If the memory manager is using paging, the linear address maps to three components: directory, table, and offset.

4. The processor uses the directory to locate the table, and then it adds the offset to produce a physical address.

The directory and table can indicate that the contents that should be in a physical address are currently not in memory, and the memory manager must load the correct physical page. This process is called *page swapping* and is the mechanism behind the swap file in use by operating systems.

Segmentation and Paging Control. An important property to understand from Figure 2.3 is the control issue. Notice that the entity controlling segmentation and paging controls the mapping of logical address to physical address. From an application standpoint, two successive accesses to the same logical address can result in two different physical addresses.

The memory manager is under no obligation to expose the complete physical address space. The physical address space in use can have holes and not allow access to specific physical address pages.

The controls that manage segmentation and paging start with Control Register 3 (CR3) and include the manipulation of the paging entries.

Front-side Bus

The connection between the CPU and MCH passes messages that allow control of the chipset and access to memory. The front-side bus (FSB) allows for the connection of multiple CPU packages onto a single MCH.

Newer platforms may use mechanisms other than the FSB to connect the CPU packages to the chipset. Other topologies are possible where the MCH is included in the CPU package. A trusted platform needs to be able to establish a trust perimeter on any bus topology.

When one looks at server topologies, there are multiple mechanisms and chipset layouts. Intel TXT will work in various topologies.

Multiple CPU Systems

When the term CPU comes up, most people think of the CPU package that is put into a platform. A synonym for CPU is processor. An Intel TXT enabled system provides support for multiple CPUs. The support ensures that all processors are operating in a consistent fashion.

MCH

The MCH connects the CPU to memory. The MCH also provides a connection between the graphics adapter and system memory. Some MCH units are actually a Graphic MCH, which has an integrated graphics adapter.

On a typical personal computer, the system has only one MCH. The MCH is not a field replaceable part and is permanently mounted on the motherboard. Some server designs use multiple MCH units to handle multiple CPUs and complex memory topologies.

Memory

All CPU requests for system memory travel through the FSB, through the MCH, and to the actual memory DIMM. The MCH can "snoop" the memory request and either block it or re-route the request to some other entity. For information held by the ICH, the MCH snoops the address, recognizes the address as one held by the ICH, then routes the request to the ICH.

Display Adapter

The MCH can either contain an integrated display adapter or it can provide a connector for a discrete display adapter. Discrete display adapters connect to the MCH on a variety of busses, the newest being the PCI Express[†] bus.

ICH

The ICH, as the input/output controller hub, provides the connections to most of the platform peripherals. Platform peripherals include keyboards, USB connections, BIOS memory, and other busses like PCI Express.

Keyboard

The keyboard connector normally uses either a USB connection or the PS2 port. Most desktop systems use the USB port for keyboard connections and most laptops provide a PS2 port for connecting an external keyboard. In the context of a trusted platform, either connector can provide the ability to protect the keyboard input.

USB

The ICH provides at least one USB controller hub. Numerous peripherals use the USB connections to attach the device to the platform.

A critical requirement for the USB connection is the need for a driver to discover and route messages to the attached devices. The driver determines which devices are visible to applications, when the devices get service, and the routing of messages from the attached devices. Requiring a driver also inhibits the use of the bus and devices on the bus during startup operations. Without a driver, the peripherals are invisible; attempting to require the device during a startup process requires some sort of intermediate driver.

LPC Bus

The Low Pin Count (LPC) bus provides a simple bus that does not require any drivers to access the devices on the bus. Typical platform components that reside on the LPC bus include the BIOS boot block and the Trusted Platform Module (TPM).

The LPC bus is a slow bus running at a normal speed of 33 megahertz. Not only is the bus slow, but the data path is narrow. The reality is that sending information to a device on the LPC bus is like sending information through a cocktail straw.

The LPC bus does have a redeeming factor: it is so simple the devices on the bus are available very early in the startup sequence. The availability of devices on the LPC bus provides an excellent location for devices that can support trusted platforms.

Current Intel Architecture Security Support

Current processors based on the Intel architecture already support some security features. Intel TXT might add additional features, but the current support is essential to enable Intel TXT.

Rings

The privilege levels, or rings, are the first instance of security support in the Intel architecture. The Intel processor manual explicitly states that rings "…protect application or user programs from each other."

(Intel 2003a) The implication is that the rings are a security device to provide domain separation. The reality is that the rings are a domain separation mechanism. Intel TXT makes use of the rings as one of the building blocks for the security solution.

Using the rings allows the user supervisor separation as requested by the early security research. Remember the 1970 task force recommendation to isolate the user program from the supervisor? Executing the supervisor in ring 0 and a user program in ring 3 provides the separation necessary for security purposes. The rings have been part of Intel architecture since the Intel 286 processor.

Protected Mode

The Intel 286 processor included another security feature: protected mode. Protected mode uses the segment register contents as selectors, or pointers, into descriptor tables. Protected mode features include:

- Descriptors that provide 24-bit base addresses
- Maximum physical memory size of up to 16 megabytes,
- Support for virtual memory management on a segment swapping basis

Protected mode mechanisms include:

- Segment limit checking
- Read-only and execute-only segment options
- Hardware task-switching and local descriptor tables that allow the operating system to protect application or user programs from each other

Protected Mode for Security

Protected mode provides security properties just as the rings do. Control of the segment descriptors allows the operating system to separate one user application from another user application.

Paging

With the introduction of the Intel386™ processor, a new security feature became available: paging. Paging provides an excellent mechanism for domain separation.

Looking at Figure 2.3 (Memory Management), notice that the entity that controls the segmentation and the page tables controls which program can access a physical address. If the supervisor properly controls the page tables, then another factor in domain separation is present.

Security Properties

With the rings, segmentation, and paging, it would appear that all is in place to provide domain separation. Well, let us update Table 2.1, creating Table 2.2, and see how the current hardware matches the trusted computing requirements.

Table 2.2 Requirements Current Supported

Requirement	Hardware Support	Comments
Isolation of programs	Paging, segmentation and paging	Support for isolation but no real support for unanticipated events
Separation of user from supervisor	Ring 0 and Ring 3 separation	Ring 0 manages the separation
Long-term protected storage		No feature supports requirement
Identification of current configuration		No feature supports requirement
Verifiable report of current configuration		No feature supports requirement
Hardware basis for protections	Yes	Whole point is that features are hardware

The support is not too bad. The requirements from the basic research are present, but the new requirements are not met. That situation would be reasonable because the new trusted requirements did not influence the original designs. Before filling in the table, the next few chapters provide detailed coverage of the current environment and how designers and attackers make use of the current architecture.

Chapter 3

The Current Environment

If you put tomfoolery into a computer, nothing comes out of it but tomfoolery. But this tomfoolery, having passed through a very expensive machine, is somehow ennobled and no-one dares criticize it.

—Pierre Gallois

Part of the inhumanity of the computer is that, once it is competently programmed and working smoothly, it is completely honest.

—Isaac Asimov (1920–1992)

In today's personal computer environment, a PC works perfectly if things are set up correctly, but if the PC is not set up correctly, you have the classic "garbage in, garbage out" scenario. Is that right? Or, can a well set up machine still give you garbage that is glorified because it came from a computer? A trusted platform believes that both situations are possible and acceptable. The rationale behind the two chapter quotes is that from a trust standpoint both quotes describe a trusted platform. Asimov really hits the nail on the head with the point that once you know what is happening it always happens in the exact same way. Gallois points out that if we do not understand what we are dealing with then the answers we get from the device are no better than tomfoolery.

To resolve these issues, the first task is to understand the computing environment of today, what works and what does not work, why we trust platforms to perform certain jobs but do not trust them for other jobs.

Platform

A platform[1] involves a combination of components. In this chapter, the discussion covers four areas:

■ *Hardware.* The CPU, chipset, and other silicon components.

■ *Operating System* (OS). The software that directly controls the hardware and provides services to applications. The OS includes drivers which extend the OS to control new hardware. The new hardware normally consists of plug-in devices.

■ *Applications.* Software that provides services to the user.

■ *Configuration.* The hardware and software have countless control options. The combination of the control choices is the current configuration.

Hardware

CPU, chipset, and other devices—the hardware provides the basic execution environment for the platform. While many think of the hardware as a monolithic entity, in reality the hardware devices are unique components, each providing important services.

The interesting issue in a security context is the fact that the hardware has configuration options. Some examples of hardware configuration are:

■ *CPU frequency.* The Intel® Pentium® processor family provides for a range of operating frequencies and voltage levels. The choice between speed, heat, and power consumption leads to a wide variety of configuration options. Some combinations of frequency and voltage can cause the processor to operate incorrectly. Most BIOS and operating systems protect from these dangerous settings, but it is possible to

---

1   Do not focus too strongly on the word "platform." The platform could be a client and as such a desktop or mobile platform. The platform could be a server and servers come in many flavors: stand-alone, branch office, blades, etc. The point to recognize here is that all platforms have the four areas under discussion.

set the values incorrectly. If the CPU no longer operates correctly, what happens to any security assurances? Checking for these types of hardware configurations is an important feature of TXT.

■ *DIMM settings.* The types of DIMM that are used and the way that the hardware controls the DIMM can also affect security. It is possible to configure the chipset improperly and cause the various FSB addresses actually to point to the same address. Validating the current settings is a large security concern.

These settings, and others, set up the hardware to perform certain operations. When some entity wishes to rely on the hardware, the current configuration is vital to any assessment of the platform.

Operating System

The operating system provides management of the hardware and a set of services for applications. The operating system also contains a wide variety of configuration options, many of them security sensitive. Some of the issues with the operating system revolve around the basic architecture of the OS.

Ring Use

Chapter 2 described the rings that Intel® architecture provides. The idea behind the CPU architects was to provide the ability for domain separation in an Intel architecture processor. Figure 3.1 shows what the Intel architects had in mind on the right and what the OS vendors implemented on the left.

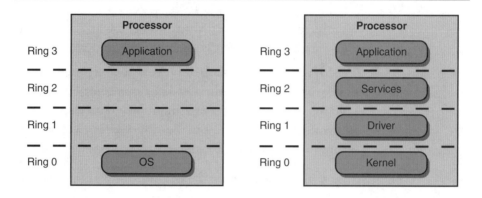

Figure 3.1   Ring Use Intended by Architects versus OS Vendors

For many reasons, the OS vendors did not use all four of the rings, they only used two. The use of only two rings, and the non-use of the other two rings, has serious security implications. By combining all of the OS activities in a single ring, all of the activities share the same security level. With a constant change in drivers, the security of the OS is constantly changing. As described further in Chapter 5, many attacks occur due to the use of ring 0 for all system-related activities.

It is possible to redesign an OS and use all of the rings; the disadvantage is that the OS, most drivers, and some applications must be rewritten. Requiring software vendors to rewrite of most of the platform software, thereby invalidating the old software, is not a viable strategy for the security initiative.

Drivers

The OS requires drivers to access hardware devices. The system has drivers for hard drives, LAN cards, graphics adapters, and other hardware devices. Most drivers require ring 0 access to properly function. Allowing multiple drivers access to ring 0 breaks any domain separation that the OS is attempting to provide. Chapter 5 shows how attackers make use of ring 0 access to perform their attacks.

Drivers also present another security problem: interactions with other drivers. Drivers may attempt to access resources that other drivers are already using and sometimes it proves almost impossible to remove the conflict.

Not removing the conflict can cause the OS to work erratically and this problem is difficult to diagnose.

Some applications require specific versions of a driver. If the user loads two programs that require different versions of the driver, one of the applications could work incorrectly.

It is possible to install two or more drivers that attempt to manage the same device. While this occurrence is somewhat rare, the correct running of the platform is almost impossible when it occurs. A user can find it very difficult to determine that the two drivers are present.

The end result with drivers is that is very important to understand the exact identity of each and every driver that is in use by the OS.

Configuration

In addition to the drivers, you have numerous configuration options in the OS. Some of the configuration options have security implications, like Internet connection options, driver load policies, and others. Installing an OS from scratch gives anyone a glimpse of the multitude of OS configuration options. These configuration options represent the executing environment of the platform, even more so than the OS code. While the code is what is executing, the configuration is the real identity.

Attempting to report the current OS configuration to outside observers is a difficult task. Many current operating systems do not have the basic design that allows for the reporting of the configuration information.

Applications

Applications mirror the issues with the OS drivers and configurations, with one additional issue: is the application even installed on the platform?

Installation

The first issue to consider—and this issue should be a simple one—is if the application is installed on the platform. Most applications leave quite visible indications that the application is present. Some applications do not.

A very interesting question regarding the installation is: what version of the application is present? The version is very important when attempting to find platforms that need to upgrade the application.

Drivers

Applications can require drivers to complete the applications' tasks. During installation, the application installer can install the required driver. The problem comes when the application installer does not properly check for a previous driver and installs a version of the driver that causes problems for other applications on the platform.

Configuration

In addition to installation and drivers, applications require configuration. The configuration choices made by the user who is installing the application can affect the security properties of the platform.

Malware

Simply put, malware is an application on the platform that performs actions that the platform owner does not like. The malware can attack the platform it resides on, or the malware can use the platform to attack other platforms. Either way the malware performs actions against the wishes of the platform owner.

Malware has code, possibly drivers, and configuration options. The malware looks like any other application on the platform. Some types of malware even appear in the installed list of applications; other malware attempts to hide its existence on the platform.

Anti-virus (AV) programs attempt to find the malware regardless of the installation method. When the culprit is found, the AV program attempts to eradicate the malware. The eradication attempt might or might not be successful. Information regarding the existence of malware on a platform allows outside entities to make trust decisions regarding the platform.

Malware Components

Malware has three basic components:

- *Distribution mechanism.* The distribution mechanism moves the malware from one platform to another. Using the human virus analogy, think of the distribution mechanism as the sneeze that distributes little viral particles throughout the room. A very common distribution mechanism is to send e-mails using the infected platforms email distribution list.

- *Infection mechanism.* The infection mechanism provides the way for the malware to penetrate the platform. Just as the sneeze only distributes the viral particles around the room and the virus needs to get inside and start multiplying, malware needs to arrive at a platform and then get beyond the protections. Programs with buffer overflow issues provide a wonderful source for malware to infect platforms.

- *Payload.* The payload triggers after the new platform is infected. The payload can be benign, discomforting, or fatal. A human virus can cause a little nasal drainage, give you the two-week flu, or be Ebola and kill you. Malware can be a nasty message on your screen, a use of all of your resources, or a reformat of your hard drive.

A specific instance of malware would pick one or more distribution mechanisms, one or more infection mechanisms, and one or more payloads. The newer forms of malware use combinations of distribution and infection mechanisms to attempt to bypass platform protections.

Break Once, Run Everywhere

Some protection mechanisms have a very undesirable property, known as Break Once Run Everywhere (BORE). A system that enables BORE attacks is, most likely, improperly designed. BORE attacks occur when the attacker, or malware, finds a shared secret. Consider a system that uses a symmetric key to encrypt messages. Normal best practice is to use some sort of asymmetric encryption to protect a random symmetric key and distribute the public portion of the asymmetric key pair. What happens if the system designer thinks: "That asymmetric stuff is just too hard, I will put the same symmetric key on all the platforms and protect the key really well." The designer might be successful in protecting the key on all the platforms, but what happens if the protection fails. If the attacker can recover the key on just one platform, the attacker has the key that works on all platforms. In other words, the attacker breaks the protections once and can now run the attack everywhere.

Notice that the designer made the decision to share a secret. Any time you have a shared secret, you have a possibility of a BORE attack. Obviously systems must share secrets; otherwise no encryption would be possible. What is dangerous is to share the same secret on many platforms.

Configurations

The thread tying hardware, OS, and applications together is configuration information. To understand what makes up the current environment, an evaluation requires the type of hardware, the operating system, the applications, and the configuration options for each one.

Changing the configuration can cause the platform to misbehave. Detecting changed, or improperly configured platforms, is very difficult. What is necessary is some mechanism to report on the environment in a manner that reflects an accurate measurement of the configuration and is verifiable by the entity requesting the measurement. Chapter 12 explains mechanisms to perform those two operations.

Finding Bad Platforms

So with all of the potential issues, how does one define a "bad" platform? The answer is that those who wish to rely on the platform should be the ones to determine what is good or bad. A platform, and the platform's current configuration, could be acceptable for one use but not acceptable for some other task. What is necessary is a mechanism that allows those wishing to rely on the platform a good view into the platform's current configuration.

Current platforms have few or no mechanisms that provide the information to outside observers. Those platforms using the Trusted Platform Module (TPM) from the Trusted Computing Group (TCG) have the ability to report information; the question then becomes what information can the platform report. The Intel safer computing initiative makes heavy use of the TPM (see Chapter 13).

Subsequent chapters build on the themes of allowing outside entities to determine their trust in the platform and providing mechanisms that allow accurate measurement of the current platform configuration.

Chapter 4

Anatomy of an Attack

So in war, the way is to avoid what is strong and to strike at what is weak.
—Sun Tzu, *The Art of War*

Sun Tzu was talking about attacking with armies. However, the principles he wrote about centuries ago are the same when discussing attacks on computers. The malware writers use the easiest mechanism available to them. We are going to create a simple application and then show how attacks can defeat the protections in place for the program. We will not show the exact mechanism used to mount the attack nor will we go anywhere near how to distribute malware. After all, it is not the purpose of this book to be a hacker's how-to manual, but show you what malware can do.

We will follow the development of an application and the programmers' response to various attacks. Our application is very simple with only one task. The application displays a special number when requested and allows the updating of the special number. For reasons that we will not try to figure out, attackers want to see the special number and some attackers want to change the special number.[1]

---

1   To be more specific, the special number can only be 42 and any attempt to change the ultimate answer should not be possible. To understand the reference to 42, the author advises the reader to read another book, The Hitchhikers Guide to the Galaxy, where the rationale for 42 becomes clear, or at least not so obscure.

From the discussion of malware in Chapter 3, the assumption for our attack is that the distribution and infection mechanisms for the attack, or the specific instance of the malware, are effective on our platform. Moreover, because the payload directly attacks our application we need to mitigate the effect of the malware's payload.

From the standpoint of our application, the malware payload provides fatal attacks. The application designer, from the standpoint of our example, is not able to defend against either the distribution mechanism or the infection mechanism. Obviously, closing the distribution or infection vulnerabilities would be very desirable in real life, but for our example, those choices are not available.

From a strictly technical viewpoint, many malware instances blend the distribution, infection, and payload components. Our example does not try to deal with those blended threats; rather the focus of this example is on the effects of the payload. Real world applications and protections are unable to make the same simplification.

Being that the author of the book is both the author of the application and the malware, the author gets to place some restrictions on the malware.[2] The purpose of our malware is to highlight issues on current platforms and to illustrate platform vulnerabilities.

The malware has one restriction: it may only use software processes—that is, no hardware modifications. While hardware attacks are certainly possible, we are not going to focus on them here. We define *hardware attacks* as those using a physical modification to the platform or use probes on the platform busses or memory. The focus on software attacks over hardware attacks comes from the responses to the following questions:

1. Have you ever been a victim of a malware process (virus, Trojan, etc.)?

2. Have you ever been the victim of a hardware attack (where the attacker actually used a probe on your platform)? [3]

---

2   Obviously, real malware has no restrictions. The author has no illusions that malware would not try to use any and all potential vulnerabilities. When looking at real attacks, the author assumes the best, and worst, from attackers.

3   If you are a current, or former, member of an agency tasked with keeping your countries secrets safe, the author assumes that some other country is very interested in what you are trying to protect.

The vast majority of users answer yes to question one and no to question two. Therefore, while we could concern ourselves with hardware attacks, the majority of users only need protection from software attacks.

Programmer versus Attacker

Let us remember the purpose of our application: it keeps track of a number, displays that number upon request, and allows for the updating of the number. The goal of the attacker is to discover what digits make up the current special number or to find a way to update the special number whenever the attacker wishes. Remember that the attacker is limited to software-based processes for the attack.

The first attack is the simplest. The malware merely reads the special number from the hard drive. Since any process can read a file from the drive, the application really has no protection against this foray.

The defense against this first attack is equally simple: encrypt the special number on the hard drive. The question to answer now is, "Where does the encryption key come from?" The most common first response to the attack would make a crucial mistake. Your first thought might be to encrypt the file using a symmetric key embedded in the program. At first blush, the new design looks like a good response because malware can no longer simply read the file and the information has protections using encryption. All attacks have mitigation. Remember the break once and run everywhere (BORE) attack described in Chapter 3? The decision to create shared secrets on many platforms was the fatal mistake. If you put the same symmetric key in every instance of the program, the design enables the attacker to break once and run everywhere. The attacker merely needs to find the key once, and then redistribute the malware with the symmetric key embedded in the malware. A very simple way for the attacker to discover the key is to run a debugger on the application and watch for the decryption process.

Well, shoot! You have an encrypted special number, but the encryption is providing no protection whatsoever. You must have a way to protect the key in the application. The normal response to this situation is: make it harder to run the debugger. The security term for this defense is *obfuscation*. Obfuscation mechanisms can be very simple or very complex. The result is the same. If one attacker is able to see their way through the obfuscation, all attackers now have the encryption key. While the obfuscation mechanism can be quite creative and make the attackers' job much harder, in the end, the obfuscation mechanism is likely to fail and allow the exposure of the file encryption key.

Obfuscation is not the answer. What you need is a different key for each instance of the application. Where does the unique key come from? The system must have a process whereby the application gets some unique value and uses the unique value, or a derivative of the unique value, as the key. Think about where you provide uniqueness to applications on a daily basis. The answer is passwords.

So, we update the application to require use of a password to obtain the encryption key. The password, or unique value, eliminates the BORE attack. Knowing the value on one platform does not allow the attacker to redistribute the same encryption key in the malware. Each platform has a unique value. Having a unique value forces the malware author to find the key for each application instance.

Normally, keys are just a random sequence of bits with a specific size depending on the encryption algorithm. Well-formed passwords do not normally fit into that definition. One method of converting a password into a key is to apply a cryptographic hash to the password. The resulting hash value has a fixed size and a nice mix of bits.[4]

The application needs a new screen for the password entry. The user enters the password, and the program takes the password as input for a two-step operation. First, it applies the cryptographic hash to obtain the encryption key. Then, it uses the encryption key to decrypt the special number on the hard drive. If the user picks a good password—that topic has fodder for more than one book—the key protects the special number from malware and no BORE attack is possible.

Application Today

Our application now protects the special number from simple reading by encrypting the special number, and it protects the encryption key by requiring a password. The elements of our application are:

---

4   Be very careful about relying too much on the fact that the cryptographic hash has mangled the password. A cryptographic hash must work the same way every time, so if your password is "pass," the result is a well-known value and everyone in the world knows the value. The hash merely converts the password into a more convenient form; it does not add additional protections.

- *Special number* that the application displays and updates
- *Special number display*, the portion of the application that displays the special number to the user
- *Update display*, the portion of the application that accepts updates from the user and changes the special number
- *Password entry*, the portion of the application that requests the users password and then applies the cryptographic hash to obtain the encryption key
- *Special number protection*, the portion of the application that uses the encryption key to encrypt or decrypt the special number

Application Components

The question we need to ask now is, "Can malware view or disrupt our application?" To answer the question, let's see how each of the components works and take an attacker's view of them. The components are:

- Display window to request the password
- Reading keystrokes for the user-ID and password
- Password processing that applies the cryptographic hash to the password and obtains the encryption key and decrypts the special number
- Decision to display the special number the decrypted special number
- Display window to output the special number
- Process to update the special number

The components combine to provide the application the ability to request from a user their password, read the password from the keyboard, and process the password to determine whether it is a correct one. The components pass information between themselves using normal internal programming mechanisms, such as shared memory, shared threads, and other such programming conventions.

Unfortunately, all of these components are susceptible to malware. Let us look at the potential malware attack points.

Display Windows

The application has three windows that it presents to the user:

■ User-ID and password screen

■ Special number display

■ Special number update

The program creates a window by using system calls to create a display frame buffer. The display adapter reads the frame buffer and mixes the information from other display buffers to create the analog[5] information that allows the monitor to display the window. The entire process uses system memory, from the creation of the display window to the frame buffer.

While each of the windows displays different pieces of information, the basic process is the same for each, process the frame buffer from system memory.

Reading Keystrokes

The user enters the user-ID and password one character at a time at a keyboard. The mechanics of this operation are:

3. The keyboard generates a scan code, a value that indicates which key was pressed.

4. Send the scan code to the keyboard driver, code that is normally part of the operating system.

5. Convert the scan code into an ASCII character.

6. Send the ASCII character to the program requesting the input.

The generation of the scan code occurs in a hardware device, but after its generation, all of the processing occurs as software processes that use system memory.

The keyboard driver, running at ring 0, provides the conversion from the scan code into the ASCII character and sends the ASCII character to the operating system. The operating system then sends the ASCII character to the application that should receive the keyboard input. The keyboard driver and the operating system reside in system memory.

---

5 Yes, we have digital display adapters now, but the real issue is taking information from the display buffer and converting the information into a format that the monitor can properly display.

Password Processing

As the user enters the password at the keyboard, the keyboard sends each individual key code, through the keyboard driver, to the application. The application takes each keystroke and builds the entire password. When the user indicates that all characters of the password are present, the program processes the characters through the cryptographic hash. Other types of processing are possible and could include making all of the characters uppercase or other such character manipulations. At this point in the process, the application has not determined whether the password is correct, just that a password is present. All of the processing occurs in system memory.

Program Decision

With a processed password, the program needs to use the processed value to continue processing. Since the processed password is the key to decrypt the special number, the program decision is easy, just attempt to decrypt the special number, and if the decryption is successful, the password was the right one. An easy way to determine whether the decryption was successful is to place some fixed values along with the special number to display in the file on the hard drive. After performing the decryption, if the fixed values are present the decryption was successful and hence the password was correct. If the fixed values are not present, the decryption was unsuccessful and the password was incorrect.

Our application uses a separate mechanism to make the decision to display the special number after decryption. While it is not necessarily the most robust mechanism, this approach highlights another type of possible attack. After the decryption, the program code contains a simple yes/no switch. The code checks for a specific value, and if it is present, the program displays the special number. If that value is not present, the code does not display the special number. All decisions and comparisons occur in system memory.

Malware Attack Points

Attacks need a vulnerability to exploit. Where are the vulnerabilities in our program? The vulnerabilities for software attacks all revolve around one main idea: manipulate memory. If the attacker can gain access to memory supposedly assigned to the program, the attacker can read or change the memory. Reading the memory would allow the attacker to disclose either the special number or the password. Changing memory would allow the attacker to change the instruction flow of the program.

The other vulnerabilities are within the input and output of information to the user. These two areas, while being susceptible to memory manipulation, get specific consideration for how to manipulate the information.

Manipulate Memory

The IA-32 ring structure provides a good protection to keep programs from accessing each other's memory. However, applications that run at ring 0 have access to all of memory, including all of ring 3. Having access to ring 0 allows an attacker to read the memory of all running programs.

Therefore, the goal of an attacker is to gain access to ring 0. Stated in the context of malware, if the infection mechanism gains access to ring 0 the attacker wins. It is possible that an infection mechanism working only in ring 3 can compromise an individual application, but for our purposes, we are considering only attacks in ring 0.

What runs in ring 0? The first, and major component, is the operating system itself. Certainly, it is possible to corrupt the operating system, but a simpler method is to install a driver. Drivers are the lifeblood of current operating systems. They allow the use of new hardware without a change to the entire operating system. The manufacturer of the hardware normally writes driver code. To perform properly, driver code normally runs in ring 0.

The attacker wants to corrupt the OS, corrupt an existing driver, or install a new driver. Any of these mechanisms allow the attacker access to ring 0. Once the attacker has access to ring 0, the attacker has access to memory. The attacker uses this memory access to read data allocated to the program.

For our sample application, the two items in memory that the malware wants access are either the password or the special number. If the malware gains access to the password, or the processed password, the malware can display the special number or modify the special number whenever the malware wishes to do so. After decryption, if the application keeps the special number in memory, the malware can search the application's memory and discover the special number.

These two attacks succeed due to the ability of the attacker to gain ring 0 access. In current systems, no mechanisms mitigate ring 0 access. The only successful defense is to ensure that nothing happens to the code running in ring 0.

Changing the Program

A related attack is for the attacker to manipulate memory and change how the program actually works. The attacker changes the op codes of the program such that the program no longer works properly. A common change is to alter the program so that it no longer makes the proper jump after evaluating the password. In this attack, the attacker does not learn the password and cannot masquerade as the true user. Instead, the program no longer works properly and treats invalid passwords as correct passwords. This attack can be somewhat mitigated by using various digital signature mechanisms on the program to ensure that no changes are made to the distributed program. These mechanisms are only as strong as the code that enforces the digital signature check, which normally consists of sections of code that run in ring 0. The signature check code itself then is susceptible to ring 0 attacks. Alternatively, one can attack the signature check code and then attack the program in question. This strategy is harder, but doable.

DMA Access

While ring 0 is the most likely place for an attack to occur, a totally separate mechanism provides access to memory. Direct Memory Access (DMA) allows a peripheral, like a PCI card, to directly access memory without any CPU involvement. The design point around DMA was to allow fast memory access to devices. It works very well. It also avoids any protections managed by the CPU. In fact, a DMA device has access to all of memory, making a DMA access similar to a ring 0 access. The attacker can manipulate the device to perform a DMA to the program's memory. The result of this attack is the same as if the attacker had access from ring 0.

An attack through DMA requires the attacker to convince the device to perform the memory access and to have the ability to communicate with the device to get the results of the memory access. This attack is very plausible.

Manipulate Input

Malware can obtain the password directly from the keyboard. Either the attack can corrupt the current ring 0 keyboard driver or it can insert a malicious keyboard driver in front of the normal keyboard driver.

Changing the Keyboard Driver

The first technique for corrupting the ring 0 keyboard driver is just a special case of memory manipulation; manipulate the current keyboard driver. The attacker would manipulate the driver such that in addition to performing the normal keyboard driver duties of accepting the keystrokes, the driver would send a copy of the keystroke to some other entity.

Chaining Keyboard Drivers

The second technique is to insert or *chain* a new keyboard driver that intercepts scan codes before sending the keystrokes to the real keyboard driver. The interception would send the keystrokes to some other entity.

Chaining drivers is a common occurrence and was a design feature of many of the original drivers. The underlying ability to chain must be a feature of each driver. In many ways, chaining is the easiest attack to perform. It provides the same information as manipulating the normal driver, but it is much easier to distribute and install. Since the information obtained through this technique is the same as the previous technique, the attacker still has to wade through all of the data, but the attacker does get the password.

Receiving Keystroke Entity

Using either of the previous two techniques, the malware intercepts the keystrokes and sends them to some other entity. The "other" entity could be a program running on the infected platform, or it could be a program running on another platform and the interception process sends the keystrokes across the Internet. The attacker might have to wade through lots of keystrokes to determine the password, but one easy mechanism to find the password is to parse the data looking for the user-ID. Once the user-ID is located, it is an easy matter to look at the keystrokes that occur directly after the user-ID. The password should be right there.

The result of the interception is the same; the attacker has access to the password. Once the attacker has knowledge of the password, the attacker can discover or change the special number at any time.

Reality of Keyboard Sniffers

An Internet search for "attack keyboard sniffer" yields over 45,000 hits. The term *keyboard sniffer* is description of the malware that intercepts keystrokes. Sniffer malware has come as greeting cards or programs to "watch your spouse." Some sniffer programs have stolen bank account numbers and bank passwords. The effectiveness of these sniffers has been outstanding with users losing information and money.

Manipulate Output

Malware that manipulates the output is trying to trick the user into entering the password into a program other than our application, to display the wrong special value, or to disclose the special value during the display.

Phishing

A phishing attack is where the attacker attempts to convince the user to perform a normal operation at the wrong time or location. An example would be creating a Web site using zero '0' instead of letter 'o' in the .com. Does one really notice the difference between .com and .c0m? The current font makes it obvious, but for many fonts, the difference is very subtle.

From the standpoint of the malware attacking our application, the phishing attack would be to display a fake screen asking the user to type in the password. Having the user type in the password to a fake application allows the fake application to forward the password on both to an outside entity and to the real program. The role of the outside entity is the same as in the keyboard sniffer attack, but here, the user kindly indicates what the password is by entering the password in the password field.

The malware must have knowledge of the application and of the display window that the application uses, but as the information is normally not a secret, it is an easy attack to mount.

A separate but related phishing attack is for the malware to display a false special value. In this attack, the malware has no knowledge of the real special value; the malware merely makes up a new special value and display the malware's guess of the special value. It's called a Denial Of Service (DOS) attack because the real user does not have use of the real special value.

Screen Scraping

Remembering how the display adapter takes information from the display buffer and mixes it to create the display information gives a hint on how the malware can obtain information. The malware locates the frame buffer, which is held in system memory, locates the special number display, and then "scrapes" the information from the display buffer. If the application displays the password on the display, the scrapping could obtain the password also.

Changing the Display Driver

Any of the previous techniques to obtain the information the malware could accomplish by changing the display driver. Just as the keyboard driver controls the input, the display driver controls the output. If the malware can corrupt the display driver, then the corrupted driver can perform phishing or screen scraping.

Reality of Output Manipulation

An Internet search for phishing yields almost 6 million hits. Some phishing schemes can fake Web sites, fake login screens, fake banks, and all sorts of phishing attacks. While mixing metaphors, phishing is a growth industry.

The Internet search for screen scraping results in 300,000 hits, with many of the Web sites offering how-to documents.

Attack Overview

Figure 4.1 illustrates the attacks in this chapter. Each of the arrows illustrates generically one of the attack vectors.

■ Arrow 1 shows an attack on the display screen through either a scrapper or manipulated driver.

■ Arrow 2 shows an attack on the keyboard driver

■ Arrow 3 shows an attack where the malware directly reads the memory of the application

■ Arrow 4 shows an attack where the malware manipulates the application and bypasses a yes/no decision

These attacks summaries are not an exhaustive list of all possible vulnerabilities. They are just examples to show the difficulties that the application has in attempting to protect itself.

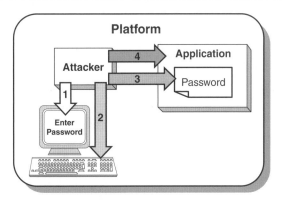

Figure 4.1   Attacks on an Application

Mitigating Attacks

Our application is under attack. We are losing control of both the special value and the application password. The attacks are coming through ring 0, with malware changing keyboard drivers, display adapters, the program itself, and through all sorts of other attack vectors. When the malware attacked our application previously, we were able to adjust the application and provide protections to the special value.

How does an application mitigate a problem with a keyboard driver? The application has no control of how the operating system installs and keeps track of drivers. If the driver is executing, it has access to ring 0 and has access to the sensitive data the application wants to protect.

No modifications are available that we can make to the application that provides ring 0 protection.

Hardware Mitigations

Without additional protections from the hardware and underlying software, our application is unable to protect itself. The purpose of a trusted platform is to provide the hardware and software necessary to enable the new levels of protection.

Our trusted platform, in order to mitigate the attacks, is going to have to protect the memory of the application from other applications, from ring 0, and DMA devices. The building blocks necessary to meet those challenges are the contents of the next few chapters.

Chapter 5

Elemental Groups

There is no logical way to the discovery of these elemental laws. There is only the way of intuition, which is helped by a feeling for the order lying behind the appearance.

—Albert Einstein

What are the elements of the trusted platform? Do the elements group somehow into blobs of like functionality? Can one even discover the underlying elements of the trusted platform?

Einstein, while talking about the physical world, was on to a very important point: sometimes you discover a law, or property, not by a logical investigation, but by a feeling that one is on the right path because things just feel right.

The elements of the trusted platform find themselves described as being an element or grouped together without an apparent logical basis or chain. We will not argue on some of them, but after discussing them and dealing with their effects on the trusted platform, we believe that these are the fundamental elements and that the groupings make sense.

Let us review, from Chapter 1, the definition of an element, where we state that an element is a functional area of the trusted platform. The example is that randomness is an element of the trusted platform. When one analyses this statement one sees that randomness is a vital and required function of a trusted platform. Security protocols require nonces to prove freshness, and key generation routines require random values to provide the appropriate level of uniqueness for a cryptographic key. Randomness has other uses on the trusted platform but one comes to the realization that without a functioning random number generator the trusted platform cannot be relied upon to perform correctly.

Element Purpose

While each element has a job to do, there has to be a rationale for including the function on the trusted platform. As it turns out, a very good rationale exists. Do you remember those attacks from Chapter 4, and the requirements to protect memory and other resources and tell the outside world about the protections in place? Well the ability to build the software that will meet those requirements is going to use the elements for their intended purpose.

To mitigate attacks, most solutions will use a combination of the elements. It is a rare problem that is directly and solely mitigated by a single element. Combining the elements to mitigate attacks is the job of the trusted platform architect and the software architects relying on the properties of the trusted platform.

Not every trusted platform will have the complete set of elements. Use models, costing, resource utilization, and other decisions will dictate that one platform not implement an element. Other platforms will decide that an element is critical and expand the resources expended to implement and instantiate the element.

Trusted Platform Elements

With the realization that there are elements to the trusted platform, let us list the elements we have identified.

- Evidence/Measurement – This element gives evidence of a static platform property or measures a dynamic component.
- Reporting/Attestation – This element distributes the evidence or measurement value to entities in a manner that allows the entity receiving the value an ability to verify the information.

- TCB Management – This element represents the ability of the platform owner to manipulate the workings of the trusted platform.

- Policy Engine – This element indicates that the trusted platform should rarely include a policy, but rather should be enforcing the policies set by the platform owner.

- PII Handling – This element indicates that the trusted platform does have Personal Identifying Information (PII) and the mechanisms of the trusted platform must appropriately handle the PII.

- Randomness – This element provides a source of uniqueness to the platform.

- Sequencing – This element provides the ability to put events into some order.

- Protected Storage – This element provides an area to store information with confidentiality and requiring some sort of authorization to use or view the stored information.

- Detection and Inspection – This element represents the ability to determine the integrity of executing platform components.

- Architectural Performance – This element indicates that platform designers must make various performance tradeoffs as they select the mix of elements on the platform.

- Isolation – This element provides the ability to separate one execution process and the resources assigned to the processes from all other processes and devices on the platform.

- Trusted Channel – This element provides the ability to connect two platform or external resources and provide integrity and potentially confidentiality to the data traveling on the connection.

- External Access – This element represents the ability to control the data flow both in and out of the trusted platform.

- Protected Execution – This element protects an executing process from corrupting itself.

The subsequent chapters will discuss each of the elements individually.

Element **Groups**

Just as elements are grouped together in the physical world, so too can the trusted platform elements be ordered into groups. Figure 5.1 shows the elements and their grouping.

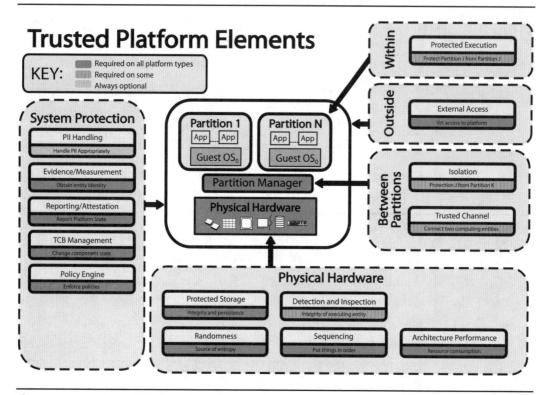

Figure 5.1   Trusted Platform Elements

In Figure 5.1, you see five groups:
- ■ System Protection
- ■ Internal Protection
- ■ Between Partitions
- ■ Outside
- ■ Inside

These groups represent an intuitive grouping, not a strictly logical grouping. Many have[1] argued about moving an element from one group to another or even about whether an element resides in more than one group. Most likely the individual is correct, but for now, and to keep the book flowing one has to accept the author's groupings[2].

If the groupings are "selected by feelings," as per Einstein, what good are they? The answer is that they provide a handle to hold on to when describing the elements. With 14 elements, trying to describe the elements quickly is very difficult. Explaining the five groups that the elements comprise is a somewhat easier task. Note that the previous sentence uses the word easier and not easy.

System Protections

The system protection group provides elements that deliver system protections visible to outside entities. The grouping is about an outward focus for the element. With an outward focus, the elements tend to have a richer API set, connections to the platform owner and/or user, and deal with more complex elements. Again, there is no reason to be hung up on the groupings, if you feel that an element in this group would be better placed in another feel free to think that way.

The list of elements in this group is:

- Evidence/Measurement
- Reporting/Attestation
- TCB Management
- Policy Engine
- PII Handling

The full description of each of these elements is in Chapter 6.

---

1   It should be noted that security architects are well known for, well, taking strong positions and sticking to their opinions. Certainly, the author is known as a very quiet person who would never argue with others regarding the esoteric placement of an element in on group or the other.

2   The author leaves it as an exercise for the reader to determine which element they would move from one group to another. It typically is easier to state that an element belongs in two groups rather then deleting the element from one and moving it to another.

Internal Protection

The internal protection group of elements is those elements that provide a base level of services for the trusted platform and other elements. The difference between system protections and internal protection is the focus of the elements, system protections tend to be outward focusing, management of the TCB, and so on, while internal protection tends to be inward focusing such as randomness.

- ■ Randomness
- ■ Sequencing
- ■ Protected Storage
- ■ Detection and Inspection
- ■ Architectural Performance

The full description of each of these elements is in Chapter 7.

Between Partitions

In the context of this description, a partition is set of assets assigned to an executing process. The process could be a complete operating system inside of a virtual machine, an isolated special purpose execution space or device, a hardware separation of processes, or any number of other types of asset collections. The point is that the trusted platform gathered the resources into a definable set and now wants to treat that set of resources differently from some other set of platform resources.

If a partition does exist then two elements would be necessary: the ability to isolate the resources of one partition from another and the ability to communicate between the two partitions.

- ■ Isolation
- ■ Trusted Channel

The full description of each of these elements is in Chapter 8.

Outside

The group only has one element, but the group still plays a vital role. Many people think of the boundary between the trusted platform and the outside world as a brick wall, nothing could be further from the truth. The wall is much more dynamic.

■ External Access

The full description of external access is in Chapter 9.

Inside

Inside represents a group with only one member, but still a very important conceptual group. The other elements focus on protection from outside influences, like trusted channel, or providing information like measurement, this group represents the elements that protect the process from hurting itself.

■ Protected Execution

The full description of each of these elements is in Chapter 9.

Chapter **6**

System Protection

"Security... it's simply the recognition that changes will take place and the knowledge that you're willing to deal with whatever happens."

—Harry Browne

It sure is fun searching the Internet looking for chapter quotes. Most likely, the work on this book would be quicker if there were no need to surf and look for quotes. This quote hits the nail on the head on what is necessary from a system protection standpoint. This group of elements attempts to mitigate the threats to the platform itself. These elements are very visible to outside entities and, in fact, provide the elements to communicate platform state to outside entities.

The elements in the system protection group are

- ■ Evidence/Measurement – The ability to collate information relative to the platform

- ■ Reporting/Attestation – The ability to tell others about the evidence collected regarding the platform

- ■ TCB Management – The ability to manage the Trusted Computing Base (TCB) of the platform

■ Policy Engine – The ability to enforce the policy wishes of the platform owner

■ PII Handling – The ability to manage Personal Identifying Information (PII)

Evidence

Trusted platforms do not exist in a vacuum, which is that other entities, locally or remotely, want "proof" that they can trust the platform. If the reader remembers any of the discussion from Chapter 1, they will remember the long discussion on trust. In fact, the TCG definition of trust is important to restate

> An entity can be trusted if it always behaves in the expected manner for the intended purpose. (TCG 2004)

The crux of that statement, for the purposes of evidence, is the word entity. An *entity* can be trusted… How does one identify the entity? Critically here if the identification is not exact, the ability to trust is not present. Think of the question like this: Program A, version 1 has a bug, and version 2 fixes the bug. Our trust statement works correctly as we state "Program A version 1 can be trusted to be vulnerable to exploit of the bug" and "Program A version 2 can be trusted to mitigate the bug." That works very well. What happens if we simply state "Program A can be…" and now we are unable to complete the sentence, as there is insufficient identification of the entity.

The evidence function of a trusted platform is there to provide sufficient identification to allow those wishing to trust the platform and the platform state the ability to make the trust decision. Evidence comes in multiple types and we are going to break down the types into three categories:

■ Properties – A property is a fixed capability of the platform that does not change over the life of the platform.

■ Measurement – A process of obtaining the identity of a platform function

■ Re-measurement – A process of determining that a previous measurement still represents the current state of the process

Properties

A fixed capability of the platform is a property. A property does not change over the life of the platform. A great example of a platform property is the chipset. After attaching the chipset to the platform, the chipset never changes.

Another example, and one that confuses people, is that the CPU is *not* a property of the platform. Why is that? The answer is that the CPU is normally a field replaceable unit (FRU). If someone on the platform can change the CPU then the CPU is not a platform property. When the CPU is a FRU, then the socket used to mount the CPU is a platform property. Moreover, the socket will limit the choices of CPU that can use the socket. The platform manufacturer can also put the CPU into the socket and "lock" the socket down such that the CPU is not a FRU. When the manufacturer does lock the CPU to the platform, the CPU does become a platform property.

Property Evidence

Once the manufacturer determines the platform properties, the manufacturer will want to leave some evidence of that property. Here the fixed nature of a property makes it somewhat easy for a manufacturer to generate the property evidence. The manufacturer makes a statement regarding the platform. For instance, a manufacturer might say platform XYZ makes use of the Intel® X48 Express Chipset. Now any entity wishing to rely on the platform, knows that the XYZ platform uses the Intel® X48 Express Chipset.

The manufacturer has a set of platform properties, what format does the manufacturer use to disseminate the properties? There are numerous choices and we will just cover the basic formats; more are possible. The formats we discuss are:

- Public statement – A public statement, like a press release, would state that platform XYZ is going to use the Intel X48 Express Chipset. For many uses, this evidence of a platform property is sufficient.

- Active Web content – Web content provides a digital mechanism that says platform XYZ has the Intel X48 Express Chipset. Providing the data in digital form allows automatic processing to occur. The automation of processing platform evidences is a critical step towards helping the relying party makes appropriate trust decisions.

There is an issue with active content: how does the party obtaining the information know that the content is fresh and accurate? The answer lies in the next format.

■ Digitally signed certificate – With a signed certificate the manufacturer provides both digital content and a way to evaluate the integrity of the statement.

Infrastructure Work Group

Providing the evidence regarding the platform is an extremely complex subject. The Trusted Computing Group (TCG) has a very active work-group, the Infrastructure Work Group (IWG), which deals with this topic extensively. The IWG provides specifications on the format of evidence, use of evidence, and the aggregation of platform properties. There will be more information regarding the IWG in the measurement section.

Manufacturer as the Evidence Designator

Using the term manufacturer in the above description is somewhat dis-ingenuous. As a platform moves from individual components to the final system presented to the user, numerous manufacturers are involved with the creation of platform properties. Any one of the manufacturing entities may wish to make generate some platform evidence. In fact the evidence may be additive, in that one manufacturer adds to a property created by a previous manufacturer. The work of the IWG considers this real life flow and allows for the addition and aggregation of platform evidence.

Measurements

Not everything that happens on the platform is a platform property; in fact, there are only a few platform properties and orders of magnitude more operating entities. These entities would include the operating system (OS), applications, installed hardware devices, really the vast majority of the "stuff" that makes up the trusted platform.

If the "stuff" is not a property, this implies that the "stuff" changes over the life of the platform. The idea of an OS changing fits into everyone's experience with an OS, on a very regular basis there are patches and upgrades available to the OS. The question then becomes how to differentiate between the various flavors of the OS, or really for any application on the trusted platform. We can differentiate by obtaining the exact identity, notice how that word identity from the statement of trust again is in use, of the entity in question. From the glossary, the term measure has the definition of taking a hash value of the entity. Therefore, if the trusted platform processes the bits of the entity a hash identity calculation is possible.

Roots of Trust. The trusted platform must provide some trustworthy processes. One could design a system where every single operation and component of the platform was trustworthy and all components always worked correctly in all combinations. The platform would cost millions, if not billions, and take years, if not decades, to build. The idea behind a trusted platform then is to create a small component, which is implicitly trusted, ensure that the small component gains control in a specified and controlled manner, and then allow the component to pass control to another platform component. While the small component, or root, has control, the root must measure the component that the root will pass control to. The ability to ensure that the root gains control at the appropriate moment is one of the critical requirements of a trusted platform.

A root has a very interesting property, which is that the root must work correctly or there is no trust. In addition to requiring the root to work correctly, as the root is implicitly trusted, the root is a property of the platform. While measurement then is a separate element, to start the measurement process, the root measurement function is a platform property. All platform properties require a statement of evidence, so the result is that the root requires a platform evidence statement. The discussion of attestation will pull all of these pieces of information together.

The platform has two types of measurement roots, the static and dynamic roots. Platforms must have a static root. The dynamic root is optional.

Static Root of Trust for Measurement. A static measurement occurs when the platform performs a platform reset. The definition of static is that the measurement occurs because of the reset and not due to any other event on the platform. The reset may be either from a no power situation or merely as the result of a reset request. The static measurement occurs when the reset mechanism ensures that a measurement is complete prior to passing control to any other component.

By way of example, the PC static Root of Trust for Measurement (RTM) is the BIOS boot block. The BIOS boot block is typically a very small section of code that does not change after the OEM ships the platform. The BIOS boot block would measure the components of the BIOS prior to actually passing control to the BIOS.

How the platform performs the boot process and instantiates the static RTM, is a critical platform property. The platform manufacturer must indicate how the RTM will function and what properties does the RTM have.

Dynamic Root of Trust for Measurement. A dynamic measurement occurs under control of a platform event that is not a platform reset. Dynamic measurements can occur numerous times without a platform reset. The example for a dynamic measurement is the Intel's TXT SENTER process. Each time SENTER executes the hardware performs a measurement of the Measured Launch Environment (MLE). Chapter 16 covers the SENTER process in detail.

The existence of a dynamic RTM is, just as the static RTM, a critical platform property that requires evidence of measurement capability. It is possible, and in fact very desirable, that the platform have more than one dynamic RTM.

What to Measure

What does the measurement process measure? The flippant answer would be whatever the RTM is pointing at, and in reality the flippant answer turns out to be the technical answer also. What is necessary is that the measuring agent has complete control of the target entity when performing the measurement. To illustrate the control issue think of a carpenter attempting to measure a board to cut. The carpenter makes sure the board is stable and uses a tape measure. If the board is loose and moving around on the ground the ability to get an accurate measurement is very difficult. The same holds true when measuring for identity. If the target is able to roll around, the quality of the measurement suffers greatly.

Executable Programs

When measuring a program the measurement occurs on the image of the program prior to loading the program into memory. The reason for performing the measurement on the disk image is the result of the load process creates a unique program image. The uniqueness comes from the "fix-up" of memory addresses in the program. If the program loads at location 0x5000 the jumps and references will be different than if the program loads at location 0x6000.

One of the goals of measurement is to obtain the identity of the measured entity. If the measurement value changes on each invocation, there is no way to relate to outside observers with a unique measurement. Measuring prior to the fix-ups then allows the measurement process to obtain the same measurement for each measurement invocation.

How Many Items to Measure

From the standpoint of any RTM, the RTM only measures one entity. After the RTM measures the component, the RTM passes control to the measured entity. There is a one to one correspondence between the measured entity and the RTM. The RTM only measures one entity and the entity only has one RTM that is capable of performing the measurement.

The platform has many more items that require measurement; those additional measurements are the subject of Chapter 14.

Re-measurement

The process of ensuring that a measured entity retains integrity as the entity executes is a re-measurement. Re-measurement is a function of evidence, but re-measurement also stands alone as a special function of the trusted platform. For this reason, re-measurement is a separate element of the trusted platform. The element re-measurement is described in more detail in Chapter 7.

Threats to Evidence

Threats to evidence are especially pernicious to the assurance of a trusted platform. If the gathered evidence is not accurate, then the platform cannot be trusted.

> The threat to evidence is when an attacker can create some evidence that does not reflect the current state of the platform.

If the attacker creates evidence that does not reflect the current platform state, the trust decision is invalid. As the evidence forms the base of the trust decision, invalid data removes the bedrock that forms the basis of the decision.

Threats to evidence can be very difficult to discover, as many times there is no mechanism to validate the evidence. Remember, evidence is a property of the platform, and a property just "is." For a concrete example consider the static RTM. The static RTM is the component that first gains control when the platform comes out of reset. No other component can measure the RTM as nothing else is executing. If one tries to measure AFTER the RTM executes than a corrupt RTM could "fix" itself up so that it looks like a good RTM and there would be no way to discover the RTM changing itself.

With the seriousness of evidence threats understood, we can now list a few of them. This list is not all-inclusive and does not purport to indicate specific threats for a specific platform; rather they represent generic attacks that are possible when dealing with evidence.

Forgery

If the attacker can forge some evidence, then those looking at the platform have an incorrect view of the platform properties. Forgeries are very disruptive if they are successful.

If the attempt is to forge a platform property, the attempt to forge is going to focus on the distribution mechanism. If the platform evidence comes from a public statement, that is difficult for the attacker to change. If the evidence is some digital content on the Web, that is very easy to change. If the evidence is signed digital content, that is difficult to change.

When forging a measurement the attacker has two potential attack paths, the measuring agent or the target. If the measuring agent is the RTM, then the attack involves breaking a platform property. We hope that breaking a platform property is difficult. If the attacker is attempting to change the target, then the defenses are the ability of the RTM to control and measure.

Distribution

If the attacker is unable to forge the evidence, they may attempt to change the reporting of the evidence. In this attack, the attacker gets in the way between the source and destination and manipulates the evidence as it travels. Protecting against this attack is a separate platform element, reporting.

Reporting

After having gathered some evidence, properties or measurements, the trusted platform now has to provide the evidence to those wishing to rely on the information. The reporting of the values breaks into two basic choices, report or attestation. A report presents evidence, typically platform properties, unaltered or verified directly to the requestor. Attestation presents evidence in a manner where the recipient can verify the source and integrity of the evidence.

From the description, it would appear that a report is not very useful and that most uses will perform attestation. Appearances can be very deceptive and while attestation is very useful, a simple report has many uses.

Report

The report presents evidence unaltered or verified. What does unaltered mean? When discussing reporting, unaltered means that whatever evidence is present, the trusted platform merely sends out when requested to by a platform verifier.

Remember our platform properties where the manufacturer produces a digitally signed statement of what the properties are. In this case, the signed statement presents a great piece of evidence to merely report. The verification is already inherent in the document; it has a digital signature from the manufacturer. The platform has nothing to add to the document, the document stands on its own; unaltered or verified, the trusted platform reports the manufacturer's evidence.

Another use of a report is when the user of the platform checks to see if the report of evidence is the same as the last time the user checked. This report is normally of a measured item on the platform. The best example here is a report on the BIOS to the user. If the BIOS measurement is the same as the previous report, the user knows that the BIOS is unchanged. The trusted platform does not verify the report, but as the user has prior knowledge, the report is very valuable.

Attestation

The key property of the report is that it is unverified. Those receiving the report have no way to validate the integrity of the report. Attestation changes that to provide a verifiable report. A dictionary definition of attestation is:

Something which bears witness, confirms or authenticates

The ability to bear witness and confirm is the exact property we want. With the platform having pieces of evidence, those wishing to rely on the trusted platform want some way to verify the evidence. Chapter 14 provides a deeper dive into attestation and the mechanisms in use to provide attestation.

Threats to Reporting

Reporting is all about getting information from one point to another. As such, the threats to reporting look very much like threats to any communication channel. We cover a couple of the high-level threats here but the complete discussion and in-depth mitigations are in Chapter 14.

Changing the Report

If the attacker can intercept the report and change the contents, then the recipient will not trust the information. The easiest way to fix this issue is to use attestation.

Denial of Service

The threat here is that the attacker blocks the sending of the report or the receipt of the report. Such threats are difficult to mitigate. Many of the mitigations depend on the channel through which the report travels. If the trusted platform receives a request for a report, the request can require a response and the trusted platform can direct the response to the requestor.

While denial of service attacks are available for almost every element of the trusted platform, the denial of service on reports is one element where attempts to mitigate some of the threats are very valuable. The reason is that without the report, there is no information to make a trust decision, and without the trust decision, there is no trust.

Trusted Computing Base Management

The trusted computing base (TCB) is all of the elements, technologies, and services that the user of the platform requires trust in. Note due to the Grandma Permission discussion[1], what the manufacturer thinks is in the TCB may be very different from what the user sees as being the TCB. No matter what the boundaries of the TCB are, the TCB needs management. That is there will be control knobs to turn, switches to set, variables to fill in, and all sorts of other decisions. These control options represent critical pieces of information that represent the current state of the platform. Even more importantly, they represent ways to control the state of the platform.

With these controls being so important it becomes an important platform element as to how the controls are set. For example, consider a switch on a platform element that enables or disables the element. Certainly knowing the status of the switch is important, but just as important is how and when the switch can change. If the switch is held on one platform in the registry of the platform with no protections and on another platform behind a cryptographic mechanism, which platform better controls the TCB? Well the answer is certainly the one with a cryptographic mechanism. It is certainly true that given a certain use case, the registry mechanism may be sufficient for some, but as a rule, the cryptographic mechanism is stronger.

Number of Control Points

The desire, from a user standpoint, will be a single control point for all of the TCB elements. Having dozens of control mechanisms makes knowing what is happening on the platform very difficult to understand. In addition, numerous control points can also make it possible for one control to affect another control, sometimes in a manner that is not readily apparent.

The other side of the argument is that it is difficult to get all platform elements, technologies, and services to agree on a single control structure. In fact given that many of the technologies and services come from different manufacturers with widely different views of what is and is not a control point, a single control mechanism is really a Holy Grail[2]. There will be multiple control points.

---

1   Grandma decides what she needs to trust the platform, see Chapter 1

2   While many of the readers will relate to Indiana Jones searching for the Holy Grail, the author's generation may think of the Grail search more in line with discussions of swallows and air speed velocity.

Threats to TCB Management

Threats to TCB management revolve around changing the settings of the control knob, or having a control knob affect some other element.

Changing the Knob

The major threat to a control knob is that some entity changes the knob to a new value. If correct operation depends on an element being on and the attacker can turn the element off, the knob is not providing any benefit but rather is providing an attack point.

The way to mitigate this threat is to provide a control mechanism that validates the authenticity of the change request. Do not assume that validate means a password. It is possible to use hardware jumpers, special bus cycles, or other platform mechanisms to authenticate.

Side Effects

While side effects show up on an operational platform, the real mistake occurs in the design of the trusted platform. To illustrate how this works consider two platform elements, one a secure storage area and the other a mechanism that provides cryptographic services. The obvious design of this platform would use the secure storage area to store the keys for the cryptographic service. If the storage area is assumed, and it is always a bad idea to assume, to always be present by the cryptographic service, then turning off the storage area forces the cryptographic service to store keys in an unprotected area. What should happen is that the design of the platform should tie the two services together such the state of one affects the state of the other. Failure to do this represents a vulnerability that attackers may find a way to exploit in a fielded system.

Policy Engine

TCB management just made the claim that there will be numerous settings for the various technologies and services on the platform. When you combine a single setting for each of the control points, you have defined a specific policy. All of the elements in a trusted platform combine to form a policy engine that enforces the defined policy. Given the number of control points on a platform, the specific policy that the platform is enforcing could be very simple or very complex. Chapter 18 has more details on policies in use on the trusted platform.

Difference between Engine and Policy

The terms policy engine and policy area going to be very prevalent in this section, they have to be that is the section subject. To ensure that you, the reader, do not get lost, we carefully describe an engine and an associated policy.

Policy Engine

The engine is the mechanism that reads, understands, and enforces a policy. A concrete example is control register three (CR3) that controls paging on Intel® Core™ Duo processors. The hardware, our policy engine, does not care[3] which memory address is in use, the OS can pick one address for one invocation of the OS and an entirely different address the next time OS runs. The OS can decide based on current operating requirements the best location for the base CR3 address. The hardware does not care; the hardware just uses the CR3 address to start the paging mechanism.

Policy

The policy for a policy engine is the settings the engine must enforce. Sometimes a policy is obviously a policy, like a statement in an application that "if A is true, the application configures the platform to do Y". Most platform observers would consider the previous statement a policy. However, look back at our policy engine example, if an OS sets different CR3 addresses based on current operating state, the OS is using a policy also.

It is simple to take each one of these individual policies and understand how the platform is working. What becomes difficult is that an outside observer is going to want to know the "combined" policy the platform is enforcing. That is to say, the observer wants to know ALL of the settings, for ALL of the policy engines. In addition, the observer wants these policy statements in a format

---

3   Within some basic requirements like page boundaries and size

that the observer can consume. This is not easy. Chapter 18 covers policy in a much greater depth.

Policy Measurement

The important point is to recognize that the platform is enforcing a policy. Outside entities are going to want to know policy the platform is enforcing. This implies that one of the jobs of the platform is to provide ways to measure the control decisions. The entire set must be measured and reportable by the reporting mechanism.

A concrete example of this is to consider a hypervisor that is managing some virtual machines. The hypervisor will have settings that indicate when the hypervisor instantiates more virtual machines, the maximum number of virtual machines, the communication paths between the virtual machines, and which input and output ports the hypervisor monitors. Next, we will assert that the choices are all the same except for the input and output ports the hypervisor monitors. Now we assert that policy set 1 does not monitor I/O port 42, and policy set 2 does monitor 42. If an attack uses port 42, then policy 1 is vulnerable and policy 2 is not. Therefore, the measurements that the trusted platform performs on the hypervisor must include the I/O port settings. Going back to our trust decision, those wishing to rely on this platform, knowing that policy 1 represents a vulnerability, have to consider is the vulnerability exploitable. If the trust decision determines that policy 1 represents an exploitable vulnerability, the decision will be that a platform that is enforcing policy 1 is not trustworthy.

Fixed Policies

As policies represent what the trusted platform is enforcing, choice appears to be a critical element. When creating a trusted platform the designer has to make some very hard decisions regarding control points.

Figure 6.2 illustrates this problem very well. The choice is to provide flexibility or remove complexity. Flexibility allows the trusted platform to support a wide range of policies and fit the needs of a wider range of customers. Complexity makes it much harder to understand the policy and all of the potential policy intersections. Complexity also adds additional attack points. How does the platform designer make the choice?

Figure 6.1   Flexibility versus Control

The platform designer needs to understand the target user very well. If the user works in a wide variety of environments, with different levels of security and trust, the design should lean towards flexibility. If the user works in a very constrained environment, with limited levels of security and trust, the design should lean towards less complexity.

Default Policies

One place where it is very important for the platform designer to make a choice is the default policy. The default policy is policy that the platform designer sets when the platform owner makes no selection at all.

Default Secure

One choice the platform designer can make is to default to a secure state. By selecting this option, the platform, out of the box, operates securely. A default secure policy requires a positive action by the user to change the option. If the user never changes anything then when the policy needs to be enforced the enforcement is towards security.

Consider the encryption of a message and an error in the middle of the encryption. If the default is secure, then it would stop the sending the message. The user would have to perform some operations to restart the conversation and resend the message.

Default Open

The other choice available to the platform designer is to default to an open system. Here the default property is to make things work smoothly for the user. Errors lead to a downgrade in security, not a blocked operation.

In our encrypted message example, an error in the middle of the encryption would result in the system sending the message in the clear and not require any action by the user.

Which Is Better?

It would be nice to state that default secure is the best way to go at all times. Unfortunately, that statement is only true from a security standpoint. Sometimes it is more important to get the job done.

The author has met this issue many times and believes that the best answer is that a default policy of default secure is only viable when policies are easy and in use that take precedence over the platform default. If there is no guarantee that user defined policies will be in place, then it is better to default to open and not cause undo operational issues for the user. The author knows that many security professionals will be saying that cannot be right, but it is normally better to sell a product than have a secure product sit on the shelf.

Threats to Policy

Threats to policy revolve around either an incorrect policy engine or reporting one policy and enforcing another. While those seem like the same, they have a slight functional difference.

Incorrect Policy Engine

Here the policy engine is enforcing the wrong policy. The policy engine reads the policy directive and acts in a manner inconsistent with the directive. For instance, the policy says turn a component on and the policy engine leaves the component off.

This is a very serious threat, because to the outside world it appears that the component is on when it really is off. The attacker has to change the policy engine or the policy engine must have a fault for this to be a viable threat.

Enforce Wrong Policy

In this instance, the policy engine thinks it is working with policy A, when it really is working with policy B. This threat means that the attacker is changing the policy after the policy engine measured the policy and reported that it was enforcing policy A.

While this appears to be the same as an incorrect policy engine, and from a result aspect they look the same, the attack is very different. The reason why is what the attacker changed. For the incorrect policy the attacker changes the policy engine to do the wrong thing, with enforcing the wrong policy the attacker changes the policy itself.

Depending on implementations, either attack may be easier on a specific system.

Privacy Considerations

The trusted platform has unique identifiers on the platform. The reporting element normally has some form of cryptographic key to report verifiable information. Other elements may also include unique identifiers. The trusted platform must appropriately handle these unique identifiers. For the reporting element, the typical implementation uses the Trusted Platform Module (TPM). The details are in Chapter 14.

The other elements though must decide how to handle any uniqueness that they include. What is interesting is the wide range of potentially identifying information.

Coverage

While it would be fun to write an entire book on privacy, many others have. This book is not going to be a complete treatise on each element, but rather an overview. With that in mind, the author will not cover the normal aspect of privacy, which is the use and protection of Personal Identifying Information (PII) but rather on some other issues that illustrate some of the underlying issues that a trusted platform can create.

Location Aware

One feature that a trusted platform may implement is the ability to locate the trusted platform in the physical world. Many technologies can provide the physical location; one of the simplest is the identity of the wireless access port that is providing access to the Internet. The author regularly connects to the Internet at the Portland International Airport, which reports your location to give you a quick reference to the nearest gates and services available. That is a wonderful service for someone new to the airport, but for Portland[4], the author has the location of all of the power outlets memorized.

Is the location of the platform a "privacy" concern? It can be if the information is available to others. If the only entity with knowledge of which wireless access port the author is using is the author, then the knowledge is of no concern, but what if the information becomes evidence, from our discussion in this chapter on evidence, and verifiably reported to outside entities? Is the fact that the author is in the airport a concern? To thieves willing to break into homes, knowledge of who is sitting in the airport might be very interesting. Note also that for a thief to be able to take advantage of this information, the thief has to be able to correlate the platform knowledge into personal knowledge. And that is the crux of when information regarding the trusted platform becomes personal. It is the ability to correlate benign technical information with personal information. The trusted platform designer has to understand the correlation of technical evidence to platform user.

Control

The discussion on location aware highlights is two important concepts; the trusted platform must control technical information and the user must control the reporting of platform evidence. The trusted platform should provide the necessary information to help the user of the trusted platform make rationale decisions regarding the evidence the trusted platform collects. Security is an area where the individual's ability to control the environment and exercise their choices has to be combined with education and supported by product

---

4   Actually, the author has the location of power outlets memorized in many airports, and no, he will not reveal those locations.

configurations (such as opting in) which enable informed decisions. In this manner, the users of technology can make choices that enhance the functionality of the platform, while minimizing the security risks and vulnerabilities.

Personal Data

It goes without saying, but the author will say it any way, that direct PII, like name or passport number, needs tight controls. The trusted platform, when it has access to PII, must allow user control of the PII. What is difficult, from the trusted platform viewpoint, is the designation of PII. Few, if any, CPU designs require the passport number of the user. In fact, the design of the CPU requires no information from the user. Certainly, software operating on the trusted platform may need the passport number, but the basic components will normally not use those values.

The basic components of the platform will however have technical information that does provide evidence. The use of that evidence can be an issue and that is why the reporting of evidence is under user control.

User Choice

Whenever the trusted platform reports evidence, the user must be able to control the dissemination of the evidence. First, the user must be able to opt-in to evidence reporting, that is the platform will not report any evidence to any outside entity without the platform owner first explicitly enabling the reporting element. Second, the user must be able to control the reporting element to turn it on and off depending on circumstances. Lastly, the user should be able to determine and filter requests from outside entities to request evidence. When the reporting element is internal to the TPM, then these controls are present.

Opt-In

As mentioned in the previous section, those elements that are privacy sensitive must be opt-in. To reiterate opt-in means that the platform owner must explicitly enable the reporting of platform evidence. The collection of platform evidence may occur without explicit opt-in, if there is no way to verify the reported evidence.

Privacy Guidelines

Privacy guidelines are available that can guide the design and implementation of elements that can affect user privacy. These guidelines include, but are not limited to, The OECD Guidelines, the Fair Information Practices, and the European Union Data Protection Directive (95/46/ECD).

Threats to Privacy

The basic threat to privacy is to have PII or platform evidence reported to outside entities without the platform owner's knowledge or approval. The attacker wants to access the information or bypass the blocks to using the information. If the attacker is successful then the platform owner may be susceptible to misuse of their identity.

In truth, all of the trusted platform elements combine to provide the protection and control of the PII. It is not a simple single control that controls the PII; rather, it is the interlocking set of all of the elements that combine to mitigate the threats to exposure of the PII.

Chapter 7

Internal Protection

Frylock: [after placing Carl's head on the machine] I give you the ultimate in military hardware! Complete with laser cannon, indestructible titanium exoskeleton, and motion activated plasma pulse rifles.

— Aqua Teen Hunger Force[1] (2000)

Frylock is talking about the latest in military hardware, here we are talking about the latest trusted platforms. Given that Frylock is in a movie, we have a high degree of confidence that the hero or villain will bypass any protection on the use of these wonderful weapons and further the plot of the movie. The trusted platform also requires some internal protection elements to help the trusted platform accomplish the role of protecting data.

The elements in this group provide services to users of the trusted platform but also to the other elements. The perfect example of this is randomness: while the platform user can and will take advantage of random variables, the other elements such as reporting rely on randomness to function correctly.

The elements of this group are:

- Randomness
- Sequencing
- Protected Storage

---

1 Nope, I haven't seen this one either but another great movie quote. And notice how I really do get it to fit into what the chapter is discussing.

■ Detection and Inspection
■ Architectural Performance

Randomness

All trusted platforms execute cryptographic operations or need to establish a shared secret with another entity. At the heart of all these operations is the ability to generate random numbers. As computing platforms are deterministic in nature, generating randomness— which is essentially a nondeterministic process—is a particularly difficult task to do correctly. Telling a bad random number from a good random number is a difficult thing to do. While it seems like a simple thing to find randomness, it is in fact a very difficult problem. John von Neumann said it best:

> Anyone who considers arithmetical methods of producing random digits is, of course, in a state of sin.

So how does the trusted platform keep itself from dropping into a state of sin? There are mounds of paper and slides with descriptions of how to create a random number generator (RNG). The trusted platform does not care about the *how* of the RNG implementation, just that an RNG *exists*.

RNG Implementation

One very good place to obtain information on RNG implementations is the NIST Random Number Generation Technical Working Group (RNG-TWG). The home page for the working group is http://csrc.nist.gov/groups/ST/toolkit/rng/index.html

Number of RNG

Once the platform has a single source of randomness that source should be sufficient for all trusted platform uses. In a perfect world that would be true. Trusted platforms do not exist in a perfect world; they exist in a world where threats are real.

Software Attacks

If the trusted platform is defending against software attacks, then a single RNG on the platform is sufficient if the RNG and use of the RNG have strong isolation. The rationale is this: if the RNG isolation keeps any other software process from seeing the results of the RNG, the next random value, and the delivery of the random value to the software process requesting the value has strong isolation, then all uses of the RNG have isolation from software attacks.

The isolation requirement is very strong here as without isolation then the attacking software process has the potential to discover the supposedly secret random value.

Hardware Attacks

If the trusted platform is attempting to mitigate hardware attacks then a single source of randomness is most likely insufficient. The rationale comes from how one mitigates hardware attacks across busses or other hardware devices, via encryption.

To make this very simple, consider two devices residing on the same platform with a bus connecting the two devices, where all traffic on the bus is extremely easy to read using inexpensive logic analyzers. The obvious first choice to mitigate that attack is encrypting the traffic between the two devices. However, encryption requires keys and a key establishment protocol. Many of the key establishment protocols require the use of random values and many of the protocols require a source of randomness at both ends of the protocol. If there is only one RNG on the platform, how does one mitigate the hardware attacks with encryption? The answer is that one does not try; it is easier to have multiple RNG on the platform and use the randomness from each of the sources to establish channels between the various devices.

Threats to Randomness

Certainly, an attacker may guess the random value if the RNG implementation is not correct. However, if the RNG is implemented correctly, then an attacker getting say 20 values prior to and after the random value gains no information by keeping track of the sequence either before or after the requested value. The lack of threat with knowledge of values previously emitted by the RNG is a basic property of an RNG and any properly executing RNG will exhibit this property.

Mechanism Attacks

The RNG is using some source of entropy on the platform. If the attacker can change that source, the RNG may not function properly. Robust RNG design will take into account the possibility that the entropy source may degrade over time or for short periods. A good example would be a temperature sensor. The RNG may only work when the temperature is within a specific range and the attacker could attempt to make the platform too hot or cold such that the sensor no longer detected changes.

Mechanism attacks have one important requirement: because they are physical attacks, the attacker must have physical control or possession of the platform to mount the attacks.

Software Attacks

Attacks on the RNG by software processes are really an example of attempts by software to break isolation. If the isolation, or separation of one process from another, works correctly, then software will not have access to the RNG values.

Persistent Storage

The definition of the platform includes the word trusted. One intended purpose of the trusted platform is the ability to keep a piece of data confidential. In other words, keep a secret. A more accurate description is that for some data the policy is to maintain confidentiality of the data and that the trusted platform properly enforces the confidentiality requirement. The requirement for confidentiality includes the requirement that the data must remain confidential even when the platform is powered down. The power requirement places requirements on both the storage mechanism and the access mechanism to the storage location.

Some data, in addition to the confidentiality requirement, has the requirement for availability. The data must persist and resist denial of service attacks. The simplest storage mechanisms are the traditional disk drives. By encrypting the content, the device can meet the confidentiality requirement. However, when adding persistence and availability requirements, the disk drive does not always meet the requirements of persistence and availability. It is difficult to ensure that no entity can erase a sector on the disk drive. Losing the sector could result in the loss of significant data. To meet the persistence and availability requirements the inclusion of nonvolatile memory on the platform is normally required. A dedicated disk drive that requires no driver would meet the requirement, as would various types of flash memory.

There is a minimum of two distinct users for persistent storage. The first distinct user is the set of services on the platform. The services keep encryption keys and other such data in the persistent storage location. The second user is the set of platform capabilities themselves. This use of the persistent storage is not visible to users of the platform and in fact requires that users have no visibility or access to the storage location. An example of this type of persistent storage would be the insertion of a key in use to tie two hardware components together with a trusted channel not visible to any outside observer.

Threats to Persistent Storage

The major threat to persistent storage is if the storage is not persistent. If one depends on a value being available and attempts to read the value but cannot, this is a serious flaw. Now one has to be careful here as a successful attack against the persistent storage area may include the use of a hammer to crush the device. Certainly, no one expects the device to survive that type of attack[2]. But realistically, it is important for the persistent storage area to resist attempts by software entities to delete or modify information in the care of the persistent store.

Sequencing

The act of putting things into some order is a basic computing necessity. The trusted platform adds the requirement that there are no methods of spoofing the sequencing. From a trusted platform standpoint, sequencing comes in three flavors: monotonic counter, tick counter, and trusted time.

---

2   Well maybe some defense agencies would like that level of protection, but that type of protection is very expensive. And if you thought that 500-dollar hammers were expensive wait till you see how expensive the hammer resistant devices are.

Monotonic Counter

A monotonic counter is the digital counterpart to the odometer on an automobile. The monotonic counter always increases and never decreases[3]. The counter value increases upon receipt of the command to increment. The monotonic nature of the count provides assurance that one event occurs after the other as the associated count is larger. What the monotonic counter does not provide is an indication of how much time passed between events. All that observers know is that the event associated with count value 2 occurred after the event associated with count value 1. There is no way to determine if 1 second or 1 year elapsed between the two events.

Tick Counter

The tick counter increments based upon a set frequency. The frequency could be very fast as in milliseconds or much slower as in seconds or minutes. The tick counter metadata must describe the frequency.

The first inclination is that a tick counter is a source of trusted time, but the inclination is incorrect. The tick counter is close but not quite a trusted time source. Notice that the tick counter increments according to a set frequency. There is no guarantee of interruption of the tick counter nor is there any guarantee of synchronization with a time source.

The requirement for the tick counter is that it must continue to increment according to the set frequency only as long as power is available. If power is lost, the tick counter will reset. When the counter resets and power is again available, the counter starts at zero and starts counting again. If the counter only had the count value, then a reset would allow for reuse of a count value and loose the ability to sequence. To avoid that problem when the counter resets and starts again at zero the tick counter mechanism associates a nonce with the tick counter. When using a tick count value the user must use both the count and the nonce. As the nonce is random, there is a mechanism to differentiate between two different tick counts of 10. A common name for the nonce is the tick era, indicating which era to associate the tick count with.

There are protocols that associate the tick count to an actual wall clock time. The association can occur at any time and associates a nonce and current tick count with a wall clock time. After this association occurs any

---

3   In the automobile case the only decreases occur with an unscrupulous used car dealer

entity can take the tick counter and determine when the count started, or what the real time was when the tick counter was at zero, and what the current time is according to the tick count.

The crux here is that when power is lost and the nonce is lost the association with real time is lost and cannot be recovered until there is a new nonce, a new tick count starts at 0, and some entity associates the tick count and nonce with real time.

Trusted Time

The synchronization of the tick counter to real time is a very desirable feature. Trusted time provides an automatic mechanism that performs the synchronization each time the tick counter resets to zero. The synchronization requires access to a real time source. This synchronization can be provided for in one of two basic ways: either include in the design the ability to connect, via the Internet, to a known time source, or include a time source in the product

The connection via the Internet works well as long as the platform has the ability to access the network. Trusted platforms may not execute in an always-connected environment. It is a platform designer decision to determine if the level of access is appropriate for the expected platform use.

The inclusion of a time source would be very expensive. The design includes both reliable power and high quality counters, like oscillation. The author really does not recommend this solution unless the platform designers want to charge a lot of money for the platform. This type of design will only make sense for customers who have lots of money to spend.

Sequencing Threats

Each of the three sequencers has some specific threats.

Monotonic Counter

The goal of an attacker against a monotonic counter is to reset the counter back to a previous value. If the attacker can perform a roll back, those relying on the counter will believe that certain events did not occur. The easiest way to understand this is to consider an application that is only going to perform an operation 10 times. The application uses a counter to count the number of operations. If the attacker uses the application 10 times and then rolls the counter back, the attacker can perform the operation as many times as they wish.

Tick Counter

The threats to a tick counter involve the two main features, the timing ticks and the nonce.

If the attacker can change the interval between the timing ticks, the counter runs either fast or slow. Changing the interval would normally involve some sort of hardware attack to change the basic property of the counter frequency. Possible mechanisms would include extreme heat or extreme cold.

If the attacker can reuse a previously used tick era by inserting a previously used nonce, the attacker can masquerade the new count as occurring at some other then when the event really occurs. This type of attack is very serious when the tick counter is in use for an audit service. If the tick nonce comes from the RNG, then the attacks have to find a way to corrupt the RNG, which should be a very difficult problem.

Inspection and Detection

In Chapter 13, where we consider attestation, there is an interesting discussion regarding the time delta between when a measurement occurs and when the attestation occurs. This gap could be quite large: consider a server that boots and runs for several years without a reboot. The question one might very well ask is, if the measurement taken at the time of boot was accurate, how do I know that the system maintains the integrity of the measured environment?

In the absence of any other facility the answer to the question is that one must depend on the protections of the platform to maintain the integrity of the measured environment. That is a hard answer to those wishing to place a very high level of trust on the trusted platform.

The solution to this problem is to reduce the time from measurement to reporting. One could re-launch the environment, but operationally that does not match the way people use systems. The answer comes from the ability to inspect and detect current integrity status.

Remeasurement

Remember from Chapter 6 the description of the Root of Trust for Measurement (RTM) and how the RTM measured some entity. We measured the entity when RTM preformed the job, hence it should be a simple task to just measure again, right? Well, no. The issue here is what to measure. The typical launch time measurement works on the disk image or file to load. There is a good reason for this. If you measure a file, then every time you measure it you obtain the exact same result, unless someone changed the file. That is the property one is looking for when dealing with attestation and reporting.

But once an entity is loaded and executing, it does not look the same from moment to moment much less day to day. The reason is how a program works, there are calling stacks, variables, load address, parameters, and all sorts of other pieces of information. Remember that with a cryptographic hash, a single bit change changes the entire output. If the program is changing many values moment to moment then there is no consistent answer.

Inspection

The first part of our remeasurement job is to perform an inspection, in this we mean obtain information from the target that allows the detection portion to make an integrity decision. What could be easier than reading memory? The reality is that this is not an easy thing to accomplish. The ability to read the target's resources are not a function of simply reading that address, because the system may be blocking access to that address. In addition, the architecture must ensure the separation of the target from the watcher; otherwise, there is the potential of an attack on the target that removes the ability to determine integrity.

The best example of the problems surrounding inspection is this one. Consider a target that has built up a secure wall around itself. No information passes in or out without direct handling by the target. Now if the inspection process by the watcher is under control of the target, then an attack on the target simply returns the "right" information to the watcher and there is no way to determine the true integrity of the target. We have then come to the requirement that the watcher needs unfettered access to the target. We just spent all of the time and effort to build a secure wall and now we want to drill a hole in the wall. In fact, we want the hole such that it reveals the most critical portions of the target, those areas that control the protections of the target. We have hole in the wall and we want to have one and only one entity make use of the hole. The issues of how to do inspection all revolve around how to drill the hole in the protections of the target.

Detection

Unlike inspection, with all of its platform-specific procedures, detection is generic; it works for all entities. That is to say, detection is generic for a specific target. The detection process for one application will most likely not work for a different application.

An example here should illustrate the issue. If we are trying to determine the integrity or a running operating system, the checks are going to look at certain modules, tables, pointers, threads, and other internal OS states. It seems very difficult to believe that a generic OS integrity checker will know the difference between Windows XP SP2, Windows Vista, and Linux. The information coming in by way of the inspection allows the detection mechanism to follow the tables and pointers in the OS to get a warm fuzzy feeling that things are okay.

Yes, you read that right; it is only a warm fuzzy feeling[4]. There is no way to check, on any reasonable schedule, the complete integrity of the target. Any target that is over 10 or 205 lines of code is going to start getting so complex all hope is lost of providing a rigorous answer. The answer is a heuristic. If these structures are intact, if this module is unchanged, and if these pointers are correct, then you assume the rest of the target is still functional. It may not be true but it is much better than having no information at all.

In the future with these services being available to applications and OS architects and developers, it is possible to conceive of targets that are capable of segregating integrity-critical information into an easily checked bundle. In this case, very complex targets could return a viable yes or no answer to the question of integrity.

---

4   For those who do not know the meaning of the term warm fuzzy it comes the contentment that one feels when things are all right, kind of like being a small child and wrapped up in your favorite blanket, that wonderful feeling of warm and security. It may have no basis in fact, but once you have the warm and fuzzy feeling things just seem better.

5   Fine, maybe that is hyperbole but hopefully you get the point—any reasonable sized application is going to be too complex to come up with a guaranteed yes or no the target has integrity.

The Watcher

The watcher combines the inspection and detection processes into one easy-to-use (we hope) package. The type of inspection access determines the inspection process and the target determines the detection process. Figure 7.1 shows the choices of where to insert the watcher. Where the watcher sits determines the type of inspection process that will be necessary.

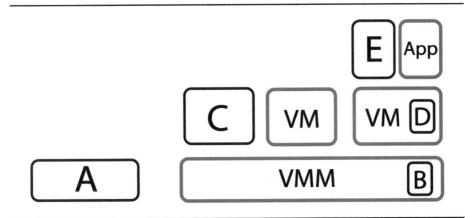

Figure 7.1   Watcher Options

Figure 7.1 shows five watchers, A, B, C, D, and E. Each has some advantages and disadvantages. First, we need to define the type of watcher.

Peer Watcher

A peer watcher runs at the same execution level as the target and requires assistance from the underlying level to allow inspection. Peer watchers are A, C, and E

Lower Watcher

A lower watcher runs at a lower execution level from the target. These watchers use services of the lower level to inspect the target. Lower watchers are B and D.

Watcher A

A is a peer to the VMM. A has the ability to look at the VMM and the resources of the VMM. The underlying level of the VMM is the hardware. This means that to run a watcher for the VMM one needs hardware assistance to create the inspection process. This is one of the hardest watchers to create. It is also the most important watcher. The reason for this is that all of the other watchers depend directly or indirectly on the VMM. If the VMM has lost integrity, the entire system is out of control.

There are many avenues to explore to provide hardware assistance when creating the watcher for the VMM. The topic is an open research project at this time.

Watcher B

B is internal to the VMM. It has the ability to look up and inspect the VM above the VMM. The services necessary to perform the inspection are all part of the VMM and no additional support is necessary.

An interesting point to clarify here is that if B were attempting to watch the VMM, note that B is internal to the VMM. That means that attacks or corruption to the VMM could potentially damage the ability of B to watch the VMM. That is why A is the better choice of a watcher for the VMM rather than B.

Watcher C

C is a peer to the VM. It has the ability to look at the VM. The services necessary to perform the inspection are all part of the VMM and the VMM controls the information flow between the VM and the watcher.

One use model for C is when the VM to watch is a special purpose application. If the VM to watch were a firewall, then the watcher would know exactly how to determine if the firewall was operating correctly. The issue here is how to distribute the watcher. If one accepts the B style watcher, then the creator of the VM has to find a way to insert the watcher code into the VMM. That may not even be possible. However, with the C model, the VM creator creates the watcher and sends the application and the watcher out as a pair, with instructions as to what access requirements the watcher has on the VMM. This model then greatly reduces the distribution requirements to send both the VM and watcher.

Watcher D

D is internal to the VM. It has the ability to look up at a specific application. The services necessary to perform the inspection are all part of the VM.

D is analogous to B; they both are peers, they both rely on the underlying layer to provide inspection services, and they both require that the watcher be internal to the layer.

Watcher E

E is a peer of the application and uses the services of the VM to inspect the application.

E is analogous to C, but is just one layer up.

Watchers Today and Tomorrow

Few watchers are available today. Most are so obscure that the public has never heard of them. As software starts to become more security friendly, more watchers will appear. Their usefulness will have as a gating function how many attacks the watcher misses. While it will be good to know what is being blocked, knowing how often the watcher can report a false negative (everything's good when really it's not) is the more important statistic.

Attacks on Inspection and Detection

The attacks here focus on the two processes, either manipulating the inspection or changing the detection capability.

Inspection

Attacks on the inspection process attempt to block access to the target or change the information delivered to the watcher.

Depending on the implementation, the ability to block access by the inspection process may be easy or extremely hard. On the easy side as a model E watcher depends on the VM, corrupting the VM allows the use of incorrect information.

On the hard side would be manipulating the hardware process in place to support model A as that attack is going to have to be one of a hardware nature.

Detection

In attacks on the detection process, an attempt to have the detection algorithm report that integrity is still present when in reality the target has lost integrity. As the detection process is a heuristic, feeding in just a little bit of false information may lead to incorrect integrity calculations.

Architectural Performance

This element of the trusted platform appears to be out of place, but the reality is that it is a critical element. The idea behind architectural performance is that security and trust are not free. One could design a system such that before executing each assembler instruction, the system checked the integrity of the application and OS. While great from a security standpoint, the system is just not going to do any real work; it will spend all of the CPU cycles just performing the integrity checks. You could build a system where 98 percent of the system cycles were in integrity, but how many people would buy that machine? If the machine is running the flight controls of the commercial airliner the author is traveling on then higher integrity is a very good thing.

What this element is pointing out is that system architects must take into account the true and total cost of the security system. In one very early Intel® TXT discussion, in fact so early it was still known as LT, an idea floated was to have the user supply a 20-byte password on each boot. Well, not just any password, but the results of a SHA-1 hash operation. Oh, and by the way, the user had to enter the same 20 bytes on each boot, including returning from sleep or hibernation. The system was secure but the cost to the user was way too high.

Similarly, the architect must consider each element as to the security provided, the cost to the platform, the cost to execution, the cost to manufacturer and deliver, the cost to install, the cost to operate, and the cost to the end user.

Neglecting these costs ends up with security systems that, while secure cost too much to use and end up never being turned on. By placing this as a real element and talking about the costs, the architects can do a better job of providing a useful product.

Chapter 8

Between Partitions

*I have only one eye, I have a right to be blind sometimes...
I really do not see the signal!*

—Lord Nelson[1]

Trusted platforms protect the execution of programs, but execution of a program is not the only element of a personal computer. As important, or maybe even more important, is the communication between the platform and the human user. Input from devices like keyboards and mice, output from devices like monitors and printers. The interesting point for a discussion of trusted computing is, "Does the input really come from the user and is the user actually seeing the correct output?" Lord Nelson, with his single eye, could claim he did not see the information[2]. What is necessary with trusted computing is to find mechanisms that ensure the input and output mechanisms. To trust a platform, the user must trust the information flowing from the user to the platform and then back from the platform to the user.

---

1   I was in England on 21 October 2005 and saw some of the festivities celebrating the 200 anniversary of the Battle of Traflgar, in which the entire English fleet saw and obeyed Nelson's commands and defeated a combined French and Spanish fleet.

2   This comment has been a classic comment from military commanders since the dawn of military activities. The essence of the comment is that if the commander does not receive additional instructions, the commander could make his own decision and do something different from wishes of the chain of command.

The trust also flows in the reverse direction. The program and the entities distributing the program want assurances that the user is providing the input and seeing the output.

When trying to provide protections between two partitions the list in this category is only two elements

■ Isolation

■ Trusted Channel

Isolation

Isolation provides the ability to separate one application from another. Figure 8.1 shows the isolation of process A from process B. The code, data, and resources associated with process A, are unavailable to process B. Various mechanisms can provide the isolation of the process A components from process B.

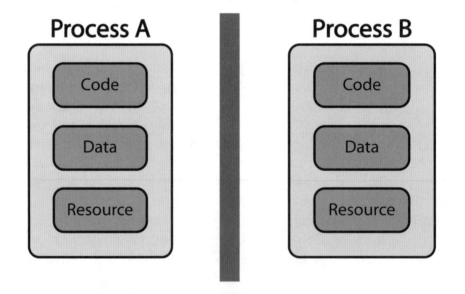

Figure 8.1   Isolation and Protected Execution

One process isolation mechanism is the paging and ring architecture. Paging and rings ensure that a process in ring 3 is isolated from other processes in ring 3. There are vulnerabilities related to ring 0 accesses and the amount of code running in ring 0. A strong OS, with a true security kernel in ring 0, can provide a high degree of isolation for all ring 3 applications. Due to the nature of device drivers and the lack of use of rings 1 and 2[3], most current operating systems do not provide an adequate level of isolation.

Another process isolation mechanism is Intel® Virtualization Technology (VT). VT provides isolation through the creation of guest partitions. No resources assigned to one partition are available to any other guest partition. VT is an excellent isolation mechanism.

VT at this time does not provide virtualization for the entire platform. Instead, VT virtualizes the CPU. VT will expand to include other platform devices through VT-d and other technologies.

The combination of paging and rings to isolate applications in a guest partition and VT to provide lots of guest partitions provides a very strong isolation solution.

Why Isolate?

The first question to ask is why even go to the trouble of isolation? What does isolation buy me? The answer comes from who you want to trust. If you believe that everyone, at all times, in all circumstances will write perfectly good code, then isolation is not necessary. The author certainly hopes you do not believe the above statement. When you look at the number of applications and drivers and extensions that are all present on a current PC platform, the idea that every single one of them is 100 percent trusted to work correctly at all times is not possible.

Attacks on Isolation

From a generic view, all attacks on isolation look the same; the attacker gains access to a supposedly isolated resource. The technique of gaining the access is specific to the isolation mechanism in use, but the underlying issue is always the same, the isolation mechanism does not completely isolate.

---

3   The lack of ring 1 and 2 support is a historical fact. The original idea was for the OS to use all of the rings but early implementations had ring transition issues and the OS writers compressed the rings into just two. Attempting change now would require rewriting all of the OS and drivers—not a viable solution.

By way of an example, consider current attacks where an application running in ring 3 has the ability to insert code into ring 0. Changing ring 0 from ring 3 is supposedly impossible, however the OS managing ring 0 has some mechanisms that allow changes to ring 0 and the attacker finds a way to misuse the mechanism.

What has to go on in the mind of the security architect is to question the isolation boundary and ensure that all possible avenues of access are isolated. This is in practice a very difficult job. As platforms become even more complex the ability to understand and manage the complete isolation set becomes even more difficult.

A well-known computer science idea provides the answer to the complexity problem; add a layer of indirection. Or in security terms, defense in depth. In this response the idea is that to isolate a resource it is better to have multiple isolation techniques rather than a single mechanism. Consider a physical memory page assigned to contain very sensitive data, like a cryptographic key. The first isolation mechanism could be ring 0 and ring 3. Next one could add virtualization so there is a difference between root and non-root mode. After virtualization, one could add DMA isolation and ensure that no external devices access the physical memory page. Note that each of these mechanisms is another layer of isolation. They focus on different access mechanisms; or stated in generic security terms, they provide defense in depth.

Trusted Channel and Trusted Path

In the security literature, you see a distinction between a trusted channel and trusted path. A trusted channel involves communication between two computing entities, like two computers. A trusted path involves communication between a computing device and a human. Here's an example to explain the difference; most Internet users know that some Web sites make a security mechanism available. The security mechanism is commonly in use during Internet shopping. The security mechanism is the Secure Socket Layer (SSL). The connection between the client and the server, the actual SSL connection, is a trusted channel. The padlock icon at the bottom of the browser indicates a trusted path between the server and the user. For a trusted path to work, the human must do something. In the SSL example, the human must look at the browser window and see the icon. Figure 8.2 illustrates the channel and path for SSL.

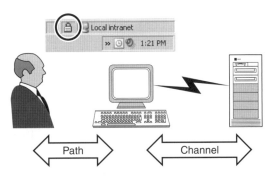

Figure 8.2 Path and Channel

Intel® TXT hardware differs in that it provides the mechanism to create trusted channels, but does not mandate trusted paths. Stated another way, Intel TXT provides the ability to create trusted channels between the platform components, but does not require any display to indicate that the channel is present. The assumption is that MLE designers create trusted paths, but no hardware requirement compels them to do so.

Why a Trusted Channel?

With the execution and storage of data protected by Intel TXT through the MLE, why do input and output present any issues? The answer lies in how an application works. The application can only work with good information—the garbage in, garbage out (GIGO) principle works here. If an application that provides protection to a digital signature key allows the key to sign anything, attackers do not have to break the cryptography. Instead, the attacker merely presents bogus information and the application signs the information.

The following list is not complete, but shows the types of problems that the MLE must consider when handling human input and output.

■ Data supplied from a secure input device, such as a keyboard, should not be readable by unauthorized applications. Obviously, this restriction is crucial for passwords or input from scanners.

■ Data supplied from a secure input device, such as a keyboard, should not be modifiable by unauthorized applications. For example, when entering financial data, the attacker should not be able to convert a user-specified amount of $100 to $234 by changing digits or to $1 by removing digits or to $1,000 by adding digits.

■ Data supplied from a secure input device, such as a keyboard, should not be *spoofable* by any application. That is, attacking software should not be able to fool an application into believing that user-generated keystrokes have occurred.

■ Data sent from a secured application to a secured output device, such as a monitor or printer, must not be readable by unauthorized applications. Such output often contains sensitive, confidential data, such as account numbers, tax records, or checks.

■ Data sent from a secured application to a secured output device, such as a monitor or printer, must not be modifiable by unauthorized applications. This restriction prevents the attacker from modifying what the user sees. As an example, in a check-signing application, the attacker could change the payee or reduce the amount of the check displayed to the user, to entice an approval for an amount other than the display.

■ Data sent from a secured application to a secured output device, such as a monitor, must not be spoofable by any application. That is, attacking software must not be able to fool the human into believing that the secured application generated the output. For example, attacking software should be unable to generate a password-entry dialog box that mimics a real dialog box. This example is a direct application of the trusted path issue; if the fake dialog box looks "close" to the real dialog box, and the user does not look closely, it is possible to fool the user.

■ The peripheral devices themselves could be a source for exposing information. Keyboards, for instance, accept the keystrokes that represent a password, so the keyboard design must not allow multiple entities access to the actual keystrokes. Saving the keystrokes in a buffer, and allowing the buffer to be read multiple times, allows an attack where the user types in their password, the attacker moves the keyboard to a new machine, and the new machine reads the keyboard buffer. Another example is a printer that buffers the last few pages of a document and allows the next printer user to reprint the pages stored in the buffer.

Trusted Channel Basics

At a minimum, a trusted channel represents a way to ensure that data travels from one computing entity to another without any interference. Most trusted channels also include the requirement of confidentiality, which means that not just any viewer of the channel can determine the contents of the channel. One mechanism that provides both properties is encrypting the data that is using the channel. Trusted channels come in two basic mechanisms: hardware or cryptography. Both have some advantages and disadvantages.

Hardware Trusted Channels

A hardware trusted channel relies on the physical nature of the platform to provide protections. A typical hardware trusted channel involves such fun things as buried traces, no visible pins, and no exposed via's. If you didn't understand those terms you are not alone, these terms are the providence of the platform hardware engineers. The underlying idea of hardware trusted channels to is prevent an entity with physical access to the platform the ability to watch or disrupt the electrical signals traveling between devices.

Two major issues with hardware trusted channels are: first the channel must be designed and built during platform manufacturing, and second, the channel is only possible with devices that are in physical contact.

The first issue of designing for the channel during platform manufacturing is not serious, if the manufacturer wants to apply the time and effort to the protections; the hardware trusted channel is possible[4]. Few commercial platforms take the time and go to the expense to create hardware trusted channels.

The second issue is much more serious. The hardware nature of the protections applies to all links in the chain between the two devices. Some devices are very difficult to physically connect and even when physically connected the attempts to provide hardware protection is impossible, or nearly so. What is necessary is some other mechanism to provide the trusted channel.

---

4   For many platforms built to military specifications, the hardware trusted channel is a requirement.

One interesting side feature of a hardware trusted channel is that the normal designs require no operational setup. With the physical nature of the channel, turning the platform on enables the protection.

Cryptographic Trusted Channels

The cryptographic trusted channel solves some of the hardware trusted channel issues while adding some new issues. The cryptographic channel solves the physical connection issue by encrypting all data traveling between the two devices. With no more worries about the physical nature of the connection, the trusted channel can span huge distances as the SSL connection between a Web site and a Web browser shows.

The issue with cryptographic trusted channels is key exchange. To provide sufficient speed and bandwidth most, if not all, cryptographic channels use symmetric encryption. Symmetric encryption requires the same key at both sides of the channel. A truly ugly question now comes up: how to accomplish the key exchange.

Key exchange is not easy. The protocols are difficult, exacting, and sometimes use lots of bandwidth. To create a channel though, the problem must have a solution. The steps to establish and use a trusted channel look something like this:

1. *Find both end-points.* It does not matter how the end-points are found; one side can look for the other. The search can be across the Internet or through buses on a platform.

2. *Say hello.* Essentially, one side sends a message that says, "I would like to start a channel."

3. *Verify the end-points.* One side verifies the identity and authorization of the other side, or both sides verify each other. The checking can be very simple or very complex. The checking can involve cryptography to validate and protect the answers.

4. *Create a session key.* The session key encrypts all data using the channel. The session key should be ephemeral, so that when the channel terminates, the session key is lost forever. Many protocols combine the end-point validation with session key creation.

5. *Establish channel.* With the session key at both end-points, all future traffic on the channel uses an encryption algorithm to encrypt

all traffic. The physical distance between the two end-points does not matter to the integrity or confidentiality of the channel. As long as both sides properly protect the session key, no intervening entity can read the data. The cryptographic strength of the algorithm and key can affect the strength property. If a reasonable algorithm, such as AES, and a decent key size, such as 128 bits, is in use, then intervening entities have a very low probability of success of decrypting the data.

6. *Terminate channel.* Either side can terminate the channel, at any time. One efficient and effective way to terminate the channel is to destroy the session key.

Trusted Channel Device Focus

Devices that support the trusted channel may also support usages without the trusted channel. Some devices must make provisions for continued use of the device when the focus changes from the trusted application to an untrusted application. One example of changing focus is the trusted channel to the keyboard. When the trusted keyboard driver has the focus, all of the keystrokes travel through the trusted keyboard driver. When an untrusted driver has the focus, the keystrokes may or may not travel through the trusted driver. Determining which entity has the focus is a critical ability of the trusted driver in order to properly handle the channel.

Attacks on Trusted Channel

The basic attack against a trusted channel is to manipulate messages traveling on the channel. If the channel is using cryptography, simple message manipulation is only possible if the cryptographic algorithm is weak.

The more interesting attack is for the attacker to masquerade as a valid channel endpoint. If the attacker can convince the trusted graphics software that another software process is really the graphics adapter, then the attacker gets to control what is sent to the real graphics adapter. Endpoint identification is a very interesting subject. In some ways this topic merges into the discussion of trusted paths. (See Chapter 1 for the quick discussion on paths.) However, endpoint identification is an inherent feature of trusted channels. One simple way to identify an endpoint is to give each endpoint a digital signature key and have the endpoint sign a message to identify the endpoint. This mechanism works great in the lab, but is somewhat difficult to implement. If each endpoint has a digital signature key, then the endpoint needs to protect the key and identify each request to use the digital signature key. In fact, the requirements for the endpoint look like the requirements for a trusted platform. And they are, so to create trusted channels you need the services of a trusted platform on both ends. Operationally will you have a trusted platform on both ends? If you do not have a trusted platform on one end, can you trust the channel you are building? These are all very good questions and ones that each use of a trusted channel needs to answer.

Chapter 9

Inside and Outside

Just left the bridge? What are we running here? A perfect stranger comes aboard the Galactica, and he's given access to a sensitive military control centre?

—**Commander Adama**, *Battlestar Galactica*

Here users of a trusted platform have to feel exactly same way as Commander Adama; they have just gone through the work of getting their trusted platform working and if anyone can just walk in and use the platform, especially if that someone is a software process, something is very wrong. The access direction is not just on the way in. If supposedly protected information travels to the outside world without any protection or vetting, the trusted platform is not really meeting the needs of the user.

This chapter discusses two groups, the inside group and the outside group. The reason for combining them into a single chapter is purely editorial; the elements inside the groups are not related. While one could imply some inference between the two with the names inside and outside, this chapter will illustrate why they are very separate groups.

The element for the outside group is external access and the element for inside is protected execution.

External Access

External access is about sending information to the trusted platform or sending information from the trusted platform.

Cell Membrane

The first thing we need to talk about when discussing external access is cellular biology. No, really. Many times when people think of "controlling" something they have the idea of some strong wall that blocks everything. The trusted platform needs something different, more like a cell membrane. Figure 9.1 gives us an illustration of this concept.

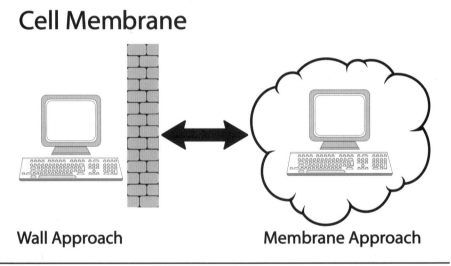

Figure 9.1   Protection Coverage versus Attack Incidents

The wall approach says that the platform blocks everything and keeps everything in. Most of us do not work in that world—we surf the Internet, do online banking, connect to the office, and thousands of other tasks and all of them can and should take advantage of the properties of the trusted platform. A simple block then is insufficient; we need a more intelligent wall.

A cell membrane has a fascinating structure. It knows what stuff it should let in, what stuff it should let out, what must remain inside, and what to block from entering. It enforces these rules and is able to change the rules on the fly based on circumstances generated both internally and externally. What a fantastic device!

Compare our trusted platform access to external entities and you see a startling similarity. The trusted platform needs to keep things in and out and let specific things in and out and the rules need to change on the fly based on both internal and external situations.

The author truly believes that this analogy holds for many of the access issues in the trusted platform. Therefore, when you see the reference to the cell membrane the author wants the reader to think of a living breathing entity that changes and protects in response to messages both from internal and external sources[1].

There is only one element in this group, external access. However, in this chapter I will treat input and output separately merely for readability.

Knowledge versus Action

This element has an interesting feature, the requirement is to know about the access points, but the complete action is a function of the services provided by the trusted platform. As way of illustration, the system documentation includes all of the access ports (knowledge) and the virtual machine monitor creates a handler and policy for each of the ports (complete action). This split makes it somewhat harder to describe in this book because the platform is really only going to provide the knowledge and the complete action comes from the software using the platform. Therefore when reading this chapter, please realize that all comments regarding actions are pointing at the software that makes use of the element knowledge.

---

1   And to top it off the author is writing the first draft of this chapter while recovering from the flu. And not one of those weak little 1-day affairs but the 5–6 day variety with a high fever all the way through. The ability of the cell membrane to change and combat a virus is simply a wonderful design.

Determining the Access Points

The first action that a trusted platform architect needs to do is enumerate the access points where data can come into or leave the platform. The first cut is easy, that network port and the floppy drive, if your platform still has one. But wait, from the platform point of view, define the network port. Is it the Ethernet cable or the wireless radio, or both? Do those network ports require different rules based on how they connect? Is there a difference in how data arrives on the network port based on the presence or absence of a VPN?

This is just the short list of questions one could raise on network access. USB is another fun access point. Consider some of these questions: Can you determine the type and use of all devices connected to the USB port? Can you really see past USB bridges and switches? What happens if the network port attaches to the USB bus, is it a wired or wireless connection, and does it matter?

The result of these questions is that determining the access points requires a complete and thorough understanding of the platform. Why is knowledge of all of the access points so important? Consider software that is managing a trusted platform that misses just one access point. Where do attackers gain access to the information to the platform? Do the attackers attempt to guess for thousands of years a cryptographic key, or do they use an unguarded access point and merely read the information. The answer is obvious. So knowledge of the access points is critical to the success in managing external access.

Inbound Data to the Platform

Inbound data represents, to the trusted platform, potentially hostile or inaccurate information. If the trusted platform accepts this information without a vetting process then the results can be catastrophic.

Trusted Channel

One way to vet incoming information is to use a verified trusted channel to the sender of the information. This type of vetting is very good when the source of the data has an identity and the trusted platform has knowledge of the source identity. A simple channel like SSL that validates both end points completely removes the chances of interception and modification of data flowing from the source to the trusted platform.

While the trusted channel alleviates the worry regarding the information in transit it does not remove the issue of the validity of the contents.

Validating the Contents

After the trusted platform entity that is managing the incoming data ascertains or fails to ascertain the source of the data, it then determines what type of data validation is necessary. This validation is source specific and is not a requirement from the services of the trusted platform, but may be a requirement from the application or users of the trusted platform.

A rational policy choice for some trusted platform implementers will be to validate all input. That policy is a very good one and represents a conservative approach. The approach also takes the most resources as input is undergoing constant verification. An opposite rational policy would be to validate input from an unknown source. This type of validation strategy is not as conservative as check everything but could make much better use of the trusted platform resources.

Open Channel

With an open channel, there are fewer opportunities to validate the source of the message. Certainly, messages can contain digital signatures or other identification and validation mechanisms, but the vast majority of messages on an open channel will not have the identification and verification mechanisms.

The trusted platform must be aware of these open channels and properly control the input of information. After receipt of the information, and the validation that the message destination really was the specific platform, the services then need to validate the message contents. As in the trusted channel case the type and amount of validation is a service of the specific platform.

Input Membrane

Going back to the cell membrane analogy, note that our input protection has to identify what should and should not come inside our trusted platform. The trusted platform then acts again as a membrane: when each piece of data enters, the membrane assures that the data has some process attached to it so that the data does not just have free reign inside of the platform.

Outbound Data to the Platform

Outbound data represents, to the platform, data that the platform will no longer control. Here the trusted platform wants some assurances, if they are available, that the destination will properly protect the data.

Trusted Channel

For sending data out of the trusted platform's control, a trusted channel is a great thing. It is even better if the channel includes attestation of the destination state. With a guaranteed delivery mechanism, the trusted channel, and the knowledge of the destination state, it is an "easy" policy decision to determine what data the trusted platform is willing to send. The easy is in quotes because any policy decision is difficult and requires lots of information and help.

Unknown Destination

If any entity asks for some information, some policy must be in place to determine what is and is not appropriate to send. Remember Commander Adama's statement; the trusted platform should not just send information to anyone. If the data is going anywhere and everywhere, which an unknown destination represents, then the trusted platform should only send information that is not sensitive. The platform and user have to determine the meaning of sensitive.

Output Membrane

To close the loop with our cell membrane analogy, note how, just as with the cell membrane, the trusted platform only allows in "good" things, and only allows out information "ready" to exit the trusted platform. The definitions of the terms good and ready are open to the user of the trusted platform and will be different for individual users and uses of the trusted platform.

Attacks on External Access

The first avenue of attack for the attacker is to locate an unprotected data port. If such a port is found, the attacker can insert into the trusted platform unverified data and potentially execute damaging programs.

After securing all of the data ports, the attacks on external access revolve around attempting to trick the trusted platform into either accepting unverified data or sending sensitive information to the wrong entity.

If a trusted platform is being conservative and validating all input, then the attacker's job is much harder as no matter the source input data still requires validation. In this case the attacker needs to find an error in the validation code to successfully insert data into the trusted platform.

If the trusted platform uses some policy as to determine which data to validate, then the attacker is going to attempt to masquerade the attack data to look like properly validated input. The strength of the source identification is going to determine the amount of vulnerability the trusted platform has to insertion of unverified input data.

For output of data, the same two previous points apply for the attacker; if full verification is present then the attacker has to convince the trusted platform to not change the data format or masquerade as a valid destination.

Protected Execution

Let us start by looking once more at the diagram used to illustrate isolation from Chapter 8, now Figure 9.2.

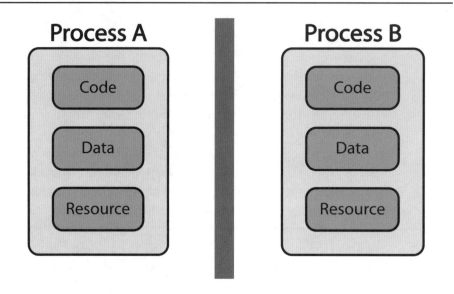

Figure 9.2 Isolation

Looking again at Figure 9.2, there is a suggestion that isolating process A from Process B provides sufficient protected execution for process A. process A now has protection at all time from all external bad things. Is process A protected from itself? Certainly, the author has never written any bad code, but others appear to ship code that is not 100 percent correct. What happens when a bug occurs in process A. Can process A protect itself from itself?

The list of things that can go wrong is long; buffer overflows, incorrect logic, bad device drivers, and a multitude of other vulnerabilities. The key question to ask here is what protections does process A have that allows it to maintain integrity?

Use What Is Available

The platform already provides a large set of protections that help mitigate potential vulnerabilities to the executable. To provide protections the application should use all of the protections on the platform. These protections include isolation through use of rings and segmentation, isolation through virtualization, and writing smaller code.

It is important to understand that using all of the protections code can be produced that is fairly well protected from modification. However, as we see from the current state of affairs, even well written code is susceptible to modification.

Execution

After using all of the current protection mechanisms, the only option left is to find mechanisms to keep the code from doing bad things. This is an area of active research and development and this description is just of the general direction.

One example of a prevention mechanism is the eXecute Disable (XD) bit. By setting this bit, the memory location does not allow execution of code. As some buffer overflows directly place executable code into the overrun area, this protection prevents the attack from occurring. It also highlights why one needs to have a defense in depth. The XD bit prevents an attacker from directly using the overrun area as executable but does not prevent the overrun from being a jump address. Therefore, the attacker looses one attack vector but still has the ability to take advantage of the overflow.

Buffer Overflow

Consistently in the past few years, a major vulnerability in code has been buffer overflows. While understanding of the causes seems high, the vulnerability continues to appear in code. Automatic testing appears to help but even with automatic checkers, some forms of overflows do appear in code.

There is very active research into this area and hopefully future trusted platforms will have mechanisms that help to mitigate buffer overflows. Without insight into the mechanism that will prevent buffer overflows the best that in this chapter we can say is that one hopes that the mitigation will allow currently written code to continue to operate.

Other Possibilities

The author spends many hours contemplating how to strengthen execution. While we could put all of the current research into this chapter, there is no guarantee that any of the ideas will work, that the ideas are implementable, and that industry will want to implement any of the changes[2]. The best advice for now is to stay tuned and look for additional books regarding this topic in the future.

Attacks on Protected Execution

This should not be a surprise to any of the readers; the attacks are what we see today, buffer overflows and other vulnerabilities that allow the attacker to take control. While the actual attacks will change over time depending on the features of the trusted platform, this will remain a target rich environment[3] for attackers.

Combined Protections

This chapter looked at protecting the platform from outside influences, external access, and internal corruption, protected execution. The combination of these two elements is an attempt to maintain the integrity of the trusted platform and the data the trusted platform is protecting. We do not anticipate that software will ever become perfect. There will always be issues with incorrect code, undefined mechanisms, incomplete requirements, new devices, and user error in configurations. The hope with these two elements is to provide defense in depth that allows the trusted platform the ability to mitigate these wide-ranging threats.

---

2   Put another way, the author and his coworkers are looking at new ideas—we are just not ready to talk about them yet.

3   The term target rich environment comes from the military and it represents an attacker who has many potential targets. A target rich environment does represent a platform that is vulnerable to attack.

Chapter 10

Trusted Execution Technology Objectives

Good people do not need laws to tell them to act responsibly, while bad people will find a way around the laws.

—Plato (427–347 B.C.)

When trying to understand security, you must properly identify the objectives of the protection effort. You must understand what is and what is not protected. No security product provides 100-percent absolute security; all products have set objectives that define the security boundaries of the product. Intel Trusted Execution Technology® (Intel TXT®) also protects some items and does not protect others. This chapter is all about the dividing line, defining what is inside the security boundary and what is not. The boundary definition comes from numerous sources and is not a bright, exactly straight line; rather the boundary line is a fuzzy curve with the final determination of the boundary being left to those entities wishing to rely on the Intel TXT platform.

Intel TXT and the Elements

The previous chapters have just done a fine job of defining the trusted platform elements. As the book now focuses on Intel© Trusted Execution Technology

(Intel TXT) the first order of business is going to be mapping Intel TXT to the elements.

Before doing that exercise we are first going to do a little definition work. The Intel TXT product includes the use of the Measured Launch Environment (MLE). When one considers the elements that Intel TXT meets does one include the MLE or not? In the previous edition of this book the distinction between the Intel TXT hardware and the MLE using Intel TXT was not distinct. As we work through this chapter we will make it explicit when we are talking about the Intel TXT hardware and the MLE using Intel TXT. Table 10.1 summarizes these distinctions.

One reason to make the distinction is who enforces what when. The Intel TXT hardware is something that should work the same way every time. The MLE using Intel TXT is software and as the system allows any MLE to execute there are no guarantees as to what features and protections the MLE provides. We will assume in this chapter a well written and full featured MLE. Arguments that a specific MLE does not provide a feature and protection, while correct, do not belong in this chapter as the assumption again is the full featured and well written MLE.

Table 10.1 Intel TXT and the elements

Element	Intel TXT Hardware or MLE	Comments
Evidence	Hardware	Providing a measurement of the MLE is the main Intel TXT job
Reporting	N/A	The TPM provides the reporting mechanism after the hardware stores the MLE measurement in the Intel® TPM.
TCB Management	MLE	After measuring and passing control to the MLE, Intel TXT does not participate in TCB management
Policy Engine	MLE	The MLE is a policy engine and enforces the policies set the MLE creator
PII Handling	N/A	The platform uniqueness is in the TPM and it controls the TPM PII. If the MLE handles other PII the MLE must manage the PII correctly.
Randomness	N/A	The TPM provides the randomness element
Sequencing	N/A	The TPM provides the sequencing element
Protected Storage	N/A	The TPM provides the protected storage element
Detection and Inspection	N/A	There is no generic Detection and Inspection element for the MLE with this version of Intel TXT
Architectural Performance	Hardware and MLE	Both look to use the platform resources in a correct manner
Isolation	MLE	The assumed MLE is a Virtual Machine Monitor (VMM) that provides isolation through the use of Virtual Machines.
Trusted Channel	MLE	The MLE, through use of the VT-D platform feature, creates trusted channels and assigns devices to specific memory addresses
External Access	MLE	The MLE manages access to the platform
Protected Execution	N/A	Other than rings and the XD bit there is no additional protected execution element.

As you can see from the elements, Intel TXT as a hardware-only feature provides two of the trusted platform elements, evidence and architectural performance. The other elements come from the MLE or other platform features. This is intentional; trying to understand the vast array of policies necessary to protect all of the platform elements, in hardware, is the reason that Intel TXT goes hand in hand with virtualization elements like VT-X.

In this objective chapter we will cover what the hardware *must* do and what the software *should* do.

The Basic Questions

When security architects gather to discuss a security issue, the first item of business is to answer the following three questions:

■ What is being protected?

■ Who is the attacker?

■ What resources does the attacker have?

When one knows the answers to these questions, defining the security objectives becomes a boundable problem.

What Is Being protected?

From the element list we know that the hardware must protect the measurement process and the MLE needs to protect data. The MLE is not going to protect all data on the platform but it will protect the sensitive data of the MLE. The assumption is that the MLE is protecting data like credit card numbers, Internet transactions, cryptographic keys, and other pieces of information.

Who Is the Attacker?

The attackers to our system have a single goal, obtain protected information. They can accomplish the goal by either recording an inaccurate measurement value of the MLE, or breaking the hardware, or by having the MLE work incorrectly, or breaking the software.

Further identification of the attacker is not necessary. He or she could be a young hacker trying their first break-in or a member of a sophisticated crime organization. From the standpoint of Intel TXT, the identity of the attacker does not matter; Intel TXT must provide protections regardless of the attacker's identity. Stated another way, Intel TXT must provide protections against the young hacker and the crime organization without knowing if the attack comes from the hacker or the crime organization. What will make a difference are the resources the attacker has access to[1].

What Resources Does the Attacker Have?

The attacker's resources break down into two categories: software and hardware. The rationale of breaking the resources down allows Intel TXT to focus on the software attacks which are the first level of attacks Intel TXT is attempting to mitigate.

Software Resources

The first, and most important, resource an attacker can have is the ability to run software processes on the platform. The processes can be user applications (ring 3) or system level (ring 0). It does not matter how the attacker delivers the software to the platform. The attack software can perform all operations on the platform or the software can use resources of remote processes.

Ignoring the transport issue for software delivery allows Intel TXT to focus on the real problem: the events that happen after the software is present. If the Intel TXT security boundary tried to keep software from actually residing on the platform, an enormous effort would go into detecting when new software arrives on the platform and into attempts to control the delivery. The Intel TXT design point is not to be executing at all times, hence attempts to restrict software delivery would be very difficult.

Hardware Resources

When using a remote process, the attacker has a large amount of computing resources available. Thus, if the attacker obtains some information on the platform, she or he can use lots of computing resources remotely in an attempt to break any protections like encryption.

Stepping up from software attacks leads to hardware attacks. To mount a hardware attack, the attacker must have physical possession of the platform.

---

1   Do not make the mistake of ignoring the fact that data owners do care about the attacker, since the data owner needs to make the decision whether the platform can properly protect the information.

While remote hardware attacks are possible, Intel TXT does not attempt to mitigate remote hardware attacks.

> **Remote Hardware Attacks**
>
> If you want to know more about remote types of hardware attacks, try a Google[†] search on "TEMPEST hardware attack" and the resulting Web sites should give the information.

With physical access, you have no limit on the types of hardware mechanisms that are available to the attacker. The attacker can open the case. With the case open, the attacker can look around and use hardware tools like the ones that are available in a high school. The attacker usually does not have access to special probes or scanning electron microscopes. If the attacker does have access to these special resources, the attacker can defeat the Intel® TXT protections.

Intel TXT is designed to provide protection from simple hardware attacks. What is the definition of a simple hardware attack? An exploit based on turning off the power and removing the battery is a simple hardware attack. Going to the local electronic store, purchasing twenty dollars worth of parts, putting the parts together and defeating the Intel TXT protections is a simple hardware attack. The Intel TXT objective is to mitigate simple hardware attacks.

Previous Platform Objectives

Platforms based on Intel® architecture have been a resounding success over the years. The addition of new features has expanded the use of the platform. The addition of security features must continue this tradition. Previous objectives of the Intel architecture platform, without regard to the security nature of these objectives, were:

■ Ease of use

■ Manageability

■ Privacy

■ Performance

■ Versatility

■ Backwards compatibility

The review of the previous objectives, and how Intel TXT affects them, leads to the set of objectives for Intel TXT.

Ease of Use

From a general viewpoint, the Intel architecture platform is easy to use. While it has some rough spots, overall many people are able to use the features and programs available on the platform. The operating system and the programs are a huge factor in this ease of use, but the underlying hardware allows the OS and programs to be written in a manner that enable easy use.

Adding Intel TXT to a platform must not make the platform that much harder to use. While some work to manage the Intel TXT parameters is necessary, their addition cannot change the users' burden fundamentally.

The best result would have a user able to purchase a new Intel TXT enabled platform and merely plug it in to find all elements would work. The OS and programs that take advantage of Intel TXT would do so in a manner that is invisible to the user. While this goal might not be 100-percent achievable due to other factors, the design objective is to attempt this result.

Manageability

In a corporate environment, the ability to manage platforms is a critical total cost of ownership issue. It is difficult for a system administrator to know what software is available on a platform and how the software is currently executing.

If Intel TXT makes the management job even harder, then IT administrators will not allow the use of Intel TXT in their networks. One can successfully argue that with the ability to control what is executing on a platform, platform identity, and the ability to report the current platform configuration, the building blocks for reducing the management load in a corporate environment are present.

Privacy

If a platform contains unique values, the system design needs to ensure that the user has control of the uniqueness. The control of the uniqueness must be such that once a user makes their choice, the platform enforces that choice upon all future boots of the platform.

An Intel TXT platform will have uniqueness on the platform. The main source of uniqueness is the Trusted Platform Module (TPM). A Intel TXT platform must ensure that the mechanisms designed into the TPM to operate properly on the TPM uniqueness are available and in use.

Chapter 6 covered the need to handle Personal Identifying Information (PII) correctly and Chapter 13 covers the TPM. While the TPM does contain unique values, Intel TXT does not add any additional unique values to the platform. Stated another way any platform uniqueness added to the platform due to the inclusion of Intel TXT is inside of the TPM. Therefore Intel TXT meets the privacy objective of proper control of uniqueness through the proper use of the TPM.

Performance

Intel has consistently provided platforms that increase in performance: not just speed, but the ability to get things done. This goal has been a driving force at Intel for many years.

You have two vectors to consider with Intel TXT and performance. The first vector is when a program is operating under Intel TXT protections; the performance of the program should be identical to a program not using Intel TXT protections. The second vector is that the overhead to manage Intel TXT should not be a major percentage of the computing resources.

The first vector implies that Intel TXT protections do not operate in the critical execution path. For example, Intel TXT should not have any affect on adding two numbers together. The objective to maintain performance while using the Intel TXT protections helps to ensure that software developers are not at a disadvantage when using the Intel TXT protections.

The second vector recognizes that all of the security provided by Intel TXT does not come for free. Security does incur a cost at some level. The Intel TXT design places the cost on the management of the security boundary and not during the execution of the protections. The time necessary to establish the protections becomes longer than the time spent if no protections were in place. Once established, the protections do not add any performance overhead, however.

Versatility

The beauty of the Intel architecture platform is the ability to allow others to innovate. The history of the platform shows that others have been able to innovate and expand what the platform can do. Intel TXT adds to this rich history.

The vision of the versatility provided by Intel TXT includes drastically different application architectures. The architects of Intel TXT do not have a crystal ball that informs them of all of the possible changes, but they hope that the basic building blocks of Intel TXT enable the new architectures.

By way of analogy, consider the history of display adapters. The author remembers the first display adapters and the beautiful green-on-green screens. To build "fancy" boxes, a programmer used the line characters amongst others. The idea of using these characters was to try to create boxes around certain areas. During programming, it was a painstaking task to count how many characters were necessary and where to put the T's to indicate sub-boxes[2].

How times change. The author is creating this book using a word processor that shows all of the diagrams in full color, with underlining, and beautiful lines and arrows. The original designers of the output systems did not foresee

---

2   Certainly, the author has counted more than his fair share of dashes, and he hopes never to count them again.

where output would go. The original designers *did* foresee that improvements would be necessary and provided hardware hooks that enabled and allowed others to innovate and create new architectures. Intel TXT is in the exact same situation. The basic building blocks are in place to provide software developers with lots of new architectures and ways to protect information.

Backward Compatibility

Although listed last, backward compatibility is a *huge* issue. In the early days of looking at what Intel TXT would be, the architects thought about an architecture that would do things in rather different ways. While the original idea had some nice security features, it did require the complete rewrite of the operating system. In addition to rewriting the OS, it also invalidated all currently written drivers. This complete change to the users of the platform was unacceptable.

The goal of maintaining backward compatibility cannot be absolute. As one adds security properties, some features do change. A good example is the restriction of no direct memory access (DMA) to pages protected by Intel TXT. Some applications that take advantage of DMA have to change. That change is the price to be paid for the additional security.

Protection and Attack Matrix

Can we answer the basic questions about Intel TXT security? Note this discussion on security involves the entire solution, Intel TXT hardware, the MLE, and applications relying on the MLE. I hope that the answer is yes. Figure 10.1 should help you to visualize what is and is not protected.

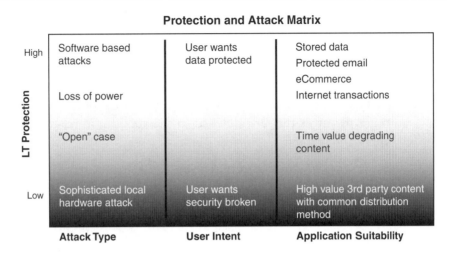

Figure 10.1 Protection and Attack Matrix

The vertical axis indicates the amount of protection that solution provides. A critical detail is that you have no definitive line between protected and not protected. This vagueness has a purpose. What constitutes protection for one user and application might not be protection for someone else. Security is not a bright line; it is a risk assessment. The idea of this matrix is to provide information that allows one to make a rational risk assessment of the protections that the solution built on Intel TXT can provide.

Attack Type

In Figure 5.1, the attack type progresses from software attack to hardware attack. We prevent software attacks and do not protect against sophisticated hardware attacks.

Software-based Attacks

Software attacks are the most prevalent attacks and mitigating these attacks will greatly increase the protections available on a platform. So, Intel TXT needs to protect against software-based attacks.

Where the software comes from should not matter to the protections provided by Intel TXT. The way a program loads, whether it comes from the hard drive or the Internet, does not affect the way that the program executes. An executable piece of code performs the same operation each time.

While data is under Intel TXT protections, Intel TXT must protect the data by preventing by any process running in ring 0 or ring 3 from attempting to view or modify the data. Protecting data is not as simple as just ensuring that a software process is unable to access a physical memory page. Numerous other resources that are attached to the application relate to the data of the application. These resources include:

■ *Registers*—the CPU has general-purpose registers, debug registers, and machine-specific registers. Intel TXT protection must ensure that only the application has access to the contents of the registers.

■ *Threads*—the application can break execution into threads. Each thread has a register set and other resources attached. Intel TXT protection must ensure that only the application has access to the threads associated with the application.

■ *Debug*—the CPU supports a rich set of debug operations. These operations include breakpoints and counters. Access to these resources by programs other than the application would leak information. Debugging is an operation that must occur at times. The design of systems using Intel TXT must be such that the application can determine whether it is accessed under a debugging environment and operate differently to avoid leaking information.

■ *Counters*—the CPU in both normal and debug mode supports the creation of counters that provide information as to how many instructions have executed. These counters provide information that makes mounting timing attacks much easier.

Timing Attacks

A class of attacks that were discovered in 1996 has a direct bearing on the software protections provided by Intel TXT. Paul Kocher, a brilliant cryptographer, discovered that small tidbits of performance information could lead to the exposure of the key for a crypto system. As Paul said:

> Crypto systems often take slightly different amounts of time to process different inputs. Reasons include performance optimizations to bypass unnecessary operations, branching and conditional statements, RAM cache hits, processor instructions (such as multiplication and division) that run in non-fixed time, and a wide variety of other causes. Performance characteristics typically depend on both the encryption key and the input data (e.g., plaintext or ciphertext). While it is known that timing channels can leak data or keys across a controlled perimeter, intuition might suggest that unintentional timing characteristics would only reveal a small amount of information from a cryptosystem (such as the Hamming weight of the key). However, attacks are presented which can exploit timing measurements from vulnerable systems to find the entire secret key (Kocher 1996).

The combination of debug registers, performance counters, and thread information can provide the resources necessary to mount a timing attack. As timing attacks can be a pure software attack, the Intel TXT protections must consider how to ensure the timing information is not available to attackers.

Loss of Power

While one might think of this event as a hardware attack, loss of power occurs in many different ways. Since many of the protections that Intel TXT provide come from internal mechanisms and a loss of power would remove those protections but not actually change what is in memory, Intel TXT needs to be robust and provide protections against this event.

If TXT is protecting memory, and power is lost to the platform for any reason, when power is again applied and the platform reboots, the platform ensures that no information leakage occurred for data protected by Intel TXT.

Chapter 17 describes the complete actions that occur on a loss of power.

Open Case

The first step of physical attacks is where the attacker has physical access to the platform. By whatever means, the attacker has the platform where the attacker can manipulate the physical nature of the platform. Nevertheless, at this point, we do not assume that the attacker has unlimited resources. Instead, we posit that the attacker has very limited resources. The attacker has the ability to add in a new device on an open bus; for example, adding a new card in a PCI slot.

With the case open, the attacker has access to the busses of the platform. From a security standpoint, the busses break down into only two categories: fast and slow.

The fast busses are the front-side bus and the hub link. The front-side bus connects the CPU(s) to the MCH. This bus is very fast, 800 megahertz in early 2004, and it should continue to get much faster. The hub link connects the MCH to the ICH. This internal bus is also a very fast connection. We do not expect an attacker who just opened the case to be able to intercept and decipher information traveling on the fast busses.

Numerous other busses are on the platform, but from the Intel TXT perspective, the bus of interest is the Low Pin Count (LPC) bus. The LPC bus is slow and very simple. The design of the LPC bus does not contemplate lots of activity or high bandwidth use. The LPC bus provides the connection between the ICH and TPM. As a low speed bus with a simple protocol, it is possible to watch the bus traffic with simple equipment. An oscilloscope and some publicly available documentation would give an attacker sufficient information to intercept bus traffic between the TPM and ICH. This "simple" attack requires a response from the Intel TXT design. Some mechanism needs to armor the traffic between the TPM and ICH. The TPM design provides for the creation of an encrypted channel between the TPM and devices using the TPM. This channel provides the armor that protects the traffic on the LPC bus.

It is difficult to launch a hardware attack without the right knowledge of the platform user. For instance, to watch the traffic on the LPC bus requires the use of probes and wires connecting the probes to some oscilloscope. I hope that the user would notice the addition of extra wires coming out of the platform. This watchfulness does not preclude the user from mounting the attack.

At the open-case level of attack, the platform should provide protections for the low-speed busses, like LPC, but it would not provide protections for the high-speed busses, like the front-side bus.

Sophisticated Local Hardware Attack

In this highest level of attack on the system, the attacker opens the case and has both the equipment and expertise to collect and interpret information from the high-speed busses. This attack represents a high level of system knowledge and monetary assets. The high-speed busses do not have protections in the first version of Intel TXT. Therefore, attackers with these resources would be able to pierce the Intel TXT protections.

Adding protections to the high-speed busses requires some very drastic changes to some basic platform components. Take, for instance, the example of encrypting information sent on the front-side bus. This solution works for the LPC bus, so why not use the same solution on the FSB? The LPC is a slow-speed bus, where data transiting from the TPM to ICH and elsewhere is a rare occurrence. In distinct contrast, for the information traveling on the front-side bus, speed is critical to the ability of the platform to execute quickly. Slow down a memory access and the system throughput degrades. Any attempt to encrypt a transaction would have throughput issues. Additionally, using more cycles to process the access can cause other devices to stall and further degrade throughput. With encryption on the high-speed bus, you also have the chance that the OS and drivers need to change. All of this leads to the fact that making a change on a high-speed bus can lead to changes in performance, backward compatibility, and possibly versatility. For these reasons, the design of Intel TXT does not mitigate this type of attack. This decision does not imply that Intel TXT would never attempt to mitigate some of these hardware attacks.

User Intent

The user's intent is critical to the Intel TXT protection matrix. If the user wants protection, the only attacks to consider are software attacks. If the user wants to break the protection, then hardware attacks are possible.

One way to look at user intent is to use the following:

■ *Protect user's data from outsiders.* The information belongs to the user and the user wants the information protected. The user does not want to attack the platform.

■ *Protect outside data from the user.* The data owner wants to protect the data from the user. The user may want to break the protections. If the user does want to break the protections, the user may use all resources available to the user.

Protect User's Data from Outsiders

With the user wanting protection, the specter of a hardware attack is gone. The user has no reason to launch a hardware attack when the user wants the data protected. The only attacks that concern the user are software attacks launched by others. The main goal of Intel TXT is to provide protection against software attacks. The goals of the user and the platform match. The data under the protection of Intel TXT would have the protection that the user wishes.

Why are the hardware attacks off the table? Assume that the user wants Intel TXT to protect the user's credit card number. The user wants to protect the credit card number from software attacks. The user has no need to apply hardware attacks to the platform when it is an easy process to pull the card out of their wallet to obtain the number.

Protect Third-Party Data from the User

User intent is critical here. If the protection desires of the data owner and the user match, then both want protection from software attacks. The user has no desire to mount hardware attacks. Intel TXT provides good data protection here.

If the protection desires of the data owner and user do not match, then the user is motivated to mount hardware attacks. The user may mount hardware attacks as the user has physical possession of the platform. With the user mounting a hardware attack, the data owner has to consider the cost of the attack and the result of the attack. If the data under Intel TXT protection has a value that is less then the cost to mount the hardware attack, Intel TXT still might provide adequate protection. If the data under Intel TXT protection has a value greater then the cost of the attack, Intel TXT most likely does not provide adequate protection.

The valuation of the attack is not the only consideration. The third party could be distributing the data to a platform of today and accepting whatever software attacks were successfully exposing the data. When Intel TXT becomes available, even though the hardware attacks are present, the increased protection from software attacks makes the use of Intel TXT an improvement over the protections of today. The very fact that to break the Intel TXT protections require a hardware attack could be a sufficient deterrent to keep the user from mounting the attack. The term in use for this deterrent is the "grandma" test. If grandma thinks the activity is bad, she will not do it. What the deterrent does is use the moral character of the user and moves an activity from where the user believes it is moral to immoral. Even though the user has the resources and opportunity to break the protections, the moral character of the user prevents them from mounting the attack.

Application Suitability

The final column in the matrix shown in Figure 5.1 combines the previous two vectors to show which types of applications are suitable for Intel TXT. Other applications can use Intel TXT, but the set of protections might not be sufficient to meet the applications need.

Stored Data

Stored data is data that is resident on the platform but not currently in use. This data is not in physical memory, but it uses some other storage medium. The typical media would be the disk drive, but other devices are possible. Stored data obtains protections from observation or use by the application encrypting the data. The encryption mechanism requires the protection of a key that can decrypt the stored data. Intel TXT provides the mechanism to protect the encryption key.

The attack points on the stored data are software attacks that try to recover the encryption key. Intel TXT provides the protections against software attack such that the stored data has protection from those software attacks.

Those entities wishing to rely on the stored data protection need to consider the potential of a user applying hardware attacks against the stored data encryption key. If the consideration is software attacks, Intel TXT provides mitigations against those software attacks.

Protected Email

Protected e-mail is a special case of stored data. The user wants to send and receive e-mail in a way that keeps other software processes from reading or modifying the e-mail. The information is specific to the user, and the user wants the information protected, so Intel TXT can mitigate software attacks. The protection mechanism would be a combination of Intel TXT memory protections and cryptography. The Intel TXT memory protection would provide coverage during the creation and viewing of the email. The cryptography would provide protection of the email during transit and storage of the e-mail.

Internet Transactions

Internet transactions represent an interesting type of data. The user might or might not want to protect the data. If the user is sending his credit card number, he wants protection. If the user is sending a confirmation of a bid price for an online auction, he might wish to cheat.

For information the user wishes to protect, an Internet transaction is another case of stored data, and Intel TXT can mitigate the software attacks.

For information that the user wishes to compromise, the grandma test works very well here. Intel TXT protects against software attacks, so the user is going to have to mount a sophisticated hardware attack. The attack mechanism would not sit well with grandma, and she would not compromise the information.

One additional type of protection that Intel TXT provides is the ability to know what application performed the operation. This is a very helpful item in a grid network. Grid networks are a combination of separate platforms that all combine to perform a single operation. In the late 1990s there were some interesting uses of grid or distributed computers. One of the big projects was a project sponsored by RSA to find the cryptographic key for RC5. The key size was 64 bits and a huge amount of computing power was necessary to find the key. To obtain the necessary computing power, a large group of interested people[3] donated their spare computing cycles to search for the key. The interesting problem the designers of the system had to overcome was how to ensure that no one who reports results is lying. As the result would reward the winner with some money, there was additional motivation for people to cheat. The designers used various techniques to isolate the application and detect cheating. The designers however were left with only performing obfuscation on the code, as they had no access to a secure area to execute a program. The designers of the software had this to say regarding their attempts to mitigate software attacks:

> Why is distributed.net still not completely open-source with all parts of its source code? Although we are providing all of the code linked on this page for public perusal, it is still necessary to keep select portions of the codebase unavailable for general distribution. Indeed, this is an aspect of our operations that we would very much like to be able to eliminate.
>
> Quite truthfully, releasing binary-only clients still does not completely eliminate the possibility of sabotage, since it is relatively easy for any knowledgeable person to disassemble or patch binaries. This is actually quite a trivial task, so we urge you not to try. Indeed, security through obscurity is actually not secure at all, and we do not claim it to be such.
>
> The source code available from this page is really all of the algorithmic code that would be of interest. The only code that is not present is the file-access and network socket code, which is not terribly interesting (nor pleasant to try to comprehend). The computational cores and platform-specific optimizations included in this package is what you would want to look at if you are interested in how the client works, or how you can increase the speed of the client for your processor.
>
> A document that discusses many of these issues at much greater depth is available for reading, and discusses the more general problem of Operational Code Authentication. (Distributed 2003)

---

3   The author was part of the group and all of the author's machines participated in the search.

If the designers had Intel TXT available to them they could have solved their problem. Notice that the designers were not interested in protecting from hardware attacks—their concern was for those who were not going to attempt to change the access or network code portions. To prevent cheating at the algorithm level, the system required duplicate attempts for the same key. The increase in computing power was offset by the assurance that work was actually being done.

Protecting the application from either manipulation or from performing unknown operations is a Intel TXT objective. Using the Intel TXT protections allow designers of these types of applications to mitigate these problems and have a higher assurance that their applications work properly in a distributed computing environment.

Time Value Degrading Content

What is time value degrading content? The best way to define this is to use an example. Consider a sporting event that is only available on pay-per-view. The providers want to protect the viewing of the event, but soon after the event occurs, the highlights of the event are available on the sports highlight shows. The value of the content degrades very quickly after the event is over. This is important in a Intel TXT context where the provider wants to use Intel TXT to protect the content. Most data loses value over time, the degradation time can be quite short or it could be hundreds of years. The value of the latest prizefight degrades quickly; the value of the United States Constitution does not degrade.

If the content provider wants to use Intel TXT for protection, the provider needs to evaluate a couple of issues. The first issue is how quickly the data degrades. In the sporting event example, the content degrades as soon as the event is over. With the degradation time so short, the protections need only be in place while the event is in progress. If the content provider believes that the Intel TXT platform can resist attacks, even hardware attacks, during the time of the event, Intel TXT provides sufficient protection for the content. If the content degrades slowly, then the attacks on Intel TXT may succeed before the value of the content reaches zero. Only the content provider can make this determination.

High Value Third-party Content with Common Distribution Method

High value third-party content is data that is difficult for Intel TXT to protect. If the data uses a common distribution mechanism, it is *very* difficult to protect. The reason is discernable by reviewing the matrix in Figure 5.1. This application is in the lower-right area, which means that the user wants to break the protection and that sophisticated hardware attacks are possible. Providing protection against sophisticated hardware attacks is not a Intel TXT objective, so this type of application may not gain appreciable levels of security by using Intel Trusted Execution Technology. Based on the grandma test or other factors, Intel TXT may provide additional levels of security that the content provider wants to use, but implying that Intel TXT will solve all of the content provider's problems is incorrect.

A serious issue for the provider if they are using a common distribution mechanism is the Break Once Run Everywhere (BORE) attack. If the attacker can mount a sophisticated hardware attack on a single system and obtain the content, the attacker then has access to any other content using the same distribution mechanism. The attacker can also distribute the BORE information and allow other attackers access to the content.

Hardware Objectives

The hardware features of Intel TXT must provide the following features:

- Accurate measurement of the MLE
- Fulfill a set of promises to the MLE

  - Consistent environment, that is when the MLE gains control the system looks the same every time
  - Controllable environment, that is the MLE has the opportunity to control the platform
  - Reset protection, if the platform resets while the MLE has sensitive data in memory, the hardware will scrub the memory prior to allowing any other process to access the memory
  - Limit the number of MLE, the hardware can ensure that only a well known MLE gains control of the platform

- Special privileges are assigned to the MLE, that is the MLE can access platform resources only available after a successful MLE measurement

- Defined set of must trust entities, the MLE will know the platform entities that must be trusted when allowing sensitive data to be in memory.

MLE Features

Objectives are great, but to meet the objectives a product or technology needs features[4]. This section is a quick introduction to each main feature of Trusted Execution Technology. Please remember that this list of MLE features are what we believe that an MLE should provide; an actual MLE implementation may or may not provide a specific feature. To make things recursive, if you want to rely on the feature set of an MLE you need to have the identity of the MLE, which means you want to rely on the hardware features of Intel TXT to perform the measurement. All of these features follow with a chapter of their own:

■ Protected execution

■ Protected memory pages

■ Sealed storage

■ Protected input

■ Protected graphics

■ Attestation

Protected Execution

Protected execution provides domain separation on Intel architecture platforms. Protected execution provides isolation of all resources associated with an application. The resources under protection include memory and internal CPU state.

To implement protected execution the majority of the changes occur in the CPU. Protected execution requires a change in the mechanisms that

---

4   Well, that is what marketing actually sells, so to keep marketing happy we need the features.

allow communication between the CPU packages and the chipsets that tie the packages together. One important piece of information the busses must communicate is the indication that all of the processors inside of a package are properly executing the domain separation feature.

Protected Memory Pages

The CPU protects the application resources using protected execution. All memory access occurs when the CPU requests access to the page using the FSB to indicate to the MCH which page to access. The CPU protections do not change what the MCH does on DMA accesses.

To protect against DMA from outside devices, the MCH has the Protected Memory Range (PMR). The PMR allows the MCH to have a view of which memory pages are under protection of the CPU. When any device other than the CPU operating in protected execution mode attempts to access a memory page, the MCH blocks access to the page.

Sealed Storage

While the CPU is executing data, it receives protection from the domain separation feature. From a platform perspective, data needs protection on a long-term basis. Storing data on a hard drive and then retrieving it needs to be a secure operation. The protected execution allows different configurations to use the Intel TXT protections. It is imperative that secrets held by one configuration are not made available to any other configuration.

The feature that provides this capability is called sealed storage. Sealed storage is a feature that the TPM provides. Intel TXT uses this feature to segregate data from one configuration to another.

Protected Input

When entering information, users need to have an assurance that only an application using protected execution can receive the keystrokes for such things as pass phrases. The traditional mechanism for creating the assurance between a device and an application is a trusted channel. Solutions built on Intel TXT have the ability to create trusted channels between the MLE and the keyboard and mouse. The MLE has complete control of the establishment and operation of the trusted channels.

Protected Graphics

Users need an assurance that what they see on a display window is truly coming from the application under protected execution control. As with input, the traditional mechanism for creating the assurance is to create a trusted channel between the application and the display adapter. Solutions built on Intel TXT have the ability to create a trusted channel to the display adapter. The MLE has complete control of the establishment and operation of the trusted channel.

Intel TXT allows for both integrated adapters and discrete adapters to participate in the trusted channels. The user sees no difference on the screen between an integrated or discrete device.

Intel TXT does not participate in the connection between the display adapter and the monitor. Previously defined protocols provide protection between a display adapter and the monitor and Intel TXT does change how those protocols work.

Attestation

Intel TXT works in a heterogeneous environment; some platforms might have Intel TXT and others might not. When an entity wants to rely on the Intel TXT features, how does that entity determine whether Intel TXT is present on an individual platform? In addition, how does the entity determine how the protected execution environment is currently executing? To answer these questions requires a verifiable mechanism that reports on the current platform configuration. The Trusted Platform Module (TPM) provides this capability.

The entire process of measuring a configuration and reliably reporting the measurement is *attestation*. Intel TXT provides the appropriate mechanisms to measure the Intel TXT configuration and store the measurements on the TPM. The TPM provides the mechanism to report on the stored measurements.

Chapter 11

Trusted Execution Technology Design Principles

I am a man of fixed and unbending principles, the first of which is to be flexible at all times.

—Everett Dirksen

Saltzer and Schroeder (Saltzer 1975) created a list of principles that security solutions should consider. The following is that list and a quick definition of each item:

- *Least privilege.* Limit access to resources to only those entities need the resource.

- *Economy of mechanism.* Privileged code should be small and easy to verify.

- *Complete mediation.* Ensure all access to the secure area is authorized.

- *Open design.* The design should not be secret.

- *Separation of privilege.* Use two mechanisms to arbitrate the access.

- *Least common mechanism.* Limit the amount of mechanisms shared between the users.

- *Psychological acceptability.* The user should want to use the system properly.

The principles overlap and sometimes appear to conflict with each other, but in the end, the principles provide an excellent starting point for the architecture of Intel® Trusted Execution Technology (Intel TXT®). By using the Saltzer security principles and the objectives from Chapter 10, one can create the Intel TXT design principles. Just as in Chapter 10, we will again differentiate between the hardware portion of Intel TXT and the supplied software for the MLE.

Security Principles

The security principles provide the framework for the overarching design. Understanding each principle individually illustrates how they combine into a coherent security design.

A critical building block for the Intel TXT design principles is the assumed heavy use of virtualization by the MLE, such as the enhancements provided by Intel® Virtualization Technology. The underlying capabilities of virtualization provide the perfect base for security operations.

Least Privilege

The concept definition is to restrict access to resources to a designated number of entities that should have access. For instance, instead of allowing all applications access to a memory page, restrict access to only the application that is using the page. The restriction comes from hardware providing services that a Virtual Machine Manager (VMM) can use to provide resource protection.

The hardware that performs the MLE measurement uses least privilege from the start. The command to start the operation is a protected command. The bus messages in use to synchronize the thread and packages are only available to the microcode that implements the command. There are other examples but following least privilege is inherent in the hardware design.

An MLE that uses virtualization provides least privilege almost by default. The VMM ensures that resources allocated to one guest are not available to any other guest, the very definition of least privilege.

The concept of locality, and enforcement of locality by the hardware, restricts access to the TPM. Locality is a projection of least privilege.

Intel TXT does a very good job of providing and enforcing a least privilege design.

Economy of Mechanism

According to the concept, privileged mechanisms are to be as small as possible. When you are trying to evaluate a mechanism for security properties, which seems more possible to evaluate, 1,000 lines of code or 10,000,000 lines of code? The answer is obvious.

The Intel TXT mechanisms do not touch the entire CPU or chipset. The domain separation comes from Intel® Virtualization Technology and does not require additional support. The launch process, while complex, uses one instruction. The chipset protection on the Intel Trusted Execution Technology Control Space (LTCS) uses a small protection engine.

Is Intel TXT as small as possible? The answer is an arguable point. Einstein had it right when he said "Make everything as simple as possible, but not simpler."[1] The question to ask is, "remove *what* to make it simpler?" Remove the launch process and it is virtually[2] impossible to measure the MLE. Other evaluators of Intel TXT have made the same comment, "Oh, this is complex." The first question back to them has been, "what should we remove?" The answer has always been "I do not see anything you can remove."

Complete Mediation

The concept is to ensure that each time an entity accesses a resource; the protection mechanism authorizes the access. To authorize an access, the protection mechanism must be able to identity the source of the access request.

For the launch process, mediation is complete. The command executes once and requires ring 0 access to launch. After the launch the hardware blocks any invocation of the launch process without first exiting from the MLE.

For a virtualization MLE, the physical page protections provide complete mediation of the access request. Any attempt by a guest to access a physical page results in the VMM gaining control. The VMM knows, from the VM exit information, the identity of the guest attempting to gain access to the page. The VMM then is able to allow or disallow the requested access.

---

1   The author of this book is also the author of the TXT security specification. So, simplifying and removing pages from the specification would be something the author would support.

2   Pun intended

Any MLE can take advantage of VT-d assignment of DMA devices to specific memory pages.

A well-written MLE should be mediating all accesses to system resources. An MLE that is not mediating is failing to provide the external access platform element.

Open Design

The open design security principle was not new to Saltzer and Schroeder. In fact, the principle is from the 1890s. The idea behind it is that the attacker knows your system, or put another way, you cannot keep your design a secret forever. If the system relies on a secret design, exposing the secret destroys the product.

The Intel TXT design is not a secret. Certainly, some information is not public, but the secrecy regarding the design is to protect Intel's intellectual property. Exposure of the design does not provide an advantage to an attacker attempting to defeat the Intel TXT protections.

The measurement of the MLE does not involve any secret values. There is a digital signature validation, but that is not depending on secrecy, rather it is depending on the protections that keep a cryptographic key secret.

The MLE would normally protect sensitive data and the mechanism to protect the data is encryption for data at rest and mediation of access for data in memory. If the MLE does an appropriate job of mediating access and ensuring only authorized access to the cryptographic keys, there should be no secret mechanisms in the design.

For both the measurement and MLE execution, the system does not use any "magic sauce" in the design.

Separation of Privilege

The design idea here is that more than one mechanism provides the protections. In some security circles, the concept is "who is watching the watcher" and "defense in depth."

The first separation of privilege that occurs with Intel TXT is the separation of the measurement of the MLE from the execution of the MLE. As the MLE will manage the system, asking the MLE to measure itself would be a violation of the separation property. The design is such that the hardware performs the measurement of the MLE before a single instruction of the MLE executes.

The second separation occurs when the MLE configures various hardware platform features to work in a specific manner. The best example of this is the MLE setting up the page tables to manage physical memory. The MLE only gets to set the policy, or how to layout the physical memory, but the MLE is unable to affect how the hardware enforces the memory layout. Once set in the hardware, the paging and segmentation mechanisms work without any additional touching.

The separation of hardware and software provides a good balance between a policy-enforcing engine and a policy. The hardware is the engine and the software is the policy, with a distinct separation between these two roles. Additional protections to be sure that the hardware works correctly or that the software has the correct policy are not inherent in the Intel TXT design. The software can easily have additional checks for the correct policy, both through attestation and additional functions. At this time, no Intel TXT design adds an additional hardware mechanism.

Least Common Mechanism

The least common mechanism is not, at first, an obvious direction. The idea is that the various mechanisms should *not* share common code or hardware. At first glance, you might think that this idea violates the economy of mechanism directive. In reality, you have no conflict. When a design shares a resource, the architecture must provide additional mechanisms to provide domain separation. If the architecture has two separate mechanisms, it becomes much easier to show the separation of the two functions.

The split in Intel TXT is between the hardware measurement and the software MLE platform management. After execution of the measurement, the code and operations are not available to the MLE. The MLE must use other platform resources to manage the platform.

Another requirement for the least common mechanism is that any common mechanism must be acceptable to all users. Intel TXT provides an excellent acceptance mechanism for the users. The measurement of the MLE allows those wishing to rely on the MLE the detailed knowledge of the exact environment they are about to accept.

Psychological Acceptability

Psychological acceptance means the technology is easy to use and easy to understand. If the user is unable to manage the system and cannot understand the protections offered, the user cannot use or properly configure the system.

Some parts of Intel TXT are very easy to understand at the user level. Stating that one guest knows nothing about any other guest is a concept that normal users accept. Trying to explain the VT-d protections for devices and DMA access is not within the normal user's realm of expertise[3].

Thankfully, the user need not know about VT-d or understand how the MLE is providing domain separation. The user does need to control the MLE, but a well-written MLE will provide adequate configuration tools that are easy to use.

Design Principles

The following requirements drive the Intel TXT design. The breakdown of these requirements is the purpose of the sections on assumptions, threats, and objectives. These high-level statements provide you with an overview of the Intel TXT design and help us to frame the questions about what Intel TXT does and does not do.

The Intel TXT hardware requires supporting software. The simple statement that "Intel TXT provides a specific protection" is not correct. Only in combination with properly executing controlling software are the Intel TXT protection capabilities available. Since the combination is the key, understanding which controlling software is executing becomes a critical requirement.

High-level Requirements

The high-level requirements for the measurement process are:

- During the launch of the MLE, the Intel TXT hardware must calculate and store an accurate measurement of the MLE.

- After measuring the MLE, the Intel TXT hardware must fulfill a set of promises the hardware makes to the MLE. (The list of promises is in Chapter 10.)

---

3   To be truthful it is barely within the author's realm of expertise

The high-level requirements for the MLE, where the MLE is protecting data, are:

■ The MLE must be able to defend itself from software-based modification.

■ The MLE must be able to protect sensitive data from access by a software process. Access is read, write, or use. The definition of data includes information and executable code.

■ The architecture of Intel TXT must allow a MLE to run different general-purpose programs concurrently.

– Note that here we are saying the architecture must not limit the MLE. It is entirely possible, and very probable, that there will be MLE that severely limit what types of services and applications the MLE allows to execute.

■ The architecture of Intel TXT should allow the use of the MLE in a wide variety of motherboard topologies:

– Multiple threads on the same CPU

– Multiple CPU packages on the motherboard

– Multiple chipsets on the motherboard

Environment Requirements

Intel TXT runs on Intel® architecture platforms. The environment of the platform creates some requirements for Intel TXT:

■ The Intel TXT architecture must enable backward compatibility.

– Backward compatibility allows the user to run legacy programs where the legacy program is unaware of any Intel TXT features. This requirement is highly dependent on the MLE implementation. The hardware can measure the MLE, but if the MLE does not support a mode or service, the legacy program will not execute.

■ Future hardware-based Intel Architecture security technologies should provide comparable or better levels of protection going forward.

User Assumptions

Both the designer of the platform and the user of the platform make some assumptions about how the user is going to interact with the platform. These assumptions drive some design principles:

- The user of a Intel TXT-enabled platform should *not* be considered an adversary.
- The user must opt in to the mechanism that provides the measurement of an MLE.
- The owner must be able to select the MLE they wish to allow to control the platform.
- The mechanisms that control the measurement and the selection of valid MLE must be easy for the end user to use.
- Third-party content protection is not a design goal of Intel TXT.

Attackers

Just as the designer makes some assumptions regarding the user of the platform, the designer makes some assumptions about those who wish to break the protections on the platform.

- The mechanism that performs the MLE measurement *must not* use a "global secret." Global secrets are vulnerable to a Break Once and Run Everywhere (BORE) attack.
  - There is no reason to use a secret mechanism to perform the measurement. Measurement is passing data to a cryptographic hash; no need for secrets. The mechanism to ensure an accurate measurement also has no need of secret values, so this requirement is very easy to meet.
- For management of the MLE, the MLE *should not* contain a global secret.
  - The distinction is that for MLE operations, there should be no global secret, but it is entirely possible, and actually quite probable, that an application will ask the MLE to protect the application's global secret.

■ Attackers with detailed knowledge of the PC platform, software architecture, and Intel TXT should not be able to launch a successful software-based attack.

■ Attackers with physical access to a Intel TXT-enabled platform may be able to circumvent protections.

Protection Requirements

The combination of Intel TXT measurement of the MLE and MLE operations are going to protect some data. These requirements though are requests for what the MLE should do. A well-written MLE will provide the following services:

■ The MLE must control access to a physical memory page such that only identified entities access the page. The example is a VMM that assigns a physical page to only one virtual machine. No other virtual machine can access the physical page so isolation of the data in the physical page from one virtual machine from the other.

■ The MLE should enable the creation of trusted channels from the MLE, or an MLE service, to the keyboard, mouse, and display adapter. This allows the system to create trusted paths that indicate the protection of the users input and output.

■ The MLE should have a mechanism that indicates to the user the state of the MLE and the state of any trusted channels.

■ The MLE needs to provide a service that enables the storage for long-term secrets. The service needs to enable integrity, confidentiality, and resistance to replay attacks to the for the information that uses the service. The assumption is that through use of the TPM seal properties the MLE can provide this service.

■ The MLE must be aware of, and be ready to respond to, various platform events like reset, power management, and BIOS configuration changes.

Upgrade Requirements

The MLE must be aware that components of the MLE may require updating. As the MLE is measured, any change to an MLE component changes the resulting measured value. As the MLE would normally make use of the TPM for sealing, a change to the MLE represents a change to the configuration that data is sealed with. The MLE must know how to apply changes and be able to recover sealed data.

What Is Not Under Intel TXT Protection

It is critical to know what items are *not* under Intel TXT protection. These items provide the basis for drawing the protection boundary. While the boundary can be somewhat soft or fuzzy, it is important to know that the boundary does not include the following items:

- The Intel TXT measurement of the MLE is susceptible to some hardware attacks.
- The MLE, while executing, is susceptible to some hardware attacks.
- The Intel TXT hardware does not provide a trusted path. The MLE using the trusted channels enabled by the hardware is responsible for displaying the trusted path.
- The Intel TXT hardware does not provide protection from all Denial of Service (DoS) attacks. The MLE is responsible for protecting the services provided by the MLE from DoS attacks.

MLE Measurement

The main job for Intel TXT is to obtain the identity of the Measured Launched Environment. The reason why the name is not Launched Environment is the desire is to know and rely on the identity of the launched environment.

Description of Measurement and Identity

A short digression is important here to define the terms measurement and identity. In the Intel TXT architecture, the identity of the MLE, VMM, or any other application, is a cryptographic hash of the module. Intel TXT currently uses the Secure Hash Algorithm version 1 (SHA-1). The calculation of the hash is the measurement. Therefore, the measurement of the MLE requires a SHA-1 calculation of the MLE code and the MLE identity is the resulting hash output.

Obtaining the MLE Identity

The difficulty with Intel TXT is ensuring that the measurement process obtains an accurate measurement of the MLE. The measurement process does not change the properties of the MLE; rather it allows those wishing to rely on the MLE the knowledge of which MLE is executing. The identity of the MLE informs the relying party of how the MLE handles the paging mechanism, how the MLE manages, DMA access, how the MLE handles communication, in fact everything the MLE does.

Figure 11.1 shows the components necessary to perform the measurement of the MLE.

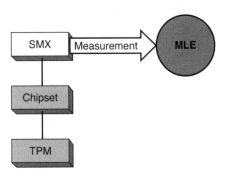

Figure 11.1 Measured Launched Environment (MLE) Measurement

The components of the MLE measurement are:

■ SMX instructions

■ Chipset hardware

■ TPM

SMX Measurement Instructions

The SMX instructions provide the ability to perform an accurate measurement of the MLE. To ensure the accuracy, the platform relies on the following components:

■ CPU synchronization

■ Authenticated code execution and measurement

■ Measurement of the MLE by the Authenticated Code (AC) module

■ Storing the AC module and MLE measurement in the TPM

With these mechanisms, the Intel TXT system provides an accurate measurement of the launching environment, the AC module, and the MLE operating environment. With those measurements, an outside entity can determine whether the system does provide the proper mechanisms to protect a physical page.

Chipset Hardware

The measurement process is not simply a CPU mechanism; the chipset must participate also. The chipset provides hardware mechanisms for the following features:

■ *The ability to accept an MLE measurement.* The chipset provides a dedicated area that is only for storing the MLE measurement. The area allows for special addressing and special processing.

■ *A way to ensure that only the SMX instructions can attempt to store the measurement.* When the chipset receives the measurement value some assurances must be made that only the CPU and an executing SMX instruction is storing the measurement.

■ *Passing of the measurement to the* TPM. After the chipset assures itself that the measurement value is coming from a valid SMX instruction, the chipset must pass the measurement value to the TPM

Storing MLE Measurement in TPM

The TPM stores the MLE measurement, and when requested, it can report the measurement value. The reporting of the MLE identity allows the entities wishing to rely on the platform the ability to evaluate the properties of the MLE.

Intel TXT does not change the TPM reporting capabilities. Storing measurement values in Platform Configuration Registers (PCR) and providing digital signatures of the PCR contents does not change in a Intel TXT platform.

Intel TXT does take advantage of the ability to report what platform entity is requesting access to the TPM. The TCG term for the access differentiation is *locality*. Intel® TXT takes full advantage of the localities to ensure the proper handling, reporting, and recording of the Intel TXT measurement.

Chapter **12**

Launched Environment

No enterprise is more likely to succeed than one concealed from the enemy until it is ripe for execution.

—Niccolo Machiavelli

Intel® Trusted Execution Technology (Intel® TXT) performs a measurement of the launched environment. If the launched environment does not manage the platform correctly, all one gains is the knowledge that one cannot rely on the platform. Therefore while Intel TXT does not directly provide a Measured Launched Environment (MLE) it is imperative that a well-written MLE exist. This chapter discusses some of the features and ideas that will create a well-written MLE.

For any MLE the basic job is going to be to isolate processes. An Intel platform provides numerous mechanisms to support the MLE in isolating operations. This chapter focuses on the idea that an MLE will be a Virtual Machine Monitor (VMM). It is not an architectural constraint that the MLE has to be a VMM; rather it appears to be the best choice to use the facilities that are available. The VMM provides the domain manager that establishes the virtual machines and manages the communication between virtual machines. For Intel TXT, it is the epitome of being Machiavellian, by concealing from the enemy the execution processes. A virtual machine can be general purpose and run an existing operating system like Windows or the virtual machine could be a specific application like a firewall. The Intel TXT system puts no requirements on the use model of a virtual machine.

The VMM has complete and full control of the processor. The VMM presents to each guest a processor abstraction and allows the guest to use the abstraction. The VMM controls processor resources, physical memory, interrupts, input and output, and communication between the guests.

VMX Operation

Intel® Virtual Machine eXtensions (VMX) provide the CPU support for virtualization. The VMX instructions do not require changes to any other platform component, including the chipset, to virtualize the CPU resources. VMX provides "true" virtualization in that the fact that the guest is virtualized is hidden from the guest. There are mechanisms that leave hints to the guest that virtualization is ongoing, so the guest may be aware of current virtualization state.

When VMX is executing, the processor is in one of two states: VMX operation or VMX root operation. If a guest has control of the processor, the processor is in VMX operation, if the VMM has control, the processor is in VMX root operation.

When a guest is operating in VMX mode, the only mode a guest can operate in, the guest believes that the guest has total control of the processor. The reality is that VMX root mode restricts what the guest can do. The restrictions include: physical memory visible to the guest, operations the guest can perform, events that execute, and instructions that work without VMX root authorization. The VMM controls the guest VMX mode by setting various options only changeable in VMX root mode. Whenever the guest performs an operation under control of the VMM, the guest exits from VMX operation and transitions to VMX root operation. Exiting from the guest uses the VMEXIT event and the VMM receives control at a predefined entry point. After processing the event, and either allowing the event or blocking it, the VMM returns control to the guest by using the VMRESUME operation.

Figure 12.1 shows the layout of the guest and VMM, the various structures, and the directions of VMEXIT and VMRESUME. The guest in VMX mode has all of the normal CPU control mechanisms available in ring 0. Those control mechanisms include the Global Descriptor Table (GDT) and Interrupt Descriptor Table (IDT). When a system is operating without Intel Virtualization Technology and a VMM, the ring 0 process has complete control of the GDT, IDT, and all other CPU control mechanisms. When Intel® Virtualization Technology is executing and the guest is in VMX mode, the guest sees a virtualized copy of the GDT and IDT. The VMM, in VMX root mode, has control of the real GDT and IDT. The virtualization of these two structures is the basic mechanism that allows the VMM to control the guest and what the guest can do.

The net effect of running in VMX operation state is to restrict or "de-privilege" certain operations of the guest, while still allowing the guest the full use and utility of the normal privilege levels, rings 0 through 3. To illustrate the de-privilege nature of a VMX operation, Figure 12.1 uses 0D and 3D. Those rings and the 1D and 2D rings not shown are in the guest. The VMM has all four rings, 0 through 3, but the rings have full privilege. The designation of "D" indicates de-privilege and "P" indicates full privilege. The current implementation of a VMM does not use the other rings 1 through 3, but they are available, and a VMM implementation could use them.

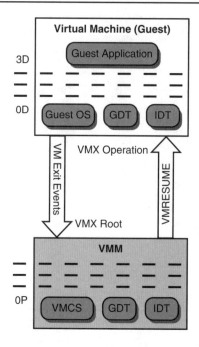

Figure 12.1 VMX Events

When the guest invokes one of the operations that cause a VMEXIT, like accessing CR3, the hardware fills in the Virtual Machine Control Structure (VMCS), passes control to the VMM, and transitions to VMX root operation.

VM Control Structure

The VMCS controls a number of functions relevant to VMX mode and to transitions into and out of VMX root operation. The VMM is the only entity with access to the VMCS; no guest can access any VMCS structure. The VMM has VMX instructions that allow the VMM access to the VMCS. The VMCS includes:

■ The *guest-state area* contains key components of processor state representing the guest's execution state and the cause of the most recent VM exit. This state is saved on a VM exit, as execution control reverts to the VMM, and this state is restored on a VMRESUME as control is passed to the guest. The VMM may modify this state to alter the behavior of the guest or to invoke a different guest.

■ The *host-state area* contains key components of processor state representing the VMM. VMEXIT restores the area when transitioning from VMX operation to VMX root operation.

■ The *VM-execution controls* regulate the processor's functions while in VMX mode. They determine, for example, which events, operations, and situations cause VM exits if they occur while the processor is in VMX mode.

■ The *VM-exit controls* determine the components of processor state to save into the guest-state area on a VM exit and certain components of VMM state that load on a VM exit.

■ The *VM-entry controls* determine which components of processor state load from the guest-state area on a VMLAUNCH or VMRESUME. In addition, they allow modification of the VMRESUME behavior, such as allowing the next VMRESUME to deliver an interrupt to guest software.

Notice that while only one VMCS is in the processor, and therefore only one guest can be "active" at any given moment, the VMM may selectively modify all guest state in the VMCS. Thus, a VMM can set up multiple guests and switch between them by explicitly saving and restoring guest VMCS state and associated controls from memory. The specific properties of such multiple-guest environments are determined solely by the VMM, which is also solely responsible for instantiating and managing each guest and its resources. It is possible to establish guests with fully private resources—that is, resources not accessible to any other guest—as well as to allocate resources to be shared between all guests or a subset of guests.

VMM Launch and VM Creation

Figure 12.2 illustrates the general process of launching a VMM, creating an initial virtual machine environment, and then adding a second virtual machine. This figure illustrates the general case, where launching the VMM occurs after an OS and its applications are already running. It is also possible to launch the VMM as part of an OS boot loader, or even during the BIOS. No architectural requirement says that the environment that initiates the VMM must be present as a guest during VMM execution. The VMM may establish a guest that contains the initiating environment or the VMM may never establish a guest that contains the initiating environment. The VMM could never establish a guest that contains the initiating environment, but when the VMM terminates, the environment to which the VMM passes control could be the initiating environment.

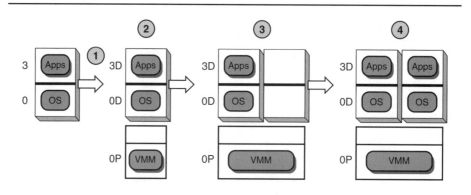

Figure 12.2 Creation of a Multi-partition Environment

The steps described here represent only an abstract view of the process. Detailed descriptions, including the specific instructions, VMCS settings, and VMM responsibilities are available in the appropriate platform manuals. Additionally, these steps identify only one process model, but multi-process variations are possible.

Step 1 in Figure 12.2 illustrates the initiating software loading a VMM into memory and the transferring control to the new VMM. Step 2 shows the VMM instantiating a guest partition with the initiating software in the guest partition. Steps 3 and 4 show the VMM instantiating another partition and loading an OS into the new partition.

On first launch, the VMM performs its own self-initialization and assumes control over critical resources formerly belonging to the initiating OS that could represent violations of the VM perimeter—for example, the interrupt table and the now-guest OS page tables, among others. The VMM also configures the desired VMEXIT conditions that cause the OS or applications in the VM to trap back to the VMM. Once properly configured, execution control may return to the now-guest OS using a VMLAUNCH instruction.

Once control returns to the guest OS in its VM, execution continues normally within that VM. As configured by the VMM, certain operations may result in traps back to the VMM. The VMM may perform the operation as specified, perform only a portion of the operation, substitute another operation entirely, or reject the operation with or without notice. As an example, an attempt by the guest OS to change an entry in the guest OS page table results in a trap to the VMM, which selectively performs or discards the requested change, depending on whether the result would violate the boundaries of the virtual machine.

At any time after the initial launch, the guest or the VMM may recognize the need to run additional, specific software in a second VM.[1] The three main ways for the VMM to establish an additional VM are:

- *Current guest loads new guest memory.* This mechanism has VM#1 load VM#2 into the memory pages in the VM#1 physical page allocation, then has VM#1 inform the VMM where the pages for VM#2 are, and finally passes control to the VMM which instantiates VM#2. When allocating pages to VM#2, VM#1 removes the pages from VM#1 control.

- *Current guest relinquishes pages.* VM#1 would release pages under control of VM#1 and have the VMM instantiate VM#2 in a separate step. VM#1 has the option to fill the new pages with information or leave the pages blank. If VM#1 places information into the pages, the VMM should validate the starting state; if VM#1 leaves the pages blank, then the VMM must provide the code to execute in VM#2.

---

1 In other models, this decision may be made by the VMM itself. In which case, the VMM requests that the guest OS in the initial VM surrender an appropriate number of memory pages, after which the VMM may install the new VM into those pages.

■ *VMM maintains pool.* In this mechanism, the VMM does not assign all free pages to VM#1. Instead, the VMM maintains a pool of free pages, and when a new VM is necessary, the VMM assigns the pages from the pool.

To manage the physical pages, the VMM can use one, all, or any of the above mechanisms that the VMM desires. Each mechanism has plusses and minuses. The use model determines what is appropriate for a VMM and the guests it supports.

The VMM, by virtue of having total control, can reject or modify the request for an additional VM. The VMM has the ability to add additional pages, start multiple VMs on a single request, or stop the instantiation of the new VM. The VMM might or might not report the reasons for denying or modifying a request for a new VM.

Once the memory pages, and optionally, other resources such as specific IO ports, have been removed from the VM#1 context and reallocated to VM#2, VM#1 no longer has any ability to touch those resources in any way. Neither can VM#2 access any resources allocated to VM#1, unless, of course, such sharing is explicitly supported by the VMM. This separation is the essence of domain separation and the underlying security assumption for TXT.

Protected Virtual Machines

Moving from just plain virtualization to the trusted platform space we now need to look at the protections available to a virtual machine. One could separate virtual machines into two classes; standard and protected. For some uses this separation is very helpful, but the separation is arbitrary. The reality is that if the VMM is protecting one VM it is protecting all instantiated VMs. The VMM may provide a different level of protection to each VM, but the cold hard fact is that every instantiated VM has protection. The guest VM and the VMM may negotiate the amount of protection necessary for the tasks the VM will execute.

Why do guests have different protection requirements? The answer lies in the task or tasks that the guest is performing. A guest that creates digital signatures and needs protection for an asymmetric private key has very different properties from a guest that manages a printer. A generic guest that operates a complete operating system has very different requirements than a single purpose guest. No one size fits all type of protection. The VMM and the guest must combine to provide the appropriate level of protection for the guest. The mechanism through which the guest informs the VMM of the protection requirements is a function of the services that the VMM supplies to the guests.

For the sake of simplicity and ease of reading, the we will discuss two types of guests: standard and protected. The definition of standard is a guest that only uses virtualization and does not attempt either to protect physical pages from DMA acces or to restrict access to I/O ports. The definition of protected is a guest that protects all resources. Numerous other definitions are possible; the point of naming them is to provide labels in the document.

The Intel TXT design places no architectural limit on the number of guests the VMM can support. The design places no architectural limit on the mix of guest protections. A VMM could support one protected and one standard guest. The VMM could also support four protected and two standard guests. Implementation issues could limit the number of guests, and they could possibly limit the protections available to a guest.

When each guest gains control of the CPU, the normal protections for the ring (0, 1, 2, and 3) are active. A guest is not able to change or manipulate the ring protections and allow a guest to bypass ring protections for memory or process resources. A guest should have no access to VMM resources. The VMM can expose services that make use of VMM resources, but not provide a direct access to any VMM resources.

History Lesson

When the author originally wrote this chapter many years ago, VMMs existed only in specialized markets and were not generally available for the PC. In 2008 this situation is changing. Commercial VMMs and some open source VMMs are now available. The models the VMMs use for security and establishment of VMM services fit into the types of models listed below. Without trying to takes sides in what VMM is the best, the author will not list any or all of the current VMMs. If the reader is interested in looking at VMM choices for services and VM instantiation the author suggests an Internet search with keywords such as "hypervisor" "virtual machine monitor" or "virtual machine kernel". Another place to start would be the Wiki article on hypervisors http://en.wikipedia.org/wiki/Hypervisor

Varieties of implementation models are possible when considering the VMM and the guests. Intel TXT does not require or enforce any specific model. The VMM designer can cooperate with the guest designer; in fact they may even be the same entity. When the VMM and guest designers cooperate they can create symbiotic models of communication and control. If the VMM and guest designers do not cooperate, either through mutual distrust or ignorance of each other, the models of communication and control are set by the VMM and the guest has no control over the interfaces. Figure 12.3 illustrates some models that can occur.

The left model, labeled A, shows a VMM that provides no services for either the standard or protected guests. A guest that is unaware of the VMM does not attempt to use any VMM services. A legacy OS would be unaware of the VMM and would not require specific VMM services to execute applications.

The middle model, labeled B, is a picture of a special purpose guest that requires kernel type services from the VMM. The kernel services could be specific for the guest or the services could be generic. A special purpose guest can be either a standard or a protected guest.

The right model, labeled C, shows a VMM that provides kernel services to guests that have their own operating systems. The kernel services in this model could provide both special and specific guest services.

The real model for a VMM is going to be the combination of all of the previous models. The VMM does support those guests that are unaware of virtualization, those guests that require a VMM, and those guests that make use of the VMM when it is present. No model is right or wrong. The system designer needs to take protection, throughput, ease of use, and other such considerations into account when deciding how to create and use the VMM and guests.

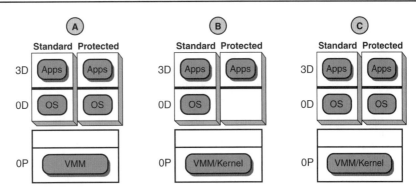

A: VMM provides no services to guest OS

B: VMM provides complete kernel services. Normally represents a special purpose guest.

C: VMM provides kernel services and guests provide OS type services. Represents a very common model.

Figure 12.3 VMM Environment Models

VMM with No Services

The VMM provides no additional services to any guest. The VMM is opaque to the guest and the guest must be self-sufficient. The VMM does provide:

- Domain separation
- Resource protection
- VM life-cycle support
- VM scheduling, though this may come from a guest
- Limited inter-VM communication

The rationale for this type of VMM lies in the simple nature of the VMM. The VMM code base is smaller than a VMM with services, and with the smaller amount of code, one might think that a security evaluation would be easier to perform. The lack of services limits the security and functionality claims of the VMM. Fewer claims and services provide developers of the VMM with an opportunity to make fewer mistakes in design and implementation.

VMM with Kernel Features

The guest must have knowledge of the VMM when the VMM provides kernel features. The VMM determines the mechanism that exposes the service to the guest. Of the many types of communication mechanisms available, the VMM may use one or more to expose VMM services.

With the VMM providing services, the ability to create special purpose guests is possible. Using the services of the VMM, the guest can concentrate on a single purpose. The trusted platform architecture does not require a single-purpose guest; it merely allows one. The VMM service of providing communication between guests now becomes a much more important service. Since a single-purpose guest only does one job, other guests are going to require the service that the single-purpose guest provides. While some services might have a low bandwidth, the assumption is that many guests have high bandwidth requirements. Hence, the communication between the guests and the VMM are critical.

The VMM is free to provide any service that the VMM developer wishes to expose. The VMM may provide services to only one guest and no other guest; the mix, content, and availability of services is a design decision for the VMM designer and implementer.

Measured Launch Environment

In the previous version of this chapter this section focused on measuring a VMM. As previously stated there is no architectural requirement to measure and launch a VMM; the environment can be any type of operating system or hypervisor. With the exception of changing the word VMM to MLE, the content of this section remains the same.

System designers can write an infinite number of MLE implementations that support the trusted platform. The variations occur due to the fact that the MLE is a piece of software and you have an infinite number of ways to write a program. Even after writing one MLE, you can update and modify the original code. Whether it is a human or a process, any entity that wishes to rely on the MLE to provide a specific set of services and assurances wants to know the identity of the MLE executing. In fact, the entity wishes to know if *any* MLE is executing. The simple answer is to ask the MLE who it is and let the MLE respond. Allowing the MLE to answer works fine when the relying party believes the MLE will not lie, but what happens when the MLE can lie? As the MLE has total control of the CPU, it is very easy for the MLE to report any identity for itself. Why would a MLE lie? Two obvious reasons are:

■ The MLE wishes to masquerade as some other entity.

■ Some attack corrupted the MLE and the attacker wants to hide.

In a world with MLEs that do and do not lie how does one tell them apart? The answer is the identity of the MLE. The MLE is just normal software with a special job to do. Creating an identity of the MLE is as simple as computing a cryptographic hash of the code. Cryptographic hashes—and from now on hash means cryptographic hash—have very interesting properties.

The interesting property that is most important to the MLE identity is: a change in a single bit of the MLE code causes a major change in the resulting hash value. One cannot change a single instruction without changing the hash value, which is an excellent property for identifying a MLE. The bottom line is that any change to the code means that the MLE has a new identity.

Hashes are very accurate in reporting the identity of the information presented to the hash. The issue is what entity sends the information to the hash algorithm. Asking an entity to measure itself does not work since that entity can present false information to the hash algorithm if it wants to lie.

Some other mechanism, one not under control of the entity to identify, must present the information to the hash algorithm.

In the Intel TXT case, the entity to identify is the MLE, but the MLE has complete control of the CPU. Some hardware that is not under control of the MLE must measure the MLE. Measurement of the MLE must occur prior to giving the MLE control of the CPU. Intel TXT provides a hardware mechanism, in use during the invocation of the MLE, which properly runs the MLE image, or binary, through a hash algorithm. The measurement process gives the launched environment the MLE name, Measured, by Intel TXT, Launched Environment.

Measuring the MLE

To have an assurance of the proper calculation of the MLE identity, or the measurement process, the measurement and launch of the MLE must meet the following requirements:

■ All measurement and storage of the measurement must occur prior to passing control to the MLE.

■ The measurement process must occur in a manner that defends against spoofing of the measurement.

■ The launch process must ensure that all processors run the same MLE.

■ The launch process must ensure that all processors start at a known entry point.

■ The MLE must complete MLE initialization prior to allowing any other entity to execute.

■ No other bus masters, processors, devices, or cache snooping can subvert the MLE measurement and or MLE launch.

■ No misconfiguration or misrepresentation of processor, chipset, or platform state must be able to subvert the launch.

Launching the MLE

When booting the platform, the BIOS performs the job of configuring the platform. The BIOS runs once and then allows the OS to manage the platform. With an MLE, a user might want to run one MLE for one task and then another MLE for another task. If the process of measuring and launching the MLE only occurs at once per boot, then to change MLE, the user would have to reboot the platform, an undesirable user experience. To avoid this situation Intel TXT provides for a "late launch" of the MLE. Late launch means that the measurement and launch of the MLE can occur at any time after platform reboot. In addition, Intel TXT contains a provision to exit from the MLE and allow another MLE to launch. A launch of a MLE can occur at any time, during BIOS processing, or during OS execution. The number of MLEs that can launch and exit is unlimited. The time between invocations of an MLE is unlimited, too. The interesting fact is that events occurring prior to the MLE launches do not affect the launch. For instance, the launch could be the first time since boot that a MLE launches or it could be the hundredth launch of a MLE; it does not matter.

Prior to the launch, the launching entity locates and loads into memory two code modules. One module is the MLE that the launch process measures. The other module verifies certain system configurations to ensure that the hardware operates in a manner that allows the MLE to protect system resources. The chipset's specific Authenticated Code (AC) module has a digital signature from the chipset manufacturer, and it executes only if the launch process can verify the digital signature.

The `GETSEC` `[SENTER]` instruction starts the measurement–and–launch sequence. The instruction broadcasts a message to the chipset and all processors. In response to this message, the other processors perform basic clean-up, signal their readiness to proceed, then they wait for a signal to join the MLE.

Once all other processors have signaled ready, the initiating processor continues the process by loading, authenticating and executing the chipset-specific authenticated code module. This module is tests for an acceptable system configuration, enables chipset protections, and provides initial DMA protection. This module then measures, registers, and launches the MLE, starting at an initialization entry point.

The MLE initialization routine completes the system configuration changes, including redirecting INITs, SMIs, interrupts, and others, and then issues `GETSEC [WAKEUP]` messages to the other processors to bring them under control of the MLE. At this point, all processors and the chipset are correctly configured.

Protecting Secrets

History Lesson on Names

The original LaGrande name for the launched environment was Secure VMM. This name came from the idea that the VMM would be secure and that LaGrande would always be launching a VMM. Well, Intel TXT does not guarantee the security of the VMM so the first name change was to MVMM for measured VMM. That name stuck for some time, until it became well known that Intel TXT did not require a VMM, it just worked very well with a VMM. So the name changes again to Measured Launched Environment (MLE) to properly reflect what Intel TXT really accomplishes.

The history lesson also shows the change in focus of Intel TXT. Early on it was to provide a robust and secure, always present, never compromised, executing environment. That was an unrealistic goal. The real goal is to allow any number of launched environments, and to identify exactly which environment is executing.

One of the promises of an MLE is that if an entity knows how the MLE acts, it is possible to believe that the MLE should be able to keep a secret. However, the Intel TXT hardware has no way to determine if the MLE can or cannot keep a secret. It is very possible for an MLE to keep a secret, but those wishing to rely on the MLE have to make the trust decision if the MLE is capable of adequately protecting the secret. The hardware can provide services to help the MLE keep a secret, think the VMX instructions, and can provide an accurate measurement of the MLE, the trust decision always comes from those wishing to rely on the MLE.

A MLE's ability to protect that secret is a major feature, and one that attackers will try to exploit. Since an MLE is software, the MLE's ability to keep secrets is not always perfect. To differentiate between MLEs, and contrast one MLE's ability to protect a secret over another MLE, is a major reason for the measurement of the MLE. Knowing the identity of the MLE allows the outside entity to understand what the behavior of the MLE will be.

The Intel TXT system needs to keep the following categories of secrets:

■ *Application secrets.* In this category, each application keeps secrets from any other application. The mechanism that allows this secret-keeping is in the ring and paging mechanisms. If the application is running in ring 3, all ring 0 processes in the same VM have access to the application secret.

■ *VM secrets.* In this category, each of the VM guests keeps secrets from all other guests running under control of the MLE. The mechanism that provides the secret protection is in the paging mechanism and the VM segregation under control of the MLE. This category assumes that the MLE is a VMM. If the MLE is an operating system this category may not be present.

■ *MLE secrets.* The MLE needs to keep secrets from all guests running under the MLE's control. Keeping this secret is a matter of keeping the MLE physical pages separate from all of the guests. In addition to keeping secrets from all of the guests, the MLE needs to keep secrets from all other possible MLEs. Keeping secrets from the other MLE allows MLE segregation. The mechanism keeps secrets across MLE invocations. In other words, if a secret is held by MLE #1 and MLE #2 executes; #2 will not have access to the secrets of #1, but #1 can recover its secrets upon invocation of #1.

The MLE can provide a variety of services to protect application and VM secrets. The ability for a MLE to provide the appropriate services is another reason to know the identity of the MLE that is executing.

The MLE secrets require special hardware support to implement. The crux of the matter is the identity of the MLE. By using the MLE identity in the Trusted Platform Module (TPM), Intel TXT provides a way to use sealing capabilities of the TPM.

An obvious way for a MLE to keep MLE secrets is to create a root key, protect all MLE information using the root key, and seal the root key to the MLE identity in the TPM. This mechanism relies on the sealing properties of the TPM; sealing information requires the exact same measurements to be present in the TPM to release the information. This property is exactly what Intel TXT provides for an MLE: accurate measurement of the MLE, and proper reporting of the measurement to the TPM. Chapter 13 contains the details on the TPM.

Establishing Secrets

With the seal property, it is easy to prove that the exact same identity is running each time. But, what informs the relying entity the first time that the environment will properly protect secrets? Here the whole stack comes into question. An application should only establish a secret if the application believes that the MLE, and any VM, will provide the protections necessary for the application to keep a secret. A VM should only establish a secret if the VM believes that the MLE will provide the protections for the VM to keep a secret. The MLE should only establish a secret if the MLE believes that the hardware can provide the protections necessary to protect the secret. This chain is a direct reflection of the previous section's comments regarding protecting secrets with the difference that the entity wants to know the identity prior to establishing the secret.

Two mechanisms are in play during secret establishment. First, measurement and launch provides the identity of the MLE in a way that software cannot manipulate. The second mechanism is the reporting capability of the TPM. The measurement process stores the MLE identity in the TPM. Using the native TPM capabilities of reporting on measurements, the TPM provides to entities wanting to rely on the platform the information necessary to make the decision to trust the platform and MLE and to allow the MLE to establish secrets.

The most important point of this process is that the Intel TXT hardware does not tell the entity that is about to use the platform to "trust me" rather the platform says "here is who I am." Then, the entity makes its own trust decision. This flipping of who makes the trust decision is critical to how Intel TXT works. By providing the identity of the MLE, the relying party can make different decisions, depending on the type of operation about to occur. The first time, the entity might trust the MLE, and the next time, the same entity might not trust the exact same MLE. Security and trust are not "pushed" from the platform; instead, the relying party "pulls" the identity and then evaluates the identity.

The actual protocols are far more complex, in part because they include mechanisms to protect the user's privacy. See Chapter 13 for a detailed description of the attestation requirements, supporting hardware and protocols.

Boundary Conditions

The MLE must maintain control of all resources, errors, or exceptions. Once measured and established, no event should be able to call into question the identity and integrity of the MLE.

Examples of such events include system reset, INIT, SMI, S3 or S4 sleep states. In any of these cases, the event may remove or bypass the protections established by the MLE launch, leaving the code and data in the formerly protected memory exposed.

As a rule, the Intel TXT Security Architecture addresses these events by:

■ Preventing the system event while the MLE Environment is launched

■ Redirecting the event handling code into the MLE

■ Confining the event-handling code to a guest VM

■ Scrubbing the system memory following the event before allowing any unknown code to execute

See Chapter 17 for detailed descriptions on the handling of each system event.

MLE Protection Boundary

After measurement of the launched environment, what does the trusted platform expect the MLE to do? In other words, what does the MLE do to protect itself from software manipulation?

This section represents what the MLE should do. An MLE writer may decide to not provide a certain protection, or rely on some other entity for protection. There are no hard and fast rules; rather the identity of the MLE allows those wishing to use the system to identify the MLE and the properties of the MLE.

The easiest way to protect information in a PC is to limit access to the physical memory page. If an application cannot gain access to a page, all of the information on the page has protection from the application. Since the MLE goal is to protect from software attacks, denying an application the ability to access a page provides the protection. While the physical memory is important, other resources require protection. These resources include hardware configuration settings, input/output devices and ports, and other system entities.

The previous discussions around requirements, design principles, and security principles point out the need to draw a boundary around what does and does not have protection. One way to describe the boundary is to use the mechanism of a Target of Evaluation (TOE) from the Common Criteria (Common 2002). A TOE produces a description of the protection boundary including the entities and mechanisms in and out of the boundary. This chapter does not create a complete TOE, but it does go into the building blocks necessary to create a TOE. The exercise of determining the components inside and outside of the boundary was helpful to the original Intel TXT architects.

From a trusted platform standpoint, the domain separation breaks when a software process obtains access to a protected resource. If a ring 3 application accesses a protected ring 0 memory page, the access represents a break. If one guest accesses the memory of another guest without permission, the access also represents a break.

Page Protections

Four mechanisms for a software process to gain access to a physical page are:

■ The software, as an application, VM, or MLE can request access to a physical page by referencing the virtual page address. The internal CPU process translates the virtual page access to the actual physical address and routes the physical page request to the memory controller. The software can be executing at any privilege level, ring 0 through ring 3.

■ The software can program a device to access a physical page. Devices access physical pages on a very frequent basis to move information from the main system memory to a storage or network device. These memory accesses do not require CPU control; hence, the paging mechanism is not in use. The term for such a direct access to memory, bypassing the CPU, is Direct Memory Access (DMA). Software configures the device by indicating which physical page the device should use for the DMA accesses.

■ Display adapters are a special case of DMA device access. Special tables are made available to the display adapter so it can create and display the output screens. The display adapter needs quick and efficient access to the display buffers so that reasonable display frame rates are possible.

■ System Management Interrupts (SMI) result in a mode switch in the CPU and the bypassing of the paging mechanism. The SMI handler code can currently run in modes that do not support paging.

The security boundary for an MLE requires the MLE to take into account all four of the physical page accesses in the previous list. Figure 12.4 shows the MLE physical page protection from a layer point of view.

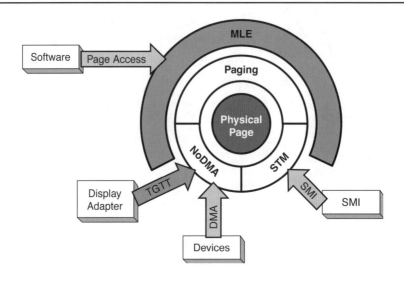

Figure 12.4 Physical Page Protections

The four boxes match the four areas listed in the previous paragraph and show the initiation of a software request for access to a physical page. The components that control the accesses are:

- MLE and the paging mechanism
- DMA access
- Trusted Graphics Translation Table (TGTT)
- SMI Transfer Module (STM)

The MLE provides a large portion of the protection as the MLE manages the paging mechanism, the DMA protection, and cooperates with the STM. The remaining sections describe the controlling mechanisms.

Paging Mechanism

The paging mechanism with a page table and ring structure has been in the CPU since the time of the Intel386™ processor. There is no change when dealing with an MLE to the paging mechanism. The paging mechanism provides separation of processes from ring to ring. The idea is that a higher-level process has no access to lower-level process information. A ring 3 process is unable to access ring 0 process information without the permission of the ring 0 process. The paging mechanism also can separate processes inside of rings other than 0; any ring 0 process has access to all of memory.

Ring 0 controls the paging mechanism by manipulating CR3, the register that contains the base address of the page directory. Any entity that can control CR3 has the ability to control access to physical memory. Operating systems control CR3 to provide process separation and to ensure that applications only gain access to real physical memory. VMX adds additional paging support. VMX allows the VMM to control CR3; the operating system in the guest only sees a virtual CR3. When the OS makes a change to CR3, the hardware causes the CR3 change request to invoke the VMM and the VMM ensures that the CR3 change is allowable. The paging mechanism also uses page tables and other controls; any manipulation of these controls by an OS requires validation and acceptance by the VMM.

The VMM control of the paging mechanism is what provides the protection from software manipulation of physical pages. All software accesses must use the mechanism built by CR3, with the VMM validating any change to CR3 and the page tables, the VMM ensures that the OS only has access to a proscribed set of physical pages. The VMM uses this control to segregate one guest from another. By assigning a physical page to one guest and never allowing the physical page to be in use by any other guest, the VMM provides the base level of domain separation. The control of the paging mechanism by the VMM is the crux of the domain separation protection. If the VMM is unable to control the paging mechanism, it cannot provide domain separation.

The MLE makes use of the exact VMX control of the paging mechanism. The VMM has complete control of CR3, and no additional controls are needed. You only need to understand which VMM is controlling CR3. The understanding requirement again points to the necessity of understanding which VMM is controlling the platform.

If the MLE controlling the platform is not a VMM, then the MLE has to handle CR3 accesses with extreme caution. Failure of the MLE to control CR3 represents a major vulnerability and would be an excellent avenue for attackers to exploit.

DMA Protections

The paging mechanisms under control of the MLE provide sufficient protections from any CPU software process attempting to access a physical page. What the paging mechanisms do not control is the ability of a DMA capable device of directly accessing a physical memory page. The original reason for DMA was to bypass the paging mechanism and allow for faster device access to physical memory. Devices that make extensive use of DMA are network cards and disk drives. Changing the system architecture to require a DMA device to use the paging tables would add an unacceptable amount of memory access latency to those devices needing direct memory access.

The issue with DMA devices is, while they are hardware, most of them allow software to configure the physical memory pages that those devices use for DMA purposes. Software configuration of the devices would allow software to break the domain separation setup by the MLE and the paging mechanism.

With no change available to the system architecture and the continued need to perform DMA access, the trusted platform needs to add a protection mechanism that limits DMA access. The protection for DMA comes from Intel® Virtualization Technology for Directed I/O (Intel® VT-d). Figure 12.4 shows that the MLE control overlapping the DMA protection. The overlap indicates that the MLE controls the DMA protection. What this implies is that while the DMA access bypasses the paging mechanism, the MLE has complete control of the VT-d configuration. By controlling the VT-d configuration the MLE controls how DMA devices access physical memory and the MLE can properly protect itself from software access.

TGTT

To create and display the screens, the display adapter needs quick and efficient access to physical memory. The mechanism in use is a special DMA access with sophisticated access patterns defined and bounded by one or more address-remapping tables. The remapping allows the dynamic change of page addresses in response to the needs of the adapter. As with any DMA device, the need to continue DMA access is critical to system needs, and changing the basic access is not possible in the Intel TXT architecture.

One change would be to indicate that the physical pages in use by the display adapter would allow DMA access. The DMA protections are binary, either no DMA or all DMA. Allowing graphic DMA access would allow any device access. One advantage that Intel TXT provides is the ability to create trusted channels between devices and drivers. One obvious device to use a trusted channel is the display adapter, which requires the creation of a trusted display channel. Many security solutions depend on the ability to create a channel between the application and the display device. The basic attacks on the display occur because the display buffers are in physical memory and susceptible to access by either applications or DMA devices. The display adapter uses DMA to gain quick access to the physical memory and create a display frame rate that is pleasing to the user's eye. To create a trusted channel the mechanism must provide both protection from software processes and other DMA devices. If the Intel TXT system does not provide these base-level protections, you have no assurance that the information on the display is what the protected application sent to the display. For all of these reasons, simply not protecting the display buffer's physical pages is an unacceptable solution.

The Intel TXT solution is to provide special frame buffers for the display and disallow any DMA access except for the display adapter. In addition, the display adapter can only communicate to the frame buffers using certain addresses. Any other attempt by the display adapter to touch other physical pages using a DMA access requires the VT-d to allow the physical page access. The Trusted Graphics Translation Table (TGTT) is the mechanism that provides the frame buffer protection.

Just as control of VT-d comes from the MLE, control of the TGTT resides in the MLE. The MLE establishes the TGTT, assigns the physical pages to the TGTT, and configures the chipset and display adapter to use the TGTT. The MLE must synchronize the physical memory pages in use by the TGTT with VT-d and the use of the frame buffers by graphics applications. Failure of the MLE to perform this task can result in the leaking of graphically protected information.

STM

The SMI Transfer Monitor (STM) provides protection of a physical page from access by normal SMI handling code. The STM is a security peer to the MLE. The STM and MLE negotiate the correct policies for what the SMI handling code should and should not do, and then the MLE allows the STM to handle all SMI events.

SMI handling code in a non Intel TXT system has access to all of physical memory. The code operates without knowledge of the OS and can manipulate any physical address. Obviously, allowing a software process this type of access does not maintain the protection boundary that the MLE is attempting to create.

The MLE cannot directly control the STM. The difference between normal execution mode and SMI is too great to allow the MLE direct SMI control. The STM is a peer to the MLE. Together, the MLE and STM establish policy that allows the STM to protect those pages from access by the SMI handling code.

MLE

The MLE is the keystone of Intel TXT security. The MLE protects physical pages by enforcing correct page tables. Without the MLE protecting the page tables and any changes to the page tables, software processes in the CPU could gain access to a protected physical page. With the MLE, software processes only gain access when the appropriate process is executing in the CPU.

The MLE provides additional physical page protection by enforcing the correlation between the page tables and VT-d. The MLE is the primary enforcer of protections from DMA device access. If the MLE allows pages under protection from CPU software access to have DMA access, the security boundary is broken.

The MLE, in conjunction with the STM, provides the protection of a physical page from SMI access. By managing the negotiation of protections with the STM, the MLE ensures that an SMI does not have access to a page under protection. As with VT-d, it is the responsibility of the MLE to ensure the proper synchronization of page under protection and SMI access.

The MLE may not directly manage the TGTT, as the TGTT could be under control of a guest partition. However, the MLE does ensure that only one guest has access to the TGTT and enforces control of the trusted configuration space.

Other CPU Resources

While physical pages represent the bulk of protections that a Intel TXT system provides, other CPU resources require protection. These resources include:

■ *Input/Output ports.* Intel Virtualization Technology provides a mechanism to control every port. The MLE gets control whenever any guest attempts to access an I/O port. The MLE must allow or disallow the access. It is permissible for the MLE to allow one guest access to a port and disallow another guest access to the port. As the protections represent a policy, the identity of the MLE allows those wishing to rely on the MLE the knowledge of how the MLE enforces and sets I/O access policy.

■ *Control registers.* In addition to CR3, numerous control registers affect the way that the CPU operates. Intel® Virtualization Technology allows the MLE to control access and provide virtualization for these registers.

■ *Machine Specific Register (MSR).* The control registers are the same on each CPU family. The MSRs are specific to a CPU family, and they might or might not be available on a previous or subsequent CPU family. The MSRs control many aspects of the platform, and some of the MSRs can affect the ability of the MLE to maintain the protection boundary. One example of the type of MSR that can affect the protection boundary is the MSR that controls the frequency and power to the CPU. Trying to run the CPU at a frequency and power level not properly tested could result in the CPU not operating correctly. Allowing software to access the MSR and change the settings could break the MLE protections. Intel® Virtualization Technology allows the MLE to provide virtualization for the MSR.

Figure 12.5 shows that Intel® Virtualization Technology provides virtualization of all of the CPU resources that affect the protection boundary. The MLE intercepts any attempt by software to access the CPU resources and the MLE evaluates the request and allows or disallows the request.

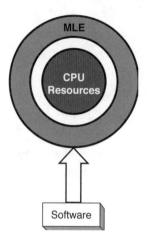

Figure 12.5 CPU Resource Protection

Keyboard and Mouse

The keyboard and mouse are special cases of input. The platform must provide the ability for the MLE to create a trusted channel from the device driver to the input device connection. Providing a connection across all connection mechanisms—that is, wired, wireless, infrared, and so on—is not a design goal of Intel TXT. If an application wants to create the trusted channel all the way to the device across multiple connections, nothing in the Intel TXT architecture prevents the application from creating the connection.

Covert Channels

A working definition of a *covert channel* is "a mechanism that can be used to transfer information from one user of a system to another, using means not intended for this purpose by the system developers." The task of defining a system that is completely resistant to covert channel attacks is nearly impossible. For example, the internal clock that the system uses for time of day and process scheduling can also provide a covert channel. Intel TXT makes no claims to prevent covert channels.

However, the MLE implementer must consider related threats. It is possible to transfer information between components of the platform using CPU and chipset control registers, status registers and I/O ports. Transfer of information can also occur using the persistent storage and state of attached devices. All of these data areas can allow the creation of direct communication channels between guest partitions. The term for this type of communication channel is an *overt channel*, which differs from the covert channel, as the covert channel does not directly leak information. An overt channel represents a security hole in the architecture. The hole allows direct guest communication outside of the physical page protections. The overt channel differs from normal guest communication because the data area's design did not anticipate inter-guest communication. Using the overt channel, an attacker might attempt to circumvent the inter-guest protections provided by virtualization and asset assignment. Overt channels are software attacks on the protection boundary of the system.

The MLE should prevent the establishment of overt channel attacks. The MLE must employ intelligent mechanisms that can monitor the complex behaviors of the previously mentioned data areas. The MLE must be able to allow a guest to manage a device or control register properly, but it also must be aware of the possibility of an overt channel.

The possibility of an overt channel exists when devices allow the routing of information between the devices without any intervention by the CPU. An example of this type of exchange is a PCI peer-to-peer data exchange. The MLE must provide the intelligence to monitor and control the data exchange, or the security policies must contemplate the potential vulnerability.

The MLE must be aware of device settings not initialized when the system resets. Some devices do not reset to default values on system reset but retain their prior settings and respond to specific reset events. The data in the device represents another potential overt channel, albeit a channel that requires a platform reset. It is the responsibility of the MLE to remove any information from these potential channels prior to MLE shutdown and to scrub the areas during MLE initialization.

The mitigation of overt channel attacks requires platform configuration and implementation-specific behavior. The definition of the specific behavior is outside the scope of the Intel TXT hardware but is within the scope of the MLE. The level of protection that the MLE provides is a design decision left to the MLE designer.

Boundary Summary

The entities to protect on the Intel TXT system include physical memory pages, CPU resources, measurements of the MLE, trusted input, and trusted output. Table 12.1 provides an overview of each of the entities and the protections for the entity.

Table 12.1 Boundary Protections

Entity	Protection Mechanisms	Function or Activities
Physical Page	Rings and Paging	Provide protection from software processes running in the same VM
	Virtualization	Provides protection between VM guests
	VT-d	Provides protection from DMA devices
	STM	Provides protection during SMI events
CPU Resources	MLE	Protects internal CPU resources from access from VM guest or DMA access
Measurements	SMX	Extensions to ensure the correct and proper measurement of the VMM turning the VMM into a MLE
	TPM	Provides a storage area for the measurements and a mechanism to report the measurements
Trusted Input	VT-d	The USB host controller provides protections for messages moving from the controller to the device driver
Trusted Output	VT-d	The TGTT provides a special buffer for the display adapter to obtain display information that has protection from VM guest and DMA access

The boundary of protected platform entities can continue to grow over time. Future versions of Intel TXT might add additional entities to protect and change the listed protection mechanisms. When the future boundary changes occur, they will add to the current boundary and not change the basic design principles. In fact, most of the design principles will never change throughout the lifetime of Intel TXT. As new threats appear, some principles may need modification, but the security principles will live on.

Requirements and Boundary Comparison

In Chapter 2, Table 2.2 lists the requirements for a trusted platform. When comparing the list to the features available on platforms today, some holes were obvious. With the Intel TXT protection boundary defined, Table 12.2 revisits the earlier table and looks at the holes. You can see that they've been plugged.

Table 12.2 Requirements Current Supported

Requirement	Hardware Support	Comments
Isolation of programs	Paging, segmentation and paging	The VMM provides both paging support and the ability to handle events issuing from the guest.
Separation of user from supervisor	Ring 0 and Ring 3 separation	The VMM is completely separate from any guest. In addition, the guests are now separate from each other.
Long-term protected storage	SMX measurement and TPM	The TPM provides long-term storage
Identification of current configuration	SMX instructions	The SMX measurement process provides for the identity of the executing VMM.
Verifiable report of current configuration	TPM attestation	The TPM provides the ability to report
Hardware basis for protections	Yes	Mechanisms are in hardware.

Chapter 13

Attestation

All human history attests

That happiness for man,—the hungry sinner!—

Since Eve ate apples, much depends on dinner.

Don Juan. Canto xiii. Stanza 99.
—Lord Byron (1788-1824)

With all of the features that Intel® TXT provides, how does an entity determine whether or not any specific platform has Intel TXT? Since Intel TXT platforms coexists with platforms that do not have Intel TXT, what provides the information that a specific platform has Intel TXT, and if it does, which indicates which MLE is executing? Finally, why should the entity requesting the information believe the response from the platform? Attestation provides the answers to all these questions.

Attestation requires roots of trust. A hardware or software mechanism that one implicitly trusts is called a *root of trust*. A platform needs the following roots of trust to be able to answer the questions posed:

- *Root of Trust for Measurement (RTM).* The RTM provides an entity that is implicitly trusted to provide an accurate measurement. The RTM can be a static entity like the PC BIOS boot block, or the RTM can be a dynamic mechanism that is provided by Intel TXT.

- *Root of Trust for Reporting (RTR).* The RTR provides an entity implicitly trusted to report information accurately and verifiably to outside entities.

- *Root of Trust for Storage (RTS).* The RTS provides an entity that can be trusted implicitly to store information without any interference or leakage of the information.

The various roots normally come as a package. The roots of trust for reporting and storage, RTR and RTS, are difficult to put into different entities on the platform. The Root of Trust for Measurement, RTM, depending on the platform, may or may not be combined with the RTR and RTS. On a Intel TXT platform, the RTR and RTS are part of the Trusted Platform Module (TPM) and the RTM is not part of the TPM.

TPM Design

The TPM definition comes in two parts, the main specification and a platform specific definition. The main specification[1], *TPM Main Spec* (TCG 2005b), defines the properties that must be present on every Intel TPM no matter what type of platform. The platform-specific definition provides the information that is necessary for implementing a TPM on a platform. The platform-specific spec on which Intel TXT depends is the *TCG PC Client Specific Implementation Specification for Conventional BIOS* (TCG 2005a)[2]. The reader needs to have both specifications available to answer any question regarding the TPM.[3]

One important piece of information is necessary to understand the *TPM Main Specification;* the specification does not mandate internal TPM design. A TPM vendor is free to implement most of the internal functions in ways that allow the vendor to differentiate the part from other TPM vendors. A good example is the speed of the device; there are

---

1 For the remainder of this chapter, the term main spec or specification refers to the TPM Main Spec. The TPM spec is now also available as ISO/IEC 11889.

2 Herein after cited as PC Client Spec

3 The author wishes to acknowledge that the development of the TPM was a group effort of the members of the TCPA and TCG TPM workgroups. Without their invaluable contributions there would never have been a TPM.

no requirements in the specifications as to how fast the TPM should perform an RSA operation. One vendor could create a part that made the RSA operation a priority and another vendor could have a part that made the SHA-1 operation a priority. Both implementations would be correct.

Figure 13.1 shows the basic TPM functions in a block diagram form.

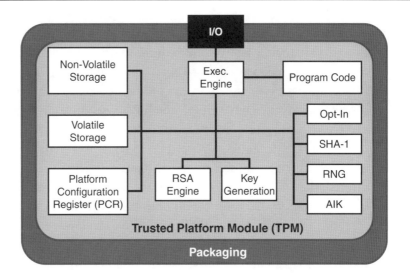

Figure 13.1 Basic Trusted Platform Module (TPM) Design

TPM Basic Components

The subsequent sections describe each of the TPM basic components.

Input and Output

All commands must enter and exit the TPM through the I/O port. The *TPM Main Spec* does not indicate what the I/O port shall be. The *PC Client Spec* identifies the I/O port as the LPC bus with a specific address on the bus.

The choice of the LPC bus is an important design decision. The bus on which the TPM resides must provide the CPU with access to the device without having to rely on interrupts or buses that require software stacks to operate. This access is very important when performing operations with an AC module that runs in a very restricted environment. The LPC bus definition includes the address for the I/O port and the registers that control the TPM communication.

The command that the TPM receives must arrive in a predefined format that includes a unique ordinal number to identify each command. For each ordinal, a predefined set of parameters provides the information that is necessary to execute the command and that must be present with the ordinal. With each ordinal, the TPM specification defines the exact bit pattern necessary to pass the command to the TPM. All TPMs, regardless of platform type, must accept the bit streams for all command ordinals. The TPM is not required to actually perform the function specified by the ordinal; the TPM only has to accept the bit stream. The TPM can return the unsupported ordinal error for all optional ordinals in the PM Main Spec.

For input and output, the Intel TPM is a slave device. The TPM never initiates any operation, but always responds to a request. Having the TPM reside on the LPC bus is a natural fit; the TPM is a slave device that always responds to commands and all devices on the LPC bus must be slave devices. The master of the LPC bus is the ICH, which controls all communication on the LPC bus. Should any device other than the ICH attempt to initiate an LPC command, an internal ICH fault occurs.

Addressing Other Platform Resources

The PC TPM, by being a device on the LPC bus, is severely restricted on what platform resources it has access to. The TPM does not have access to main system memory; the ICH blocks such accesses. In fact, the TPM has no access to any resource using a memory address—the ICH blocks the memory request.

Changing Execution Flow

With the TPM as a slave device on the LPC bus there are major restrictions on what the TPM is capable of doing. Combine the memory restrictions and the response nature of the TPM and there is no way for the TPM to alter the execution flow of the platform. Stated another way, there is no way for the TPM to change how the platform boots, or how an application executes. There is a way for some portion of the BIOS, or application, to take information from the TPM, make a decision based on the information, and change the execution path. The subtle difference is that the entity using the TPM is making the determination about what to do; the TPM itself is not initiating the change.

The distinction between the TPM forcing the change and the calling entity is very important. The TPM receives a command to perform one of the defined TPM commands; the TPM executes the command and returns the result. The TPM has no knowledge of which entity is making the request[4]. The TPM performs the operations the same way each time the request is made. If the caller wishes to make a decision based on the TPM supplied information, which is fine, the TPM itself will not have made the decision nor will the TPM have made the entity do something different.

Execution Engine

Upon receipt of a command in the input buffer, the TPM needs to determine the proper formation of the command. The execution engine parses the bit stream to ensure a well-formed command. After validating the structure of the command, the engine locates the appropriate code according to the command ordinal. Depending on the internal structure of the TPM[5], the execution engine locates the program associated with the command ordinal. After locating the program code, the execution engine passes control to the specified ordinal program code.

---

4   Almost no knowledge: see "Locality" later in this chapter.

5   Remember that TPM vendors have the ability create TPMs with different internal control mechanisms

The execution engine ensures that the distribution of commands occurs only for valid TPM commands. This assurance of proper distribution provides a level of security that guarantees only TPM-defined commands execute on the TPM.

Program Code

The program code for a specific ordinal, located by the execution engine, provides the logic for the ordinal. The code performs the following tasks:

- ■ *Validate the entire command bit stream.* While the I/O and execution engines perform some bit stream validation, the program code needs to complete the command validation. This activity includes determining the size of the command, which is ordinal specific, and checking for optional parameters.

- ■ *Validate each parameter.* The program code knows about the form and type of each parameter. The program code validates those parameters capable of validation. Since some parameters pass in user data where the structure of the data is unknown to the TPM, not all parameters are capable of an internal validation. When passing this type of information, the caller is responsible for validating the parameter before sending the information to the TPM.

- ■ *Validate the command authorization* if the command needs authorization. See "Authorization Values" in this chapter for complete details.

- ■ *Perform the ordinal logic flow specified in the TPM specification.* Each command has a defined set of actions to accomplish. These actions describe the exact details of what the command does and does not do[6].

- ■ *Create the response packet.* After performing all of the actions, the program code creates the response packet. If the command was successful, the content and format of the response comes from the actions. If the command was unsuccessful, the program code creates an error response according to the rules for errors.

---

6   Well actually, it is close. As one TPM vendor told me, "David, we treat the order of operations as advisory." The point was that the exact order of operations in an ordinal is not mandatory and that there is more than one way to get the job done. Again the flexibility for the TPM vendors is present and the vendors make use of the flexibility.

While the program code must perform all of the previous operations, the TPM manufacturer may implement the operations in any logically consistent fashion. This flexibility allows the manufacturer to build a TPM that meets different criteria. A manufacturer can create a TPM that is faster but costs more, or a manufacturer can build the cheapest TPM.

Non-Volatile (NV) Storage

As the Root of Trust for Storage, the TPM must provide some long-term values. The requirement in the TPM is that the information must be available when the TPM boots and that the information not be affected by power cycles. Non-volatile (NV) storage is the most typically used mechanism. When creating a TPM based on silicon, the TPM manufacturer will typically use a manufacturing process that allows for information to be stable when no power is available on the TPM.

Two uses of the non-volatile storage on the TPM are internal TPM values and defined ordinals.

Internal TPM Values

The TPM maintains two 2048-bit RSA keys internally: the endorsement key (EK) and the storage root key (SRK). These keys provide the essence of the Root of Trust for Reporting, the EK, and the Root of Trust for Storage, the SRK. The EK is set once, and under normal circumstances[7], never changes for the life of the TPM. The SRK would change when, and if, the platform changes owners.

In addition to the RSA keys, the TPM holds additional values necessary to manage the TPM state. Some of these values are permanent and some update on a limited basis. An example is the settings that the user selects for opt-in.

---

7   Like many of the TPM absolutes there are mechanisms to actually change the EK. The results of changing the EK are very large and many TPM vendors and platform users of the TPM may not expose the ability to change the EK.

Defined Ordinals

Along with the internal use of the NV storage, the TPM provides a set of ordinals that allows outsider entities to use NV storage. NV storage in the TPM is not cheap. Other mechanisms provide NV storage at a much lower cost so the NV storage in the TPM needs to provide some extra value. The value that TPM NV storage provides is that the TPM authorization mechanisms validate each and every access to the TPM NV storage area. The TPM provides a small NV area. The assumption is that between the platform manufacturer, CPU manufacturer, and the OS vendor, little or no NV storage area would be available for general applications.

Burn Issues

NV storage has an interesting property; the NV area has a lifetime number of write operations.[8] Most NV storage manufacturers specify the maximum number of writes as some value around 100,000. While no counter stops the TPM from working at 100,000, the result is that the writes start to take longer and longer to execute. At some point, the attempt to write a new value takes longer than the timeout value for the command and the write fails. The number of reads to NV storage areas is not restricted.

With this limit, the TPM needs some mechanism to control when and how the NV storage is in use. The TPM provides that all writes to the NV area have an authorization that limits any entity's use of the NV area.

Volatile Storage

With the limit on writes to the NV storage area, the TPM needs storage that has no limit on the number of writes, and the volatile storage area fills that need. The volatile storage is used internally by the TPM for the following things:

---

8   To be 100-percent technically accurate, the operation that causes a problem is changing a bit from 1 to 0. Some implementations take advantage of this fact and optimize how and when the device performs the erasure. While TPMs might use this type of optimization, in the context of this book, a write operation equates to an erase cycle.

■ Keeping track of current internal TPM state

■ Providing an area for cryptographic keys (not the EK or SRK)

■ Authentication sessions

■ Transport session

■ Other sessions

The volatile storage could also provide program code space for very large commands. The TPM manufacturer decides how to use the volatile storage. Outside entities have no direct connection to the volatile storage, other than access to the results of various operations.

The volatile storage area does not persist across power cycles, so any information that needs to be persistent must have an external storage location, like a hard drive, or the information must reside in the NV storage area. It is possible to move information from one area to another, but the restriction on use of the NV storage area would require use authorization.

Secure Hash Algorithm 1 (SHA-1)

Secure Hash Algorithm 1[9], or SHA-1, is a cryptographic hash algorithm. Hash algorithms take a string of arbitrary length and produce a fixed-length output. Given the resulting output value, it is computationally infeasible to calculate the input. Also, hash algorithms are order dependent; that is, hashing A then B results in a different value than if one hashes B then A. The SHA-1 output is a 20-byte value.

The TPM makes extensive use of the SHA-1. Some of the functions that use SHA-1 are:

■ Authorization values

■ Binding together of structures

■ Hashed Message Authentication Code (HMAC) validation

■ Creation of XOR strings

---

9   The author is fully aware of the issues with SHA-1. The TCG is also fully aware of the issues and is looking at ways to change the TPM reliance on SHA-1.

Authorization Values

The TPM requires authorization of many commands and uses knowledge of a value to prove authorization. The authorization value held in the TPM is a 20-byte value, its size chosen intentionally to match the SHA-1 output size, based on the assumption that the authorization value would be some pass phrase passed through a previous SHA-1 operation.

Binding Structures Together

The structures in use by the TPM contain both sensitive information and information that needs integrity protection. Many times the combination of sensitive information and information requiring integrity protection becomes too large a structure to encrypt in a single operation. The solution is to take a hash of the information needing integrity protection and include the hash value in the sensitive information. When checking the integrity later, the hash of the TPM calculates the hash of the integrity area, and then compares the resulting hash value with the hash value stored in the sensitive area. A single bit change results in a new hash value and represents a failure to validate.

This use model represents a basic construct that many applications use. An area that needs integrity protection has a hash value stored and protected by the TPM. When validation is necessary, TPM recalculates the hash value and compares it to the stored hash value.

Hashed Message Authentication Code (HMAC) Validation

When performing authentication checks, the internal mechanism that the TPM uses is the HMAC calculation. The HMAC definition is *RFC 2104-HMAC:Keyed-hashing for Message Authentication* (Krawczyk 1997). The HMAC calculation is

```
H(K XOR opad, H(K XOR ipad, text))
```

where

H	is the SHA-1 hash operation
K	is the key or the authorization data
XOR	is the xor operation

opad   is the byte 0x5C repeated B times

B   is the block length and the block length is determined by the algorithm in use

ipad   is the byte 0x36 repeated B times

text   is the message information and any parameters from the command

RFC 2104 requires the selection of two parameters to define the HMAC in use. These values are the key length and the block size. The TCG choose to set the values such that the HMAC calculations for SHA-1 are very easy. The resulting sizes are: key length (K) of 20 bytes and a block size (B) of 64 bytes.

Creation of XOR Strings

The TPM provides encryption using an XOR mechanism. The XOR mechanism needs an encryption string the exact same length as the plain text data. The TPM uses the *PKCS #1: RSA Encryption Standard, Version 2.1* (RSA 2002) and the Mask Generation Function (MGF) to create the encryption string. MGF generates a string using SHA-1, a shared secret, and a counter. While not particularly fast, MGF does provide a reasonably secure encryption algorithm.

Continued Use of SHA-1

The spring of 2005 saw the publication of some SHA-1 vulnerabilities. The TCG is aware of the SHA-1 vulnerabilities and future versions of the TPM are likely to add additional hash algorithms to the TPM.

Platform Configuration Register (PCR)

The PCRs are storage areas that keep track of measurements reported to the TPM. The *TPM Main Spec* (TCG 2005b) does not specify the number of PCRs, while the *PC Client Spec* (TCG 2005a) specification mandates that the TPM must have a minimum of 24 PCRs. Reading and writing to any PCR requires special TPM ordinals and the PCRs are never directly written to.

Extending the PCR

When an entity wishes to store a measurement in the TPM, the entity wants an assurance that no other entity can change the measured value. The TPM provides this assurance by not allowing any entity to write directly to the TPM; the entity "extends" the specified PCR. The extend operation concatenates the current PCR value with the new value and performs a SHA-1 on the concatenated value. The resulting hash value is the new PCR value. Graphically, the extend operation looks like this:

PCR = SHA-1(PCR old value, new value)

Using the extend operation has some interesting properties. First, a single PCR can keep track of an unlimited number of measurements. Since each extend operation results in a 20-byte hash value, it makes no difference to the PCR storage requirements whether that value is for one measurement or one hundred measurements.

Second, the extend process uses the ordering property of SHA-1. To recap, ordering provides for a different hash value when hashing A then B, against B then A. This is the property you want when keeping track of measurements on a platform. With the extend process order dependency, an entity cannot pretend to occur after a certain event. The ordering is automatic.

Finally, the extend process also prevents an entity from attempting to create a log that essentially removes the entities own measurement from the log. Assume that entity A measures entity B and stores the measurement in a PCR. Entity B wants to hide, so B makes it appear that entity C is currently executing. Entity B has to find a value that, when extended, results in the same value for entity C. This operation is computationally infeasible.

PCR Event Log

The PCR only contains the results of all of the measurements. The list of measured events is not available inside of the TPM. If the event log was internal to it, the TPM would need to reserve enough internal resources to hold the entire log. This problem becomes unbounded because the PCR can contain an unlimited number of measurements. The solution is to hold the log externally to the TPM. The log provides all of the measured values that extend into the PCR. Any verifier can validate the contents of the log by performing the extend operation in software. The resulting hash value matches the PCR value if the log is correct. When the log is incorrect, the verifier knows only that the log and PCR do not match, with insufficient information to determine why the log and PCR are out of sync.

Reporting the Current PCR Value

With the measurements held in a PCR, entities outside of the TPM require a way to validate the TPM report of PCR value. The TPM provides a digital signature of the PCR value that a requesting entity can verify is correct and fresh. The correctness comes from the format of the digital signature and the ability to validate the key that creates the digital signature. The freshness comes from the inclusion of information from the verifier. Typically, this information would be a random number, but it could be other types of data. The freshness prevents an attacker from replaying a previously good measurement report.

Resetting of PCR

A PCR can be static or dynamic. The difference between static and dynamic is when and how the PCR can be reset to its default value. A static PCR can reset only when the TPM itself resets. As long as the TPM is active, the PCR value continues to extend. The PCR cannot be reset independently without resetting the TPM. This property provides an excellent way to measure and keep track of events that occur during the boot of the PC and do not change after the PC is executing. The best example is information relative to the boot of the platform like the BIOS and OS loader.

A dynamic PCR can be reset independently of the TPM, so long as the process that resets the PCR operates under sufficient controls that an attacker cannot reset the PCR and supply incorrect measurement information to the PCR.

Random Number Generator (RNG)

Randomness is critical in a cryptographic system. The randomness provides a way to generate keys, both symmetric and asymmetric, and is a source of nonces that provide freshness. A nonce is a random number used once. While it seems like a simple thing to find randomness, it is in fact a very difficult problem. John von Neumann said it best:

> Anyone who considers arithmetical methods of producing random digits is, of course, in a state of sin.

The RNG requirement for the TPM is to avoid any sin and use mechanisms that can produce random numbers. The actual implementation of the RNG is a manufacturer-specific option. Sources of entropy allow a device to harvest the entropy, run the entropy through some processes, and output a random number.

Note   *A considerable body of literature is available to tell you how to create a valid RNG. Various software implementations are available for downloading. In addition, you can find reports on how to harvest entropy from various sources. Several of these resources are listed in "References" for your convenience.*

RSA Engine

Asymmetric algorithms break key usage into public and private components. The TPM uses RSA for encryption and digital signatures. The standard key size for most keys is 2,048 bits. When used for internal encryption the TPM must use 2,048-bit keys.

When performing RSA encryption the TPM enforces the rules established by PKCS #1 V2.1. These rules require randomness (provided by the RNG) and masking (provided by SHA-1). The rules set forth by PKCS #1 provide mitigation against all sorts of esoteric attacks. By following these rules, the TMP uses a well-known algorithm and protocol and avoids the necessity of performing additional cryptographic evaluations.

When performing RSA digital signatures, the TPM provides for a couple of standard digital signature schemes. These schemes allow for the digital signature on a wide variety of internal TPM and external data. The schemes also provide for mitigation against attacks.

Key Generation

Applications using the TPM are not all going to want to use the same key. In fact good security practice demands that the applications use different keys. Some key will provide data protection and other keys will provide digital signatures. It would be nice to predetermine how many keys the TPM requires but one is now in the child's game of "Pick a number. 21? Okay, I pick 22. I win!" where whatever number is picked will be wrong for someone. The end result is the requirement that the TPM have the ability to generate RSA keys on demand. All information necessary to generate the key must come from internal TPM resources[10]. The process for generating the key is:

■ Obtain two random numbers. While the TPM could go looking for a source of randomness, one of the major reasons that the TPM has a requirement for an internal RNG is to provide the randomness for key generation.

■ Determine whether both the numbers are prime numbers. This is the fun part of creating an RSA key. For the typical key sizes, the numbers are around 1000-bits. While knowledge of prime numbers has been around for thousands of years, and tests for determining if a number is prime area available, to perform an exhaustive test on the two numbers could take days. Obviously then the TPM does not do an exhaustive test but performs some sort of statistical test to gain an assurance of that the number was prime.

   – The normal method is to first make the number to test odd, as the only even prime number is 2, and 2 has only 2-bits not the 1000 bits we are looking for. The TPM then uses the statistical tests to determine whether the number is prime. If the number is not prime, the TPM could add 2 to get to the next odd number, and try the tests again. If, after a certain number of tries, the TPM does not find a prime number, the TPM could discard the original try and get some more randomness from the RNG.

---

10 The entity requesting the new key certainly provides the key type, protection or signing, key size, and other pieces of information, but the randomness must come from the internal TPM RNG.

- The testing for a prime number is not deterministic. That is, no one can tell you how long the TPM will take to find a prime number. While it would be great if we had some way to put a bound on the process, with today's processors and mathematical knowledge, prime number testing is going to take some indeterminate amount of time. Because of the indeterminate time necessary some TPM vendors "cheat,"[11] whenever the TPM is idle, the TPM is creating a list of prime numbers. Now, when the TPM gets a request to create a new RSA key, the TPM merely picks the next two prime numbers from the list and performs the rest of the math. If too many requests for new keys arrive in a short amount of time, the prime number list could be exhausted and the TPM would need to find a prime number in real time.

■ With two prime numbers, the TPM would perform the other mathematical operations necessary to create a RSA key pair.

Opt-in

The TPM contains a unique value, called the *endorsement key*. The platform owner must have an assurance that the EK is only in use for those operations that the platform owner authorizes. The authorization provides protection against the improper use of the uniqueness. Improper use of the uniqueness could create the ability for outside entities to correlate two different uses of the uniqueness, resulting in a loss of privacy.

The TPM is an *opt-in* device. Opt-in means that the platform owner must take specific steps to turn the TPM on. When shipped, the TPM is not operational. The TPM must have a mechanism that stores and keeps secure the platform owner's selection of the state of the TPM.

The opt-in mechanism must include some physical mechanism that an operator at the platform must manipulate to indicate that a human is operating the platform. This physical presence mechanism, when asserted, allows the TPM to validate that requests to manipulate the permanent state of the TPM have authorization from a human.

---

11 Actually, I don't think of this proactive number generation as cheating. It is rather an excellent way to use the limited TPM resources.

Attestation Identity Key

The Attestation Identity Key (AIK) provides a mechanism for establishing that an entity is communicating with *a* TPM but not for determining *which* TPM. This distinction is very important when discussing privacy issues. If the requesting entity can determine from the key in use which TPM is in use, the entity could correlate uses and cause a loss of privacy. The EK is the Root of Trust for Reporting, but if every single report used the EK, then the correlation would be very easy.

The AIK provides a mechanism to report on TPM internal information like the status/content of a PCR, but not to use the EK directly.

Authorization

The advantage that the Intel TPM provides to entities wishing to rely on the TPM is that many operations require authorization to execute. From the standpoint of the TPM mechanisms, there needs to be a mechanism that can prove to the TPM that the entity requesting the operation has the authority to do so. While it would be nice for the TPM to put up a dialog box or use a voice request, those options really are not possible. The HMAC mechanism provides a way to authenticate TPM requests.

The authorization of a command wants to use a shared secret, which is, both sides of the communication know the shared secret, one side wants to prove to the other side knowledge of the shared secret, and neither side wants to transmit the shared secret over the communication medium. HMAC provides the mechanism to do that.

When an entity creates a new key, or other resource requiring subsequent authorization, the creation process includes the authorization value. When the entity wishes to use the resource, the request to use the resource includes the HMAC of the request and the authorization value, or shared secret. The TPM must associate with the resource and permanently keep track of the authorization value.

A security concern, not just a theoretical one but a practical concern, is that some attacker could capture a request to use the resource and replay the HMAC calculation. With the request being the same and the authorization being the same the HMAC calculation would result in the exact same value. To mitigate this vulnerability the calling entity places into the request some randomness and includes the randomness into the HMAC calculation. This way, the caller knows that the command sent to the TPM and the response from the TPM, which also uses the randomness, is fresh and not a replay.

TPM Functionality

The value of a TPM comes not from the basic building block features of the PCR or the RNG, but from combining the building blocks into new functionality.

Transitive Trust

The idea of transitive trust is to provide a way for relying parties to trust a larger circle of entities from a single root of trust. The process for establishing transitive trust is:

1. *Measure the next entity.* Measurement is the process of taking some data and performing a hash on the data. For transitive trust, the program code is the value under measurement. A quick example is the BIOS could measure the OS loader.

2. *Store the measurement.* The storage location is a TPM PCR and the measuring agent uses the TPM_Extend command to extend the PCR with the new value.

3. *Pass control to the measured entity.*

Figure 13.2 shows the process by which trust is extended.

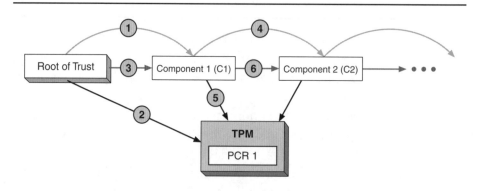

Figure13.2 Transitive Trust

Combining the Root of Trust for Measurement (RTM), the PCR, and the Root of Trust for Reporting (RTR) allows a challenger to gain a verifiable picture of the current platform state. When the RTM measures the next component to gain execution control, any challenger can be assured that the measured component was in fact the component next in the execution path. This assurance comes from the challenger's dependence on the RTM. If the challenger trusts the RTM, the measured component really did get control.

Measurement Chains

When attempting to evaluate the trust properties of a platform, the entire transitive trust chain of elements is important. The first component will perform a measurement on a second component, the second on a third, and so on. The issue is that all components of the chain are actually the policy engine and the policy being enforced.

Measurement Atomicity

Whether a static or dynamic measurement chain is created, much stock is placed in how the first measurement in a chain is produced as this is the bedrock for all other measurements that take place. So from a platform perspective, the first measurement must be viewed as an atomic operation, which cannot be interrupted or interfered with. To do so would undermine the value in the trust chain. Like Randomness trusting this atomicity is implicit in trusting the platform.

Order

The measurement process, by virtue of using cryptographic hashes, is order dependent. That is measuring entity A then entity B results in a different result from measuring entity B then entity A. The ordering property is very important when attempting to evaluate the current state of the trusted platform.

One aspect of the ordering property is that if the chain one is trying to measure is not order determinate, the resulting chain is very difficult to evaluate. With only 3 components being order independent, 6 chain values are possible. Lengthy chains could have thousands of potential combinations. It is a basic property of the trusted platform to attempt to limit chain sizes by keeping the number of components to a minimum and to help ensure order dependence such that the measurements can be performed in only one way.

Chains can be very short or very long. The length of a chain does not necessarily represent the trustworthiness of the measured system. For instance, measuring 10 items that represent a government certified high security system can represent a more trustable chain of then a chain with 2 measurements that identify a known weak system.

Freshness

After a measurement is complete, an interesting property now comes into play. The strength of the platforms protected execution. To see why this is true consider a static measurement that assures any outside observer that DOS 3.1 was successfully launched. But DOS 3.1 has no internal protections and any program can edit the "list of lists" in DOS 3.1. The OS really has no real control of the system. The end result is that saying that the platform successfully launched DOS 3.1 two days prior really says the current state of the platform is unknown.

Figure 13.3 shows the freshness issue. There is a concern that between time 0 and time Y, corruption of the entity is possible.

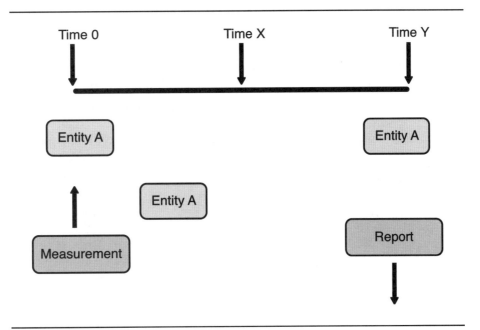

Figure 13.3 Measurement Freshness

At time 0 the measurement agent, RTM or some other entity in the trust chain, measures entity A. At that moment the measurement of entity A is accurate and the measurement agent stores the measurement value in the TPM. At time Y the TPM reports the measurement value stored in the TPM. The TPM does *not* perform a new measurement on entity A; it merely reports the stored value in the TPM. The entity receiving the report must make a determination if the measurement value is actually reporting the current state of the platform.

There are numerous ways that the platform can assist the relying party as to the veracity of the report. These ways include:

■ Better isolation

■ Stronger protected execution

■ More measurements

Better Isolation

If the platform has a weakness in isolation, then those entities evaluating the trust chain and the potential for corruption after the measurement will discount their reliance on the reported measurement value. If the isolation mechanism is strong, the relying parties will not believe that outside entities could have affected the measured entity.

There is every reason to believe that the isolation provided by Intel TXT and VT are sufficiently strong that relying parties will not believe that corruption is possible from the hardware of Intel TXT and VT. Relying parties will closely evaluate the MLE that is providing the configuration of the platform hardware as it is very probable that there will be MLEs that do not properly control a platform. If the MLE loses control of the platform or more accurately allows pages and resources to be improperly shared between guests, then the potential for corruption of a measured guest is quite probable. To provide a high level of assurance that inter-guest corruption is not occurring, trusted MLEs will undergo a high level of evaluation. The type and extent of the evaluation is determined by the needs of the entity attempting to rely on the MLE and may include formal evaluations like Common Criteria or informal code reviews.

Stronger Protected Execution

The concern from an outsider's point of view is that the measured entity has become corrupt. If the isolation protections are secure then the only way for an entity to become corrupt is for some sort of internal fault or bug to occur. Preventing internal faults is the type of issue that protected execution is designed to address. The stronger the protections are the higher assurance there is that the entity remains exactly as it was when measured. The best assurances come from protections provided by the hardware.

The trusted platform element Inside is exactly the answer for providing additional protections for the MLE.

More measurements

Without changing the isolation or protected execution mechanisms one way to obtain more accurate measurements is to measure more often. More often however is a difficult proposition. The static measurements occur at reset, so the only way to obtain a new static measurement is to reboot the platform. In reality the only way to obtain a new dynamic measurement is to initiate the event that performs the dynamic measurement, a process on many platforms that is the moral equivalent of reboot. With no way to measure from the root of trust there must be another way to measure the current environment.

The trusted platform element of Inspection and Detection is the ability to again assure that the integrity of the measured entity remain intact.

Combination

The solution to freshness is the combination of all of the previous mechanisms. Strong isolation, protected execution, and more measurements all give outside observers the assurance that the identity of the entity is correct and current.

Evidence Services

An evidence service periodically checks on some other platform entity and reports the health of the reviewed entity. An evidence service is normally specific to the reviewed entity. The reason for the specificity is the need to intimately understand what represents a healthy entity.

An evidence service is not a base capability of the platform. There are two reasons for this. The first reason is the specificity of the evidence service. While it might make sense for an evidence service, putting a service that is specific to a single entity is obviously not useable for any other entity and the evidence service may not ever be used.

The second reason is even more compelling; the evidence service is just that, a service. Being a service, it is instantiated after the base capabilities are executing and hence would be a measured entity.

Sealed Storage

Sealed storage provides a way to combine measurements and protection of external data. To help keep track of which thing is which, the following terms are in use for this section.

Data refers to the external information that the TPM is going to protect. *Value* refers to the current value inside of a PCR register. While it is possible, and normally desirable, to use more than one PCR register in the seal process, for this section all references to PCR refer to only a single PCR.

The idea now is for the TPM to provide protected storage of *data* combing the Root of Trust for Storage (RTS) and the *value* in a PCR. The protection uses encryption, the RTS, and measurement values, the PCR. Protecting the data is *Seal* and recovering the protected data is *Unseal*.

Sealing

The seal process takes the external data, a requested PCR value, encrypts the data, and creates a sealed data package. The TPM returns the sealed data package to the caller and the caller is responsible for keeping track of the package and presenting the package back to the TPM when the caller wants to recover the data.

The seal process, internal to the TPM, ensures that only the TPM that creates the sealed package can unseal the package. The TPM ensures this type of behavior by including in the sealed package a nonce known only to the individual TPM. During the unseal proces, the TPM validates that the correct nonce is present in the sealed package. Figure 13.4 illustrates the seal process showing the external data, the measurement values, and the sealed data package.

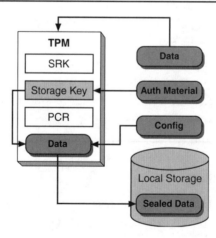

Figure 13.4 Sealing Data to the TPM

Of note is the actual key in use to encrypt the data. The key is a storage key that forms part of the Storage Root Key (SRK) tree. The key could use the SRK directly or a storage key many layers away from the SRK. For the seal process internal to the TPM, the key that performs the seal does not really differ from the other keys. From an application standpoint, you could have an operational difference, but the end result is a sealed data package that the application must keep track of.

The TPM does not perform any validation or checking of the PCR value during the seal process. The caller can specify any PCR value that the caller wishes. The platform may or may not be in the configuration that the caller is specifying for the unseal configuration, and that is intentional—the TPM only enforces the requested configuration during the unseal process.

Unsealing

While the obvious description of unseal would be that is was the reverse of the seal operation, the obvious is not correct. While any entity can perform the seal operation, the purpose of the seal process is to *restrict* the unseal operation. What is necessary to define is what the restrictions are and when does the TPM enforce the restrictions.

Before enforcing the restrictions the basic unseal operations must occur. The basic operations are to decrypt the sealed package using the indicated storage key and validate that the decryption was successful. The decryption reveals all of the internal information and the external data. The validation ensures that the package information was not modified.

The first restriction is that the sealed package is only useable on the TPM that created the sealed package. The TPM enforces this restriction by ensuring that the TPM nonce included in the sealed package matches the internally held nonce.

The next restriction is the PCR value. The TPM compares the current value in the TPM PCR to the requested value in the sealed data package. If the two values do not match, the unseal operation aborts.

The combination of the restrictions is that the external data is only available to a caller when the correct measurement value is in the specified PCR. Any entity wishing to rely on the use of the data to a specific platform configuration can use the seal property and have a high degree of assurance that only in the right configuration does the data become available.

Transport Session

Assume that you have just executed an unseal command and the TPM is returning the sealed data back to the caller. The TPM_Unseal does not provide any protection to the returning data; any entity with access to the communication channel can see the unsealed data. If the data was an encryption key, having outside entities view the key might be a very bad thing. As callers to the TPM could be sending information across the Internet, numerous entities could potentially have access to the data.

The transport session is a response to the issue and a way to protect information traveling to and from the TPM. The transport session provides for the confidentiality and sequencing of information traveling from a requestor to the TPM. The basic features of the transport session are:

■ *Confidentiality.* The transport session can encrypt data sent to and from the TPM. The mandatory encryption algorithm is XOR using MGF; however, individual Intel TPM manufacturers can support a wide variety of additional algorithms such as AES or 3DES.

■ *Sequence of commands.* The transport session groups a set of commands and provides a digital signature on all of the commands in the group. This grouping allows an entity to prove that a sequence of commands actually occurred. The sequencing can also include timing information that can show the exact time that the commands executed.

■ *Total control.* The transport session can be exclusive, such that any command outside of the transport session causes the session to terminate.

Locality

One Root of Trust for Measurement (RTM) on a platform performs measurements from the boot of the platform. The normal designation of this RTM is the static RTM, or the RTM that keeps track of the information that statically defines the boot of the platform[12]. Other mechanisms could provide an RTM on the platform. Intel TXT has another RTM, called the dynamic RTM.

The dynamic RTM is a critical component of Intel TXT. Later chapters describe the actual dynamic RTM mechanism. What the TPM needs to understand is when the dynamic RTM is communicating with the TPM. An unspoofable hardware mechanism that the TPM can interpret must provide communications from the dynamic RTM. The TPM uses locality to provide this mechanism. The *Intel TPM PC Client Specific TPM Interface Specification* (TCG 2005c) defines locality as:

> A concept that allows various trusted processes on the platform to communicate with the TPM such that the TPM is aware of which trusted process is sending commands. This is implemented using dedicated ranges LPC addresses and a new LPC "start" field. Six localities are defined: numbers 0 – 4 and Legacy.

The TPM definition provides for localities or indications of specific platform processes. The *TPM Main Spec* (TCG 2005b) makes no reference to what the localities are; the actual locality definition for the PC is in the *PC Specific Specification* (TCG 2005a). The TPM has five localities 0 through 4. Each locality has a specific meaning.

■ Locality 4—Trusted hardware. The platform hardware ensures that only trusted processes have access to locality 4. Locality 4 assertions should be made by the hardware dynamic RTM. The locality 4 assertion allows the TPM to respond appropriately to dynamic RTM requests for measurement and resetting of PCR.

■ Locality 3—Auxiliary components. These components are optional and represent processes that gain control after the trusted hardware at locality 4 but before the normal trusted process runtime has control. The auxiliary component may or may not be part of the dynamic RTM.

12 Review the TCG documentation for complete details on the static RTM.

- Locality 2—The normal trusted operating system, as the trusted OS, gains control after the locality 3 and 4 processes have properly initialized the platform.

- Locality 1—An environment set up by the trusted OS. The trusted OS does not have to use locality 1, but if the trusted OS desires, it may provide access to locality 1.

- Locality 0 provides access to the TPM for the static RTM and any other processes operating after the static RTM.

- Locality legacy. The 1.2 TPM provides for backward compatibility with version 1.1. Since 1.1 did not have locality and did not have a standard communication mechanism, the ability to communicate with the TPM using old drivers is available. The legacy locality is the same as locality 0.

The chipset provides the locality mechanism. A reserved set of addresses correlates with the localities, as shown in Table 13.1, and it is the responsibility of the chipset to protect those addresses from any process that does not match the locality.

Table 13.1   Locality Addresses

Locality	System Address	LPC Address
0	0XFED4_0xxx	0x0xxx
1	0XFED4_1xxx	0x1xxx
2	0XFED4_2xxx	0x2xxx
3	0XFED4_3xxx	0x3xxx
4	0XFED4_4xxx	0x4xxx

Note: System address is permanent address on PC

Attesting To Information

The PCR contain the results of measurements provided by the RTM and other entities on the platform. The seal property makes use of the PCR and ensures that data is only available when the specified set of measurements is present. The unseal operation proves to the entity using the unseal operation that the correct configuration is present. But if the outside entity has not performed a seal operation, how does one prove to the outside entity that a current configuration is present? The answer is attestation.

Attestation is the process of providing a digital signature of a PCR or set of PCRs and having the requestor validate the signature and the PCR contents. The process is very simple, the entity wishing to validate the current platform configuration, requests the TPM_Quote command specifying an Attestation Identity Key (AIK) to perform the digital signature, the set of PCRs to quote, and a nonce to ensure freshness of the digital signature.

The TPM processing is also very simple; validate the authorization to use the AIK, fill in a structure that shows the set of PCR to be quoted, and perform a digital signature on the filled-in structure. The TPM then returns the digital signature as the output to the TPM_Quote command.

The entity requesting the attestation validates the digital signature by using the public portion of the AIK, validates the AIK by interpreting the AIK credential, and now evaluates the current configuration. If the configuration represents an acceptable configuration, the requestor can rely on the platform configuration[13].

Measurement Agent

When attempting to rely on the attestation from a system, the evaluation of the "accuracy" of the measurement is vital. The RTM is suppose to provide a high degree of assurance that the start of the measurement chain is valid. The degree of difficulty here is that the RTM is a component outside of the TPM; the RTM is a *platform* component. How the platform is put together directly

---

13 That paragraph certainly compresses lots of information. The validation of attestation values is a subject for an entire book, and is the current focus of the Trusted Computing Group Infrastructure Work Group. The ability to determine what an acceptable configuration is can be simple or complex and, as just stated, outside the scope of this book.

affects the ability of the RTM to start the chain of measurements. The purpose of Intel TXT is to provide a dynamic RTM that outside entities can rely on to accurately measure the MLE and truly move the MLE to an MLE.

Use of the TPM

The TPM is a key building block of an Intel TXT platform. The TPM provides two roots of trust on the platform; the Root of Trust for Storage (RTS) and the Root of Trust for Reporting (RTR). The TPM is bound to the Root of Trust for Measurement (RTM) and the RTM uses the PCR to store measurements.

The PCR and the RTS combine to provide the seal capability, a key component in the ability of the TXT platform to provide long-term protected storage.

The PCR and RTR combine to provide the attestation capability, which allows outside observers the ability to determine the current platform configuration.

The RTM, static or dynamic, provides the measurement values that drive the PCR contents.

The bottom line is that the TPM truly is a key building block for the Intel TXT platform and the TPM provides key services that allow Intel TXT to properly initialize and accurately report the current platform state.

Chapter 14

Intel® Trusted Execution Technology Architecture

Architecture starts when you carefully put two bricks together. There it begins.

— Ludwig Mies van der Rohe

The architecture of Intel Trusted Execution Technology (Intel® TXT) starts putting together the bricks available on the platform. The requirement is to protect software and use domain separation to provide the protection. Figure 14.1 shows the basic picture of Intel TXT.

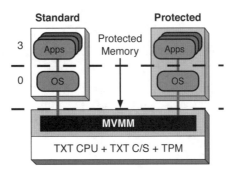

Figure 14.1 The Basic Intel® Trusted Execution Technology Architecture

The architecture has three main features:

- The *standard partition* or the left-hand side (LHS), of the diagram is an operating environment such as one sees in non-Intel TXT platforms. This part is the execution area of today.

- The *protected partition* or the right-hand side (RHS), of the diagram is the protected environment. This area is under the protection of Intel TXT. All applications running in the protected partition have protection from software attack.

- The *Measured Virtual Machine Manager (MVMM)* provides the controlling entity that manages all partitions.

The protected partition and the MVMM reside in protected memory.

The Naming of the Sides

In the early days of Intel Trusted Execution Technology project, a small task force of security architects was working on the design of Intel TXT. The groups output was going to be a specification that defined Intel TXT. The name of the specification was going to be something like "Intel TXT Security Architect Specification." As that moniker was much too large, the acronym of Intel TXT SAS appeared, which was finally shortened to SAS. The series of meetings to work through the various sections of the document are known as the SAS meetings. The SAS continues to meet,[1] albeit with a larger group now, defining the security properties of Intel TXT.

When the SAS started on the task of defining what worked with what with whom and when, it became very apparent that some sort of naming convention was necessary. As the conversation went back and forth, covering items like protected or unprotected, known and unknown, secure and insecure—they all got mixed up. Someone would ask, "Where is the item at any point in time?" The diagram in Figure 14.1 was up on the white board constantly, and one of us would point to the left or right side and say "there." Figure 14.1 soon became "standardized" in that the standard partition was on the left side and the protected partition was on the right. The shorthand soon became to say simply left or right, and everyone in the room knew whether or not the information was under protection.

This shorthand worked very well for the security architects in the SAS. In fact, as the architects talked with others working on trusted computing projects, the terms left-hand side and right-hand side became the standard. For those working on these projects for any length of time, left-hand side always conjures up the image of something not under the protection of the platform, while conversely right-hand side always implies something receiving protection. The terms were so prevalent that the definition of the acronym of Left Hand Side (LHS) and Right Hand Side (RHS) are in the specifications.

Not surprisingly, marketing people feel that the terms LHS and RHS are not appropriate to use for a major new technology. Without the background of Figure 14.1, LHS and RHS do not really impart any information to a listener. When I gave the first presentation of Intel TXT at the Intel® Developer Forum (IDF), the marketing team asked me not to use LHS and RHS as the terms were just too esoteric. The LHS became the standard partition and the RHS became the protected partition. While the terms are much more descriptive of the type of partition, they do not have the ease of use the LHS and RHS do. Having briefed many people on Intel TXT, I still use LHS and RHS. When I communicate with other security architects who work for OS vendors or other hardware manufacturers, we continue to use LHS and RHS. I am going to attempt to keep the marketing folks happy in this book and use the approved names, standard and protected. The reader must know though that when they hear or see someone talking about the LHS or RHS, the speaker is referring to Figure 14.1.

---

1   I was the chair of the TXT SAS, a role I both loved and hated. The meetings are known to have lots of discussions with many twists and turns. The normal SAS time slot is two hours and many a new person has come to the SAS with a 15-minute topic—leaving two hours later a better and wiser person.

Actual Use

A funny thing happened with the architecture diagram: everyone realized that the diagram was really incomplete. One must come to grips with two realities when looking at Figure 14.1.

First, the diagram does not actually represent what most MLE vendors are likely to implement. Intel® Virtualization Technology allows for an almost unlimited number of partitions. Why should Intel TXT limit the possibilities to only two? The answer is that Intel TXT does *not* limit the number of partitions; the MLE can have one, two, or twenty partitions.

The second is that the difference between protected partition and unprotected partition is arbitrary. All partitions automatically have protection between each other that is a function of Intel® Virtualization Technology. The real protection attribute comes from individual page protection that prohibits DMA access. Certainly, the MLE would normally provide protection for itself from DMA, but individual partitions could easily have a mixture of protected and unprotected pages.

With these two issues, it becomes very difficult to differentiate between the partitions again. So, for the sake of sanity, the terms protected partition and unprotected partition continue to be used throughout this book. However, the reader is admonished to remember that the designation is only one of convenience and real partitions have a mixture of protected and unprotected physical pages.

Measured Launched Environment

The MLE is the controlling software in a Intel TXT system. The MLE provides:

- Memory arbitration
- Resource assignment
- Communication channel
- Partition lifecycle

You must remember as we discuss the MLE that the MLE is just a *Measured* *Launched Environment*. With the assumption[2] that the "normal" MLE is a Virtual Machine Monitor (VMM), the basic capabilities and responsibilities of a VMM do not change when the VMM becomes an MLE.

Memory Arbitration

The MLE provides control of all memory and resources in the system. If an application needs access to a physical memory page, the application uses a memory address. Using the page table entries, the CPU evaluates the address and converts the virtual address into a physical address. The setup of the page table entries is under complete control of the MLE.

Memory arbitration is the basic building block for guest partition isolation. Ensuring that each and every memory access complies with the policy set by the MLE, and that the CPU enforces the memory access policy, is the crux of MLE protection capabilities.

Memory arbitration is an inherent feature of any VMM. The MLE adds no real additional properties to the memory arbitration feature of the VMM.

Resource Assignment

The MLE controls, in addition to physical memory, all resources of the platform. Disk drives, display adapters, USB devices, and any other device one uses on the platform are all under control of the MLE.

All memory-mapped resources are very easy for the MLE to control; they appear as memory addresses, so the MLE treats the address as a protected page. The entire MLE page controls map onto the controls for the resource.

Resources that are not memory mapped require specific support from the MLE. The MLE must be aware of how entities communicate with the resource and then the MLE must be able to intercept, or virtualize,[3] the access.

---

2   Remember from chapter 12 that we are going to assume that most MLEs are VMMs. This does not preclude any other type of MLE construct, it just makes writing the book tractable.

3   Chapter 21 talks about possible future enhancements, such as the handling of resources.

Communication Channel

Guests are going to want to talk with each other. While it is certainly possible to simply require guests to have an Internet connection and use the Internet for inter-guest communication, the reality is that direct guest-to-guest communication is mandatory. The MLE has complete control of how each guest communicates with any other guest.

Partition Lifecycle

A major feature of the MLE is the ability to launch and terminate a guest partition. The MLE contains either explicitly as a standalone entity or implicitly as part of the code, the policy on when and how to launch and terminate guest partitions. Entities wishing to rely on the MLE and its guest partition lifecycle management policy must have the ability to obtain validation of the currently enforced policy. For MLEs that have the policy implicitly embedded in the code, attesting to the MLE identity also confirms the guest partition lifecycle management policy. For MLE that have explicit policy statements, the MLE must be able to show which policy the MLE is enforcing and how the MLE loaded the policy.

Standard Partition

Defining the LHS as a standard partition implies that the LHS is the normal situation that a user expects. This is correct. The standard partition does run standard operating systems and applications. The OS and applications need no modification to run in the standard partition.

The standard partition provides protection from software attack. Information held in the standard partition has the exact same areas of exposure that the information does today on systems without Intel TXT. If the application designer wants or needs protections, they will have to use some component that resides in the protected partition. The next section, "Protected Partition," explains how to design an application that takes advantage of the protected partition.

Operating System

The OS is any standard operating system like Windows† XP, Windows Vista, Linux, or a home-grown OS. The specification places no restrictions the type of OS that runs in the standard partition. If the user runs a particular OS today on their platform based on Intel architecture, the OS would still run in the standard partition. Certainly, if the OS in question is very old, its ability to run using new hardware may be questionable, but not due to Intel TXT. The OS probably would not understand the newer hardware.

The OS does not need any knowledge of the MLE. Certainly if one were to run DOS 3.1, the OS would have no knowledge of the MLE. DOS 3.1 would run correctly, but a direct knowledge of the MLE would be impossible.

The OS can be aware that the MLE and protected partitions are operating and available. A new OS can understand the hardware nature of a Intel TXT platform and provide the new services that the hardware allows.

Application

In the standard partition, you can run a normal application such as Quicken† or a user-written application. The application makes use of the OS services and executes without any knowledge of the MLE or the protected partition.

For applications running on an OS that has no knowledge of the MLE or protected partition, the application's ability to use the protected partition is limited. Unless the protected partition provides a communication mechanism that is publicly available and discoverable by the application, the application is unable to use any services of the protected partition.

If the OS is aware of the MLE and protected partition, then the OS can expose to applications the services exposed by the MLE and protected partition.

Protection Partition

All software in the protected partition receives protection from software attack, with no difference in the protection whether the application is running at ring 0 or ring 3.

Kernel

The kernel provides the services for applications running at ring 3. No requirement states that a protected partition must use both ring 0 and ring 3. It is entirely possible to create a domain that only uses ring 0.

The kernel can provide a rich set of services or it can provide limited services. When more code is in the kernel, it becomes harder to evaluate the security properties of the kernel. From the standpoint of security, the kernel should be as small as possible. From a service standpoint, the kernel should provide a wide and deep set of services. Since these two views conflict with each other, the kernel designer must weigh these two issues and make the appropriate choice for the use model.

Rich Service Kernel

One way to provide a rich service kernel would be to use a current OS like Linux. While this certainly provides a rich set of services, most existing operating systems are very large and difficult to evaluate. Nothing in the Intel TXT architecture prevents someone from using an OS as a kernel in the protected partition. The ability to show the properties of the OS is very difficult.

A rich service kernel is possible and desirable when the use model allows for user written applets that provide many user services. Carefully creating and adding the necessary services to the kernel can result in a rich kernel with services that enable a rich set of applications.

Limited Services

A limited service kernel can be either general purpose or designed to support a special application, which would seem to be an oxymoron. However, by providing a controlled set of services, the limited kernel actually provides a better trust boundary. The rich service kernel described earlier provides lots of services that a special purpose application would not need. By providing only the services necessary for the application, the amount of code that requires validation is smaller.

Another way to provide limited services and keep the kernel small would be to select a set of services that the majority of applications relying on the kernel would need. For instance, providing memory management, trusted input, trusted output, and general thread handling could possibly provide services for a wide variety of applications. While the extra special fancy stuff may not be available, the ability to create trustable applications may be greater.

Applet

The term applet is a very specific label. The idea is that applications using ring 3 in the protected partition are not the rich applications that one sees in ring 3 for the standard partition. Protected partition applications are *applets:* small, single purpose, and capable of being evaluated.

Take an application that does online stock transactions. Most of the application could be a ring 3 standard partition application—that is, parts that display the choices, allow the user to determine what to buy, and create the buy order. The only portion of the application that must be in the protected partition is the component that allows the user to verify and digitally sign the order request. This type of requirement defines an applet very well. The applet does four things:

■ Receives XML string

■ Displays XML string using trusted output

■ Receives user OK through trusted input

■ Signs XML string using a digital signing key protected by the trusted platform

The application then uses a simple applet and the applet only requires a limited service kernel. While it is not the only use of an applet and kernel combination, this use does represent a valid combination.

Application

There is no requirement that entities in the protected partition must be applets. Applications are possible also. The difference between an application and applet is that an application is standalone not requiring any outside help, while the applet is a component of a larger application.

Applications will come in all of the varieties that are available today. Large applications with thousands of options and abilities and small single-purpose applications that do their job quickly and efficiently are all possibilities.

Partition Communication

No direct communication occurs between any ring 0 or ring 3 process in the standard partition and any ring 0 or ring 3 process in the protected partition. The communication vector is the MLE, which has the responsibility to expose interfaces to the standard and protected partitions such that the two partitions can communicate. The MLE is under no obligation to provide the communication path, and if it does not, the partitions must communicate using some outside path such as a network or files.

If the MLE does provide a communication path, it can take any form that the MLE wants to provide, using a standard protocol or creating a special protocol.

Communication between two processes normally occurs as an Inter Process Communication (IPC) or a Remote Procedure Call (RPC). The mechanism that an MLE could expose is closer to an RPC than an IPC.

IPC

The IPC mechanisms normally take into account the use of internal resources to make the transfer faster. The activity of two processes mingling some internal resources is the exact type of behavior that a trusted platform should prevent. It is possible for a MLE to create mechanisms that look like IPC interfaces but that do not mingle process resources. If the MLE wants to implement pipes, the MLE could create a system that allowed a partition to establish a pipe to another partition. The actual implementation of the pipe would be a pipe from the establishing partition to the MLE and then an MLE-managed pipe from the MLE to the destination partition.

The creation of a direct pipe between two partitions would be illegal.

Partition Communication

The previous sentence highlights one of the main learning's over the years with trusted platforms and Intel TXT. The sentence, as originally written, reflects a view of the world that Intel TXT controls all. While the sentiment is nice, the reality is that Intel TXT only measures the MLE and the MLE provides control of the platform. While the architects of Intel TXT can make assumptions about what the MLE will do, there is no guarantee that a MLE will perform a certain way. In addition, consider a MLE that is creating two partitions that need a fast channel between the two partitions. A direct pipe might be the exact answer necessary for that use model. Calling that pipe illegal is attempting to force a set policy onto the users of the trusted platform and does not represent how the platform is used in the real world.

With the new understanding of the promises made by Intel TXT and the MLE, the above sentence becomes, "Any communication between partitions must be established and monitored by the MLE." Note now that the MLE sets the rules for how to establish and monitor. The job of Intel TXT is to measure the MLE such that outside entities can identify the MLE and know the policies the MLE enforces for partition communication.

RPC

The RPC provides a communication mechanism that requires some sort of arbitrator in the middle. The RPC mechanism then matches what the MLE needs to do to provide communication between the partitions. The MLE may choose any of the numerous RPC mechanisms that are currently available or it may design a new one. If the MLE is attempting to hide the protected partition, an RPC could be an appropriate communication mechanism.

Other Mechanisms

IPC and RPC are not the only mechanisms that are possible. While many applications today use IPC and RPC, other mechanisms provide good functionality for specific purposes.

One extremely easy method is to simply have a shared buffer between the two partitions.[4] One guest writes to the buffer, the other guest reads from the buffer. The implementation may or may not cause a security concern; only an evaluation of the MLE would be able to properly alleviate any security concerns.

The OS, MLE, and Kernel Interaction

Who must build the various base components? You have five combinations and each has some advantages and disadvantages.

OS, MLE, and Kernel from Same Vendor

Advantages are:

■ When all of the components come from the same vendor, you have some wonderful opportunities for collaboration. The OS and kernel know about each other and can optimize communication. The range of services can be tuned to the services the OS and kernel want to expose.

■ The MLE provides the glue and understands what the OS and kernel require. The communication mechanism can be configured so the normal transfer of information occurs in an efficient manner.

■ When the vendor wants to perform an evaluation of the security properties of the system, the combination of all of the components provides an easier base to show what the component can and cannot do. Being able to show the exact duties of a component in a security evaluation makes it easier to make and prove security claims.

Disadvantages are:

■ The major disadvantage is that the vendor has to supply two complete operating systems, standard and protected, and the MLE. The amount of code is large.

■ A negative perception could also be that if one vendor does all of the work the result can lead to security problems.

---

4 As this is a very easy mechanism, you should expect to see this mechanism in actual use.

MLE and Kernel from Same Vendor

This combination provides the security components from the same vendor but allows any standard OS to execute. This combination could be the same as all three components coming from the same vendor.

Advantages are:

■ The MLE and kernel understand the use models of the OS and provide for the most efficient use of the resources.

■ The MLE and kernel combination would also support the use of an old OS that had no knowledge of the MLE and kernel. This approach works very well when the communication mechanism is a RPC and both the OS and applications think that the protected partition resides on some other platform.

Disadvantages are:

■ Most of the normal application processing occurs in the OS, so you have no way to build efficiencies into the OS-to-kernel communication.

■ Also you could not design the OS to handle itself efficiently because the MLE design must allow for all operating systems.

OS and MLE from Same Vendor

This combination is a strange one. The vendor creates the standard OS and the MLE but does not provide any protected partitions. This situation combines the worst features of all the other combinations. As the MLE and kernel provide security, any evaluation of the two would be very difficult. In addition, the combination relies on the ability of the MLE to properly setup communications, and while all combinations do rely on this ability, this setup would assume that the MLE has no visibility into the kernel, making the communication mechanism difficult. While strange, this combination is not illegal.

OS and Kernel from Same Vendor

This situation is certainly possible. Think of the OS and kernel as being identical. Nothing requires the OS and kernel to be different. Therefore, in this model the MLE merely starts two instances of the same OS and places security around one of the instances—you really have to think standard and protected partitions now. The beauty of this approach is that the operating systems already know how to communicate with each other through some sort of RPC. The MLE exposes the RPC for use by the two operating systems and it all works from the start. The trick here is to consider whether the OS is robust enough to protect information. A simple OS that provides no internal protections does not give the protected partition the kernel support that is necessary to protect the applets.

The MLE in this case provides an RPC and the normal resource protections. This MLE could be a generic one that is designed to work with any OS or it could be one that is written by a separate vendor to support a specific OS. If the MLE is small enough, it would be easy to evaluate.

VMM Models

In 2008, this model appears to be the model of choice for commercial vendors. The ability to host Linux or Windows[†] in multiple virtual machines is a common feature and represents the use model under consideration.

All Three Components from Different Vendors

The combination of all three components from different vendors is possible. Any attempt at efficiencies is a very difficult task. Some efficiency would be possible, but nearly everything needs to be written to the lowest common denominator, forcing the design to avoid efficiencies and do tasks in a simple manner.

Simple and slow is not always a bad thing. Components that are simple and slow might have simpler designs, and simpler designs equate to easier to evaluate and maintain. Therefore, the simple design could result in a slower use model but one that provides a higher level of security assurance.

Standalone Applications

When creating applications that are single purpose and that require no help from any outside partition, the end result is potentially three components from different vendors. The assumption that the application vendor is related to the OS and MLE vendors is not necessarily a correct one.

A good example of a standalone application would be an Internet firewall. The firewall has a specific purpose and only needs OS support to perform certain operations. In some instances, the firewall could even work in an environment where the firewall itself makes no communication with the outside world, removing the requirement for input and output support. The firewall vendor could build the application on top of a specific OS, or a custom OS, and there would be no relationship whatsoever to the MLE. The chances that all three vendors were different would be quite high.

Application Design Options

Application design can be unaware of the protected partition, make use of a small component in the protected partition, or be an application totally consumed by the protected partition.

Unaware Applications

With the application unaware of the protected partition, no direct communication occurs with any applets in the protected partition. The application must make use of some library function that is dynamically linked or that is provided by the OS.

The example in Figure 14.2 shows an application that makes use of a service provided by the OS. The application makes a normal system call to obtain the service. Updating the service to run in the protected partition requires an RPC stub in the standard partition and the actual service running in the kernel. The design could have the server run as an applet, but this example does not illustrate that use.

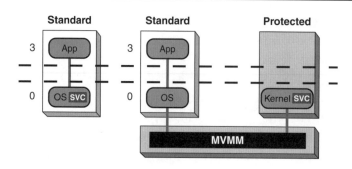

Figure 14.2 Application Unaware of Protected Partition

When the service was in the standard partition, the application made a system call to obtain the service. With the service moved to the protected partition, the application still makes a system call to a service in the standard partition. Instead of performing the actual operation, the service uses the communication mechanism provided by the MLE and sends the operation request to the protected partition. The protected partition service performs the actual operation and then returns the answer to the application through the MLE and the OS service.

Protected Component

From a component perspective, the layout is the same as in the previous example with the unaware application. The application does four things:

- The application calls a service.
- The service uses the MLE to communicate to the protected partition.
- The applet in the protected partition performs an operation.
- The applet sends a response back to the standard partition through the MLE.

The difference between this situation and the unaware application using a protected component lies in the application being aware of the protected component. With this design, the application can pick the components that need protection. The application can place more of the process in the applet.

Verification Model

The verification model is possible with the protected component option. In this instance, the application can perform whatever operations the application requires and then pass the result of the operation to the protected partition for verification. Figure 14.3 shows an example of a stock market purchasing transaction using the verification model.

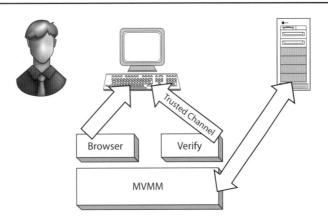

Figure 14.3 Verification Model

The standard partition performs most of the work of the stock transaction. In the standard partition, the user does four things:

1. Browses for possible stock purchases

2. Locates a stock

3. Indicates how many shares to buy at a stated price

4. Creates an XML request to send to stock broker

The sequence is the same for an application without verification, but the verification model adds the following steps:

1. Send the XML request to the protected applet

2. Applet displays request using XML viewer in a trusted output window

3. Applet requests user verification of transaction

4. User okays transaction using trusted input (mouse or keyboard)

5. Applet performs digital signature on XML transaction

6. Applet returns digitally signed transaction to the standard partition

7. Standard partition sends transaction to broker

The stock broker now receives the transaction, just as they do normally. The difference is that the broker can apply some additional trust to the transaction. The broker knows the following:

■ The platform in use has Intel TXT. The proof of the platform claim comes from the attestation the broker performs on this transaction or a previous transaction. The broker can also determine the exact version of the MLE and applet in use to protect the transaction and display it to the user.

■ The key that signs the transaction requires specific authorization to use it. This proof comes from the keys that are available for use either on the TPM or by the applet. The private portion of the key is always under protection and should not be available to any software process to either steal or misuse.

■ The user saw the transaction. The proof that the user saw the transaction comes from the fact that a Intel TXT platform can create a trusted channel to the display adapter, that the applet creates a trusted path to the user, and that the applet uses the trusted window for the

XML viewer. If the proof does not include verification of a Intel TXT platform, then the broker has no way to be sure that the trusted output was in use. The broker also validates that the XML viewer properly parses an XML string and that the applet requires the use of the XML viewer.

■ The user authorized the transaction. The proof of user authorization comes from the use of the protected input. The user either used the mouse or entered a value from the keyboard and a trusted channel handled either of the inputs.

■ It is now difficult for the user to make a claim that the user did not see what the transaction was or that the user did not explicitly authorize the transaction.

The verification model provides an excellent way to use Intel TXT without making major changes to an application. The verification model works on many types of transactions. Applications making use of the verification model can even be unaware that the verification is taking place, by having the verification process take over the normal process of merely transmitting the transaction.

The verification model is not the only model that can use protected components. Many more models are possible, and as the Intel TXT architecture becomes available, these models are likely to emerge. It is certainly possible that entirely new models of use could appear.[5]

Contained Application

The contained application lives solely in the protected partition. The actual implementation would normally be an applet, but a service of the kernel is possible. The applet may not even have interfaces available to the standard partition but be solely for the use of the MLE or other protected partition applets.

---

5 I always liked the verification model because it shows what Intel TXT can do but it does not require huge changes to existing applications. In fact many of us already execute in the verification model. When we do purchases on the Web, we go through the browse and select phase and then the check-out phase. In the Intel TXT model, the check-out phase would move to the protected partition.

A contained applet could be a user agent. Assume a stock agent that the user sets up to buy and sell stock without any interaction once established. The user would set the parameters for what stocks to buy under what conditions. The user would know that the applet would only run in the exact same environment, so any change to the environment, including the parameters, would invalidate the applet and it would no longer run. The design requires the applet to seal the parameters for the MLE and applet.

The contained applet could be something very different from an agent. The applet could be a firewall or virus engine. The sky is the limit for the design of applets.

Application Use

The previous sections have put the Intel TXT building blocks to use. Applications make use of the protected partition with various communication mechanisms. Nothing in this chapter should limit what designers do. They are free to use the Intel TXT building blocks and design applications that use both the standard and protected partitions.

This is a really good time to reiterate the comment from the "Actual Use" section. While this chapter uses terms like standard and protected partitions or LHS and RHS, normal use would be a combination of protected and unprotected physical pages in the guest partition. The mix of protected and unprotected physical pages is an MLE and guest partition policy decision and not a fixed and unchangeable setting. If the guest partition has a mix of protected and unprotected physical pages, the applications themselves will make use of these protections in interesting ways. No attempt is made to prejudge or define how applications make use of the Intel TXT protections.

Chapter 15

Late Launch

A slipping gear in your M203 grenade launcher can cause it to fire when you least expect it. This could make you very unpopular with what is left of your unit.

—Unknown, Army Magazine of Preventive Maintenance

For effective security, knowing what causes the launch of the protected partition is vital. To prevent slipping gears from causing the exposure of protected information, the launch of Intel®Trusted Execution Technology (Intel®TXT) must ensure that the CPU protection modes receive proper initialization. In general, TXT uses the Safer Mode Extensions (SMX) and Virtual Mode Extensions (VMX) as the gears and controls them through the CPU commands of GETSEC [SENTER] and GETSEC [SEXIT]. GETSEC is the CPU instruction leaf that implements the SMX instructions. To shift these gears smoothly you prepare for GETSEC [SENTER] execution, load the MLE, pass control to the MLE, and finally remove the MLE through GETSEC [SEXIT].

Launching the Protected Partition

Figure 15.1 illustrates the typical technical discussion at the "…and magic happens here" point. On the left, you see no protected domain; on the right, the protected partition is executing. Some process changed the state to enable the protected partition. Who waved the proverbial magic wand? What was that process? When did the process occur? [1]

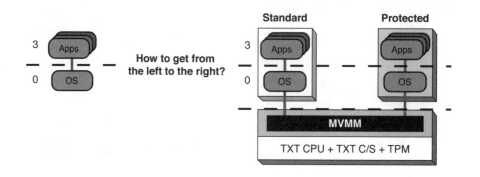

Figure 15.1 The Launch Sequence

The answers to the first set of questions are:

■ Who? A platform component will issue GETSEC [SENTER]. The component could be the platform user or the component could be an automatic process.

■ What? The GETSEC [SENTER] process.

■ When? GETSEC [SENTER] can occur at any time.

Those were the easy questions and the answers merely point to the GETSEC [SENTER] process. Pointing to the GETSEC [SENTER] process slows the hand waving2 down to a slower speed and bounds the further definitions.

A History of SENTER

Deciding the properties of the protected partition was the first order of business for the security architects. It was "easy"—well at the time it was very hard—to specify the protection boundaries of the partition. Many times

---

1   "Where" is not forgotten, but the "where" is always platforms with Intel®Trusted Execution Technology.

2   The realm of hand waving includes the hummingbird effect. The hummingbird effect occurs when the hand waving is so vigorous that the hand waver levitates off the ground and the hands are no longer visible. When discussing Intel ®TXT, and the discussion is at Figure 14.1, the individual leading the discussion would be demonstrating the hummingbird effect.

the team did a hand wave[3] and said, "Let's worry about the initiation of the partition later." Well, later finally came and hand-waving wasn't enough. The time for a definition of the secure entrance into the protected partition was upon the team.

On one difficult day, after many hours of discussion, the team kept coming back to the same simple fact: to have a chain of trust that would ensure the proper launch of the protected partition, you had to have a platform reset. However, the team did not want to require a platform reset because everyone felt that the user experience would be terrible. The team was at an impasse. But, you repeatedly heard the comment that a platform reset was necessary.

The mantra of needing a reboot led the team to ask the question "can we create a reboot without doing a reboot." Said another way, the question is, could you have a disruptive event that looks like a reboot but does not trigger a complete reset of the CPU internal state? The disruptive event could occur at any time and would not rely on any prior event. The term in use for the disruptive event was a *secure enter*[4] into the protected environment. As all architects want to use abbreviations, secure enter became SENTER. The term *late launch* comes from the ability to issue SENTER at any time.

A disruptive event is the design principle for SENTER: the system must cause one, control the results, and record the software and hardware that participated. The objectives for the disruptive event are:

■ Initiate the protections at any time and allow for removal of the partition.

■ Make sure that all CPUs participate.

■ Detect any tampering with the launch process.

■ Allow multiple invocations of the protected partition without requiring a platform reboot.

■ Ensure properly configured hardware.

---

3   These hand waves were so vigorous that the speaker would sometimes pass through the hummingbird effect and initiate the typhoon phase of hand waving where huge amounts of air are being moved.

4   As my editor points out secure enter is not grammatically correct, it should be secure entry. However, to be historically accurate, the term really was secure enter; the architects were just not concerned about grammatically correct phrases. Heck, we were simply happy to solve the problem.

Initiate the Protections at Any Time

Launching the protected partition with a reboot was the initial design. However, the final design uses late launch. The difference lies in the approach to control and measurement.

Launch Control

When people first hear about the protected partition the assumption is that controlling the process from reboot is the easiest. The idea is attractive... but wrong. Directly out of reset, the CPU is a clean slate. The CPU internal state and the settings for the platform all require initialization. The initialization of both areas comes from the BIOS sequence. The code includes BIOS boot block, main BIOS, Option ROMs, Master boot record, and the OS loader.

To provide a secure launch, every line of the boot sequence must be trustable. Option ROMs come from multiple vendors. The master boot record resides on the hard drive with little protection. The OS loader is provided by entities other than the BIOS and Option ROMs, and the BIOS itself is available to update via flashing. The code in some of these entities is years old and the coders did not consider security to be an issue. Requiring the providers of the code to rewrite the entire suite to meet the security requirements is not viable. As a result, the secure launch must not rely on the code in use for reset.

Measurement

Along with controlling the launch process, the design has to meet a requirement to measure the code involved in the launch. In particular, the code that executes as part of the SENTER process must have an accurate measurement. By controlling the launch process, it becomes possible to provide an accurate measurement of the launch code.

Disruptive Event

With SENTER providing the disruptive event for the launch, the process has no tie to platform reset. However, SENTER is a disruptive event that does not need any prior activity to operate. With no prior requirements, other than VMX not being on, SENTER can execute at any time.

Partition Removal

SENTER occurs at any time after platform reset and launches the protected partition. The partition executes until the receipt of a request to remove the partition. If the partition shutdown is complete and leaves no internal state resident in the CPU, then a subsequent SENTER executes correctly. The design allows for multiple invocations of SENTER with different parameters and settings without requiring a reset of the platform.

Many of the same issues that define the launch process are also present in the shutdown process. The name for the shutdown is secure exit or SEXIT. GETSEC[SEXIT] is a disruptive event to ensure the complete removal of all CPU state associated with the protected partition.

Trust Framework

SENTER removes all reliance on the reset process for the launch of the protected partition. Use of a disruptive event provides the framework for both trust and security. The SENTER and GETSEC[SEXIT] provide the mechanism that controls and measures the launch process and the subsequent protected partition.

Ensure that All CPUs Participate

Chapter 14 provided a definition of protected execution and showed that one of the main protection mechanisms was the internal CPU protection of physical pages. When one looks at a platform, what is the definition of a CPU? Multi-core packages and Intel® Hyper-Threading Technology (Intel® HT Technology) makes a CPU definition very important.

CPU Definition

This chapter is going to use a definition of CPU as a computing thread. A device that implements Intel® Hyper-Threading Technology (Intel® HT Technology) would have two CPUs. Intel® Trusted Execution Technology (Intel TXT) treats the device with the two CPU threads as two entirely different devices.

If the platform includes two or more packages—and think of packages as the actual physical device one places on the motherboard—then the number of CPUs is the total of all CPU threads. If the device did not implement

Intel®HT Technology, and there were two packages on the platform the count of CPU threads would be two. If the devices did implement Intel HT Technology, and there were two packages on the platform, the count of CPU threads would be four, the four coming from two CPU threads on each package and there being two packages.

Multi-core packages add an additional dimension to the CPU thread count. A multi-core package provides complete CPU cores in a single package. Assuming that the multi-core package has two cores and both cores implement Intel HT Technology, the CPU thread count for the package would be four. A platform with two packages, both packages with two cores and all cores Intel HT Technology enabled would have a CPU thread count of eight.

The current limiter to the number of packages supported by Intel® TXT is the chipset. A Intel TXT platform only operates with a single chipset.[5]

CPU Synchronization

One can ask, "Why the focus on how many CPUs are present?" The answer[6] involves the GETSEC [SENTER] disruptive event, which has a main goal of gaining control of the page tables. What happens with multiple CPUs if the page tables and protections do not match? If one CPU says protect page 22 and the other CPU says page 22 has no protection, you face a very real possibility that software could expose data that is supposedly under protection. The physical pages are just the tip of the iceberg; unsynchronized CPUs could expose numerous items.

The goal of GETSEC [SENTER] is to force a mechanism, like reset, that requires all of the CPUs to have a consistent view of the platform. The mechanism must contemplate the addition or removal of a CPU from the platform.

Be Sure that the Launch Can Detect Any Tampering

In addition to the hardware mechanisms for GETSEC [SENTER], the launch process has software components that are susceptible to tampering during the

---

5   Chapter 21 talks about the future of Intel TXT and possible extensions.

6   Another answer might be that we know what is good for the system. But that answer is so short, one might not be motivated to purchase this book.

launch process. The GETSEC [SENTER] process does not protect the software components from tampering. Instead, the process ensures that the measurement process detects any tampering of the software. In addition to detecting tampering, the measurement process provides the building block for the next objective: knowing the identity of the protected partition.

Knowing the Identity of the Launched Environment

What does identity mean in relation to the protected partition? Intel TXT defines identity to be the software that is in use during the protected partition launch. Identity corresponds to the protected partition environment. To provide the identity value, the launch process obtains the digital hash of the code. An inherent property of a hash algorithm is that a single bit change in the input should result in at least 50 percent of the output bits changing. If the hash output represents the identity of the launched environment, and it does, then the single bit change, and the resulting new hash output value, represents a new identity. The new identity based on a single bit change is the exact property desired of the launching and measuring process.

Ensure Properly Configured Hardware

Just as the software identity is important so is the configuration of the hardware. Some hardware configurations can cause the protected partition to assume that certain protections are in place when the hardware is unable to actually provide the protection. Chapter 16 describes these concerns in detail. Part of the configuration verification uses the secure initialization (SINIT) module.

The GETSEC [SENTER] Sequence

To accomplish the launch of the MLE the GETSEC [SENTER] process follows a set sequence. Figure 15.2 illustrates the SENTER sequence.

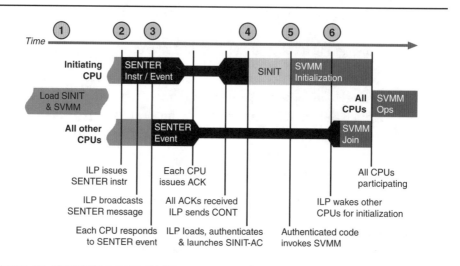

Figure 15.2 The SENTER Sequence

To understand the sequence, you should be familiar with the following definitions.

- The definition of CPU thread as defined earlier in this chapter.

- A processor is a CPU thread; a processor is not a package. While the equivalence of processor and thread can create some ambiguity, both terms have been in use for many years. Both terms are used to describe a CPU thread.7

- Initiating Logical Processor (ILP) is the processor that starts the GETSEC [SENTER] sequence. The ILP must be the same processor as the Bootstrap Processor (BSP).

- Responding Logical Processor (RLP) is any other processor on the platform other than the ILP. The "responding" aspect reflects the fact that all other processors must respond to the messages from the ILP.

---

7   I understand fully the possible confusion between thread and processor. My early background was in software and thread has a very specific meaning there.

- Broadcast is the mechanism whereby the ILP sends information to all of the other processors.

- Sleep is where the processor is performing no operations other than looking for a wakeup message.

Figure 15.2 illustrates the GETSEC [SENTER] process. The numbers refer to points in time and where specific actions take place. The following sections describe each step and the rationale behind it.

Loading the Modules

Before actually executing the GETSEC [SENTER] instruction, the entity currently controlling the CPU must locate the SINIT and MLE and load them into memory. The controlling entity could be an operating system or the BIOS. The type of controlling entity makes no difference to the GETSEC [SENTER] process. Any software that has control of ring 0 can initiate the GETSEC [SENTER] process.

The controlling entity loads the SINIT module and the MLE into memory. Neither the SINIT module nor the MLE has any protection against modification at this time. The design of Intel TXT does not require any protection to the modules, and if modification does occur, the GETSEC [SENTER] process detects the tampering.

The SINIT module must reside in a contiguous section of memory. The MLE uses a page table to indicate the physical pages that contain the MLE.

SINIT Module Size Requirements

The SINIT module's address and size are parameters of the GETSEC [SENTER] command. The ILP evaluates the address to be sure that the address is on a modulo-4,096 boundary, and the size is 0 modulo-64. Furthermore, the size must be larger than the minimum and smaller than the maximum. The minimum and maximum are specific to the processor type. Any errors result in a general protection violation.

MLE Layout Requirements

The MLE uses physical pages and a page table to indicate the location of the MLE. The page table must follow the rules for page tables on the current platform.

Executing GETSEC [SENTER]

With the SINIT and MLE in memory, the stage is set to start the sequence. The ILP issues the GETSEC [SENTER] instruction. GETSEC is the new instruction that implements all of the SMX commands.

It is important to differentiate between the GETSEC [SENTER] process and the SENTER message. The GETSEC [SENTER] process is part of the GETSEC instruction. The SENTER message is a result of the GETSEC [SENTER] process.

Before invoking GETSEC [SENTER], the following conditions must be present:

- The processor must be executing in Ring 0.
- The processor cache must be available.
- A Intel TXT enabled chipset must be present.
- The Trusted Platform Module (TPM) must be present.
- No MLE can be executing, therefore only one MLE can execute at any one moment in time.[8]
- The processor cannot be in authenticated code mode.
- The process cannot be in VMX mode.
- The ILP must be the boot-strap processor (BSP).
- No outstanding machine-check error conditions exist.

If any of these conditions are not true, the GETSEC [SENTER] process signals a general protection violation. After validating all of the preceding conditions, the ILP issues the SENTER-ACK message.

With the preceding group of requirements and the fact that the GETSEC [SENTER] process takes time, it is a requirement on the invoking entity, OS or BIOS, to ensure the proper environment. The invoking entity should

---

8   Do not confuse the restriction on concurrent MLE execution with sequential MLE execution. It is possible and desirable to execute one MLE, terminate the MLE, and then execute a separate MLE.

ensure, with all reasonable checks that the GETSEC [SENTER] process would succeed.

Issuing SENTER-ACK

The issuing of the SENTER-ACK message starts the disruption that the architects designed into Intel TXT. Before the SENTER-ACK message is sent, errors would result in a general protection violation. After issuing the SENTER-ACK message, errors result in a TXT-shutdown. You can find the complete details of the TXT-shutdown later in this chapter.

The ILP issues the SENTER-ACK message on the front-side bus. All other processors, such as the RLPs, must respond to the SENTER-ACK message. The RLPs respond to the SENTER-ACK on the next instruction boundary, so the time before all RLPs respond is variable.

> **Moving to Intel® QuickPath architecture**
>
> The FSB is dead, long live Intel QuickPath architecture. This new interconnect changes the bandwidth and speed properties of the conection between CPU packages and the chipset. From the standpoint of Intel TXT, there is no real functional difference between FSB and Intel QuickPath architecture. Both provide a connection between the devices, both transmit the SENTER messages, and both allow for the synchronization of CPU packages and threads.
>
> Certainly there are operational changes as the interconnect moves from a bus to a point-to-point architecture, but functionally the new interconnect provides the same features for Intel TXT. We will continue to note the differences between FSB and Intel QuickPath architecture, but please remember these are really just operational differences.

Enumerating the RLP

The ILP needs a mechanism for collating all of the responses from the RLPs. Putting the mechanism in the CPU requires entirely new logic in the CPU. The chipset already has a mechanism that keeps track of individual processors in the system, the bus-agent ID. The chipset assigns to each processor a bus-agent ID and uses the ID to route messages on the front-side bus.

When the chipset receives the SENTER-ACK message, the chipset requires a response from every previously identified bus-agent ID. When a response is present from each RLP, the chipset sets a flag to indicate that all RLPs received and responded to the SENTER-ACK. The ILP polls the flag and waits until the flag is set. Failure to set the flag within a time-out period results in a TXT-shutdown.

Each RLP upon receipt of the SENTER-ACK, issues the response to indicate to the chipset the acceptance of the GETSEC [SENTER] processing. The RLP only indicates acceptance of the SENTER-ACK on the next instruction boundary. Only responding at instruction boundaries allows the RLP to treat the SENTER-ACK as an interrupt. This approach simplifies the new code necessary to handle the SENTER-ACK.

> **RLP enumeration**
>
> Identification of packages is very different in Intel QuickPath architecture. The responsibility to identify the packages, keep a count of the packages, and then ensure a response from all of the packages does not change.
>
> The basic SENTER-ACK messaging remains the same with the chipset just identifying the packages differently.

RLP Sleep

After responding to the SENTER-ACK, the RLP moves into an SMX sleep state. The sleep state places the RLP into a mode where the RLP waits for the ILP to indicate the successful completion of the ILP GETSEC [SENTER] process.

The SMX sleep state is an important piece of the GETSEC [SENTER] puzzle. By placing the RLP into SMX sleep, the RLP is not executing any instructions. With the RLP not executing, the RLP makes no attempts to access any platform resources. The most important resource the RLP does not access is physical memory.

Ensuring Processor Participation

A major result of the SENTER-ACK and the RLP sleep is the assurance that all processors are participating in the GETSEC [SENTER] process. With all RLP responding to the SENTER-ACK, the design provides a hardware mechanism that ensures GETSEC [SENTER] participation of all platform processors.

ILP Processing

When the chipset indicates to the ILP the receipt of the acknowledgement from all of the RLP, the ILP continues the GETSEC [SENTER] process.

Inhibit External Events

Issuing the SENTER-ACK causes the ILP to mask external events. The RLP mask external events upon receipt of the SENTER-ACK. The events masked include INIT, A20M, NMI, and SMI. Under normal conditions, event handlers process the event. The secure environment needs specific handlers that ensure handling of the event does not leak secrets. Once the secure environment establishes handlers for these events, the events are unmasked. The A20M event remains masked during the entire duration of the protected partition.

Validate Chipset and TPM

The ILP now validates that no outstanding valid uncorrectable machine-check error conditions are present. Prior to issuing the SENTER-ACK, the ILP did the same validation. The second check ensures that no error occurred in any of the RLPs while the RLPs responded to the SENTER-ACK message. The response to the machine-check being present is not a general protection violation, but the more serious TXT-shutdown. Here's the reason: after sending the SENTER-ACK message and having all of the RLPs in a sleep state, no execution environment is available.

Verify Power Management Settings

The ILP verifies that the current power management settings are appropriate. The ILP determines appropriateness by looking at the current voltage ID and the bus ratio values held in the GV3 model-specific register (MSR).9 If the values are not appropriate, the ILP attempts to change the values. If the attempt fails, the ILP issues a TXT-shutdown.

---

9   The majority of the power settings are in the GV3 MSR; however specific devices and platforms may have additional MSRs that the SINIT code needs to check. The inclusion of device-specific checks is one advantage of the SINIT ACM.

Power settings are important to the protected partition because a processor running at power settings that are on the edge of the power envelope could execute unpredictably. Unpredictable execution could lead to an exposure of memory under control of the protected partition. Once the MLE has control of the system, the MLE could decide to allow power settings other than the defaults set by the GETSEC [SENTER] process. This change to the settings is permissible as the MLE can report what the MLE allows or rejects.

Lock the Chipset to the ILP

A major security tenet is that of defense in depth. Depth of defense means that the design should contemplate more than one attack. The only devices on the front-side bus are CPUs. Every CPU other than the ILP is an RLP. All of the RLPs are in the SMX sleep state. No accesses should be occurring from these processors. To ensure that this is true, the ILP locks the chipset so that only accesses from the ILP are valid. The ILP uses the ILP bus-agent ID to indicate to the chipset that only accesses with the specified ID are permissible.

The lock remains in effect until the ILP specifically releases the lock. The ILP keeps the lock on until the MLE needs to activate the RLPs.

SINIT Processing

The ILP has assurance that the RLP are sleeping, that only the ILP can communicate with the chipset, and that external events are masked. The ILP now needs to validate various hardware settings. The ILP performs these validations using the SINIT module. The ILP must locate the SINIT module, load it, validate it, and then execute it.

SINIT Load

The SINIT code, loaded by the OS or BIOS, still resides in the same physical memory location. Nothing in GETSEC [SENTER] or the SENTER-ACK processing made any changes to the SINIT code. Up to this point, the hardware provides no protection to the SINIT code. Any RLP, prior to the SENTER-ACK response, or any DMA device could manipulate the SINIT code. SINIT is an ACM to mitigate the vulnerabilities that unprotected code enables.

The GETSEC [SENTER] instruction, takes as one parameter, the location of the SINIT module. The ILP now uses that location to load SINIT into the ACM execution area.

The ACM area provides protection from external bus snoops and the memory type must be WriteBack (WB). If the ILP finds that the WB condition is not present, the ILP forces a TXT-shutdown.

Once SINIT is in the ACM execution area, the ILP ensures that the ILP executes in a mode where internal and external events do not disrupt the execution of SINIT. The protections are an inherent feature of ACM, but they have a direct security benefit: the SINIT code executes without any interference. Knowing that the SINIT code runs without interference allows the SINIT code to validate portions of the current hardware configuration. Chapter 16 discusses the platform issues under review by SINIT.

Authenticate the SINIT Module

The SINIT module is a normal ACM module, and ACM modules require a specific format and details of the format are available in the Intel TXT documentation from Intel. The important part here is that the ACM has three main sections:

■ Module header

■ Internal working scratch space

■ User code and data

Module Header

The module header contains information necessary to allow the ACM authenticated code processing to validate SINIT module. The chipset manufacturer is the entity that must vouch for the SINIT module and perform a digital signature on the module. The chipset contains the hash of the public key that can validate the module. An improperly formed SINIT header results in the ILP issuing TXT-shutdown.

The ILP obtains the hash of the signing key, from the chipset, using special Intel TXT front-side bus cycles. The module header includes the public key that signed the module. The ILP then calculates the SHA-1 hash of the public key in the module header. The ILP compares the hash from the chipset with the calculated hash and if they match, SINIT load continues. A mismatch results in a `TXT-shutdown`.

Validating the Module

With the public key validated, the ILP can now validate that the SINIT is the proper module. The validation involves performing a digital signature validation of the ACM. The ILP calculates a SHA-1 of the appropriate area and then performs a digital signature validation of the module.

The digital signature validation fails with a change to a single bit. Since the SINIT module was attackable until loaded into the ACM execution area, this signature validation is critical. It proves that the SINIT module has no modifications. Any attempt to modify the SINIT code results in the digital signature validation failing. The digital signature validation failure results in a TXT-shutdown.

As SINIT is an authenticated code module, an attacker cannot modify the SINIT code in a manner that allows the SINIT code to pass the digital signature validation. The validation detects any tampering with the SINIT module, thus meeting the requirement for tamper detection.[10] The Intel TXT hardware enforces the validation and provides assurance that the SINIT code does validate the hardware settings properly. Using the hardware to perform the digital signature validation enforces a model that allows only SINIT code from the chipset vendor to execute.

After validating the signature, the ILP places the 20-byte SINIT module hash in the first 20 bytes of the scratch space. The ILP does not save the 20-byte hash of the signature key.

Storing SINIT Measurement

Attestation requires an accurate measurement and the proper storage of that measurement. The ILP just completed an accurate measurement of the SINIT module. The result of that measurement is the 20-byte hash value in the scratch space. The TPM is the attestation device on the platform so the ILP needs to send the 20 bytes to the TPM without any interference.

---

10 The requirement is not to stop tampering, just detect the tampering.

TPM Bus Considerations

The ILP needs to move the SINIT measurement from the currently executing GETSEC [SENTER] instruction to the TPM. The measurement has to travel from the CPU to the MCH over the FSB[11], from the MCH to the ICH over the hublink, and from the ICH to the TPM over the LPC bus.

It was tempting to consider using a bus like USB, but these busses present some major problems. The first problem is that the processors are masking all events. Therefore, any bus requiring an interrupt cannot work. The only executing processor is the ILP; and the ILP is executing AC code, which has a size limit of around 32 kilobytes. A USB handler and the code to perform the hardware validation would not fit in that size. The bus cannot be a complex bus requiring software handling. The next issue with the bus is the ability to indicate to the TPM that the GETSEC [SENTER] microcode has control of the CPU. A bus like USB does not have the ability to ensure that no other device can generate the signal.

With the USB bus ruled out, and like busses also, the requirement remains of moving the measurement from the CPU to the TPM. The bus of choice is the LPC bus. The LPC bus is available at all times and does not require any interrupts. Another nice feature of the LPC bus is that addressing is available with memory maps. When and how Intel TXT uses the features of the LPC bus is revealed in the rest of the GETSEC [SENTER] process.

Setting the PCR

The ILP needs to send the SINIT measurement to the TPM via the indicated busses. The ILP uses TPM commands and special addresses to indicate the CPU control. Figure 15.3 provides the illustration of the process for storing the measurement in the TPM. Please read FSB to also include Intel QuickPath architecture.

---

11   Or the new Intel QuickPath architecture

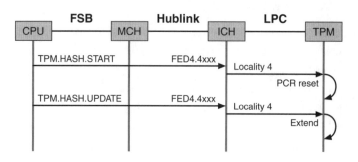

Figure 15.3 TPM.HASH.START Process

The ILP issues a TPM.HASH.START command by issuing a single-byte write to the TPM.HASH.START port. The definition for the TPM.HASH.START command is in the TCG PC Specific Specification (TCG 2005a). The TPM.HASH.START port is a memory mapped address at location 0xFED4_4xxx. The ICH reserves the 0xFED4 range for TPM access. Locality 4 access occurs in the 4xxx range. The ICH blocks all access to 0xFED4_4xxx unless the CPU indicates that the GETSEC [SENTER] microcode is executing.

The ILP uses special FSB cycles to indicate the execution of the GETSEC [SENTER] microcode. When receiving the command, the special FSB cycle sends the command to the ICH using special cycles on the Hublink. The ICH accepts the command and writes the command to the TPM on the LPC bus using the 0xFED4_4xxx address.

The TPM only accepts the TPM.HASH.START command on the 0xFED4_4xxx address range. Using any other address for sending the command to the TPM results in an error condition in the TPM. The combination of the ICH enforcing the protection on the address and the TPM only accepting the command on the address produces an assurance that the TPM.HASH.START command only arrives at the TPM during the GETSEC [SENTER] process.

TPM Response to TPM.HASH.START

Upon receipt of the `TPM.HASH.START` command, the TPM performs two critical operations: resetting of the dynamic PCR and setting the mode of the TPM to accept any measurements.

Resetting the dynamic PCR involves the TPM setting the PCR to their default values. The TIS specifies that the default value is `0x00` for all bytes in the PCR. The PCRs that are reset using `TPM.HASH.START` are PCRs 17 through 20.

The TPM sets the internal state of the TPM such that the TPM is ready to accept the bytes of the measurement. The TPM clears the TPM input buffer and locks the TPM such that only commands from locality 4 are acceptable.

ILP Measurement Transmission

The PCRs are at the default values and the TPM is awaiting further locality 4 commands. The ILP sends the 20-byte hash value stored in the scratch space by looping through each of the 20 bytes, starting with the least significant byte of the hash. The ILP uses the `TPM.HASH.DATA` port to perform the writes.

The ILP then performs four single-byte writes of the contents of `EDX` to the TPM using the `TPM.HASH.DATA` port. The contents of `EDX` provide a proof of the parameters set when invoking the `GETSEC[SENTER]` command. The parameters provide an indication of the level of functionality enabled for use by the protected partition.

The ILP terminates the SINIT measurement by performing a single-byte write of a `0x00` to the `TPM.HASH.END` port. Upon receipt of the `TPM.HASH.END` command, the TPM takes the information in the TPM input buffer, which is the SINIT hash value, and the contents of EDX, and performs a TPM_Extend operation to PCR 17. The TPM now contains the SINIT measurement. The Intel TPM provides the protection on PCR 17.

The `TPM.HASH.xxx` commands bypass the normal TPM interface protocol. protocols. The bypass allows for ILP microcode that is simpler and smaller.

Initialize ILP State

With the SINIT measurement safely reported to the TPM, the ILP can now make ready to pass control to the SINIT. The ILP needs to initialize the ILP internal state to allow the execution of the SINIT module. A complete resetting of the ILP state is not needed, but certain registers and tables need initialization. The information as to how to set the registers and tables comes from the SINIT module header. A partial list of the items set is:

- Global Descriptor Table Register (GDTR)
- Registers CS, DS, SS, and ES

Unlocking the Chipset

The chipset locked down various areas upon receipt of the SENTER-ACK message. The ILP now needs to start opening the locked down areas of the chipset. The ILP issues the TXT.CMD.OPEN-PRIVATE message. The message informs the chipset that the SINIT begins executing soon and the SINIT needs access to chipset resources. The ILP issues the TXT.CMD.OPEN-PRIVATE message to the chipset using special FSB cycles. The cycles ensure that only the ILP can properly issue the message.

In addition to unlocking the chipset Intel TXT private space, the ILP also unlocks the chipset locality 3 TPM address of 0xFED4_3xxx. This space is available to the SINIT module and allows the SINIT module to identify itself to the TPM.

GETSEC [SENTER] Completion

At this point, the GETSEC [SENTER] instruction is complete. The ILP has loaded and authenticated the SINIT module, and it has set the ILP internal state such that SINIT execution is possible.

The ILP and RLPs that were once active now assert an indication that the processor is executing in SMX mode for all bus memory read transactions. This assertion continues until the execution of GETSEC [SEXIT]. The mechanism in place to make the assertion is to use signals on the FSB on all bus memory transactions. Failure to assert the signal when attempting a bus memory transaction results in the chipset issuing a TXT-shutdown.

SINIT Execution

The ILP passes control to the SINIT module now. The SINIT code has the following main objectives:

- Test for proper hardware configurations (See Chapter 16 for a detailed explanation of the test)
- Initialize the SMM handling
- Enable the DMA handling
- Load and measure the MLE
- Store the MLE measurement in the TPM
- Pass control to the MLE

Initialize SMM Handling

The MLE has a peer monitor that manages System Management Interrupts (SMI). This peer monitor is the SMI Transfer Monitor (STM). Chapter 12 discusses the SMI handling model. The STM has some configuration options that the SINIT module must validate to ensure proper connection to the MLE. If the processor MSEG MSR indicates the enabling of the STM, the SINIT code validates the following actions:

1. Read the chipset TXT MSEG.BASE and SIZE registers.

2. Compare the processor MSEG MSR address field to the chipset MSEG.BASE. Addresses that are different indicate a configuration error with the STM. In that case, the ILP issues a TXT-shutdown.

3. Read the STM header, which is located at the base of the MSEG. Extract the STM image size from the header.

4. Beginning from the base of the MSEG, read the STM image up to the size specified in the header. Add each byte of the image to an SHA-1 hash.

5. Starting from the end of the STM image size, write zeros into the remainder of the MSEG region. Writing in these zeros prevents attacks where non-STM code was present in the scratch or data areas of the STM,

which later allows some attack mechanism to be invoked by the code.

6. Complete the SHA-1 operation and obtain the 20-byte hash value.

7. Using `0xFED4_3xxx`, locality 3, issue a `TPM_Extend`[12] operation to PCR 17 with the hash value that was created in the previous step. PCR 17 now contains the values of both the SINIT and STM.

STM and DMA

The MSEG area is part of protected memory just like the MLE. The MSEG area does not require the setting of any additional DMA protections. The chipset automatically blocks all inbound access to SMRAM, and SMRAM includes the MSEG.

Enable DMA Protection

With the ILP CPU memory protections turned on, the SINIT code needs to enable the chipset protections against DMA accesses. Enabling the chipset to provide DMA access protection allows the use of main system memory for protected operations.

While the CPUs—that term includes the ILP and all RLPs—are quiet, DMA devices have no such restriction. A DMA-capable device could initiate a DMA access during the `GETSEC[SENTER]` process.

The chipset is responsible for ensuring that pages marked as needing protection from DMA have DMA protection. There is the need to resolve potential race conditions where there is a request to protect the page that arrives concurrent with a DMA request for the same page. The chipset handles these and other synchronization issues internally without any need for assistance from the CPU or other platform components.

The chipset may support caches or manually created hash tables. These changes could result in better performance. If the chipset supports the improvements, the SINIT code is responsible for setting the controls correctly.

---

12 While we attempted to minimize the TPM-specific code in the microcode during the storage of the SINIT measurement, the SINIT code itself can use the normal TPM commands.

SCLEAN Validation

Chapter 16 discusses the issues of ensuring proper cleanup after resets or other events. One of the mechanisms performs a "scrub" of memory. Scrubbing involves writing a zero to every byte of memory. SCLEAN is the authenticated code module that performs the scrub.

SINIT needs to validate the installation of the correct SCLEAN module. The TPM holds the module identity in either a PCR or a NV storage location. SINIT loads the SCLEAN module identity and then validates that the SCLEAN is an appropriate module. If the validation fails, SINIT terminates with a `TXT-shutdown`.

MLE Loading

The SINIT now loads and measures the MLE. The basic process is to protect a page, read the page and then measure the page.

The first item to find is the MLE heap. The chipset holds the information in the `TXT.HEAP.BASE` and `SIZE` registers. The MLE then adds these pages to the PMR region. With the heap protected, the SINIT can now load the MLE page table.

The MLE page table is at a specific offset in the MLE heap. The SINIT verifies that the MLE page table follows some basic rules. The rules may be processor specific, but generically they are:

- Page table entries go from low memory addresses to higher addresses.
- The page table entry type is fixed for all entries in the table. The actual type is processor specific.

If the page table does not follow the rules, the SINIT initiates a `TXT-shutdown`. SINIT now performs the following actions for each page in the MLE page table:

1. Add the page to the PMR Protected Region. Adding the page to the PMR region also invalidates any cache entries for the page ensuring that the next read of the page, which occurs in the next step, actually reads the physical page.

2. Read the page.

3. Add the page contents to a SHA-1 hash.

After protecting, reading, and hashing all of the MLE pages, the SINIT module completes the SHA-1 hash. The resulting hash value is the measurement of the MLE. The TPM needs to receive the MLE measurement. The SINIT extends PCR [18] using the TPM locality 3 port. Locality 4 is not available to the SINIT module.

The MLE digest value is in a different PCR than the SINIT identity. This separation is not an issue as when using the TPM, the sealing entity can specify both PCR and ensure that the entire environment (SINIT, SCLEAN, STM, and MLE) are identical.

Passing Control to the MLE

The PMR region table is protecting all of the MLE pages; the TPM holds the MLE identity so the last action of the SINIT module is to pass control to the MLE. The MLE entry point is part of the MLE header structure. The SINIT extracts the MLE entry point and then far-jumps to the entry point. The SINIT uses the GETSEC [EXITAC] instruction to perform the jump.

The GETSEC [EXITAC] instruction automatically changes the paging mode, sets CS:EIP and SS:ESP and returns the processor cache to normal operation.

MLE Execution

The MLE now has control of the ILP and needs to complete the GETSEC [SENTER] process.[13] The initialization process, while complete from the GETSEC [SENTER] standpoint, is still a long way from being able to execute user code. The MLE has to re-enable interrupts, enable the SMI Transfer Monitor, and rendezvous the RLP. After accomplishing the rendezvous, the MLE can then perform any additional MLE initialization.

Enabling Interrupts

Interrupts disabled during the activities of the GETSEC [SENTER] instruction now need enabling. The MLE establishes an IDT entry and enables the ILP to take interrupts. Having the MLE allow interrupts implies that the MLE

---

13 The MLE initialization steps are all MLE specific. While Intel proposes that the MLE properly perform the steps, it is the responsibility of the MLE to actually complete a valid initialization.

is sufficiently initialized to handle the interrupts when they occur. The MLE does not enable the RLP to take interrupts at this time. The only process able to take interrupts is the ILP.

The MLE interrupt handler must be able to accept and handle all interrupts properly.

Enabling SMI

With normal interrupts enabled, the MLE now needs to start accepting SMI. It is possible that platform implementations could enable SMI prior to this time. The MLE must be aware of how each specific platform handles SMI. The MLE must not ignore SMI as these events can be benign events like requests to change the screen brightness or critical events like thermal warnings that should turn cooling fans on or handling of device specific errors. Turning SMI back on is a critical issue and the MLE writer must examine carefully the guidance in the MLE writers guide.

Secure Launch Recap

On numerous occasions when teaching this concept, I have teased audiences that seem to be slightly confused:

> I do not understand why you are confused. I have been working on this for many years and I just do not understand why you cannot pick it up in an hour or so.

Anyway, maybe a short recap is in order. The secure launch performed the following steps and operations:

- *Rendezvous all processors, physical and logical.* The rendezvous ensures that all processors are aware of the GETSEC [SENTER] process and all processors will enter the MLE environment.

- *Select the ILP and put to sleep the RLP.* The ILP is the only processor executing and the sleeping RLP ensure that no extra transactions occur on any bus.

- *Protect against outside events.* Outside events, like interrupts, could disrupt the ability of SINIT to properly determine the state of the platform and discover potential hardware mis-configuration.

- *Load and verify the SINIT module.* The SINIT comes from the chipset manufacturer, is specific to the current platform hardware components, and no tampering of the SINIT code occurred.

- *Store the SINIT measurement in the* TPM. The SINIT identity, stored in the TPM, allows for both SEAL operations to protect long-term secrets and the attestation of the SINIT code executed.

- *Establish the NoDMA table.* Protect the MLE from software attacks launched by entities other than a CPU.

- *Protect and measure the MLE.* Protecting each MLE page allows the MLE to protect itself. The MLE measurement, in conjunction with the SINIT measurement, provides the exact MLE environment that is executing.

- *Store the MLE measurement in the* TPM. The stored MLE measurement enables both SEAL and attestation of the MLE environment.

- *Launch the MLE.* The MLE can now control the platform.

GETSEC [SEXIT] Processing

The late launch premise is that the protected environment can successfully terminate without requiring a reboot of the platform. The operand for this command is GETSET [SEXIT]. The GETSEC [SEXIT] command works in the reverse of GETSEC [SENTER].

Just as GETSEC [SENTER] needs all processors to rendezvous and have a consistent view of the protections, GETSEC [SEXIT] needs all processors to rendezvous and release all protections. Having one processor still believe that memory has protection results in the exposure of protected information.

GETSEC [SEXIT] does not have the complication that GETSEC [SENTER] does in that no validation of the hardware configuration is needed. Also, you have no need to bootstrap a protected environment as the protected environment is already running. Without these needs, running an authenticated module during GETSEC [SEXIT] is unnecessary.[14]

GETSEC [SEXIT] Initiation

To start the protected environment, any ring 0 code can call GETSEC [SENTER], as shown in Figure 15.4. The reverse is not true for GETSEC [SEXIT]. The MLE controls the issuing of GETSEC [SEXIT] and the MLE can block issuing of the command. The MLE is the only entity on the platform that can issue GETSEC [SEXIT].

---

14 While the current implementation does not support the GETSEC [SEXIT] SINIT parallel ACM, Chapter 21 does discuss what the future may hold.

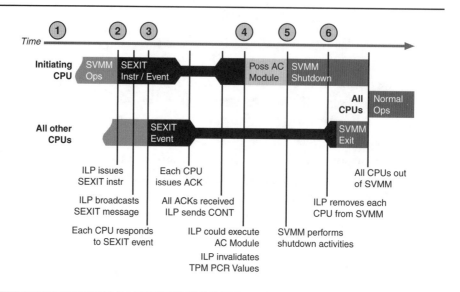

Figure 15.4 The GETSEC [SEXIT] Sequence

Once the MLE issues the GETSEC [SEXIT] command, the following sequence occurs:

1. Validate that the MLE issued the command.

2. Broadcast a message to rendezvous the processors.

3. Ensure that all processors respond to the broadcast.

4. Shut down the MLE.

5. Remove all protections and allow normal operations.

GETSEC [SEXIT] Validation

The processor receiving the GETSEC [SEXIT] must be the BSP, which becomes the ILP for the GETSEC [SEXIT] process. The ILP validates the GETSEC [SEXIT] command came from an executing MLE. The various flags and modes must be present to continue GETSEC [SEXIT] processing. If the MLE did not issue the GETSEC [SEXIT], the ILP issues a general protection violation.

GETSEC [SEXIT] Rendezvous

Just as the ILP issues the SENTER-ACK for GETSEC [SENTER], the ILP issues the SEXIT-ACK message for GETSEC [SEXIT]. The mechanism is the same for GETSEC [SENTER] and GETSEC [SEXIT]. After the ILP issues the SEXIT-ACK, each of the RLP responds to the message such that the chipset knows that all processors responded.

The same restrictions apply for GETSEC [SEXIT], the bus-agent ID identifies the processor, and the chipset matches responses to known ID's and failure to have all processors respond results in a TXT-shutdown.

After the rendezvous, the GETSEC [SENTER] starts and executes an authenticated code module. The GETSEC [SEXIT], being already in a protected environment, needs no authenticated module.

MLE Shutdown

The MLE has ultimate control of the platform. While requests to start the MLE can occur from any ring-0 process, termination of the MLE environment is under control of the MLE itself.

Outside entities can make requests to the MLE to terminate, but the MLE has the final say to actually execute the GETSEC [SEXIT] command. The MLE, when requested to terminate can refuse the request and continue operations. The MLE can accept the termination request, but prior to the termination; perform other operations prior to the MLE termination.

After all protected environments are shut down, the ILP sends the SEXIT-CONTINUE message to each RLP. The RLP accepts the command, removes all protections in the platform, and moves to execute the next instruction. The next instruction was designated as the instruction to execute upon receipt of the SEXIT-ACK. The setting of the next instruction is one reason that the MLE must control when the GETSEC [SEXIT] operation is valid. The best practice would be to put the RLP into some sort of sleep state. After the GETSEC [SEXIT] execution, the operating system would then wake up the processors.

TXT-Shutdown

Many times in this chapter, the issuing of the TXT-shutdown is the response to an error. TXT-shutdown is a special error that makes sure that the error condition does not result in the exposure of protected information.

TXT-shutdown first writes to the chipset's TXT.CRASH register the TXT-shutdown error code. The error code indicates the type of TXT-shutdown that is occurring.

The processor then writes to the TXT.CMD.SYS-RESET register, the system issues a Intel TXT special cycle to initiate a platform reset. All processors, in response to the special cycle, enter a shutdown sleep state. The sleep state masks

■ External pin events

■ Intel TXT bus events or error events

■ Machine check signaling

■ Other internal state

Only the assertion of a platform reset takes the processor out of the sleep state. The reset does not clear the TXT.CRASH register, so the cause of the TXT-shutdown is available after the reset.

The TXT-shutdown can occur as part of most of the GETSEC leaf functions when recovery from the error would not result in a reliable state. Reliable state would include the inability to complete the GETSEC [SENTER] process.

Legacy IA-32 triple-fault shutdown conditions covert to a TXT-shutdown. This conversion generally occurs in the state between GETSEC [SENTER] and GETSEC [SEXIT]. If the processor is in VMX mode, and the triple-fault causes a guest to exit back to the MLE, the exit to the guest supersedes conversion to a TXT-shutdown. If the triple-fault occurs in the MLE, the conversion does occur.

Chapter 16

Configuration Concerns

Where large sums of money are concerned, it is advisable to trust nobody.
—Agatha Christie (1890–1976)

One could instantly trust the hardware of a platform with Trusted Execution Technology (Intel® TXT), but is it possible that troubles could lurk in the hardware? The answer is yes; some hardware configurations make it difficult for the hardware to mitigate threats to a protected partition. The configurations that can cause these problems are discoverable, and during the protected partition launch, the launch process verifies the state of the hardware.

Intel TXT works in the Ronald Reagan mode of "Trust but verify." Various components on the platform set up the hardware to operate properly. The configuration of the devices occurs when a protected environment is not available. The protected environment assumes a proper hardware configuration and attempts to verify the current settings.

Intel TXT Chipset

A Intel TXT platform requires the presence of a Intel TXT-capable chipset. The CPU and chipset work in concert for numerous operations, and if the chipset is not capable of supporting Intel TXT, the CPU must not start the protected environment.

The GETSEC [SENTER] operation validates the existence of a Intel TXT capable chipset. The validation occurs at the very start of the GETSEC [SENTER] operation. If GETSEC [SENTER] determines that no Intel TXT chipset is present, the GETSEC [SENTER] process terminates with a general protection fault. The error does not cause a TXT-shutdown because the chipset check occurs prior to any broadcast messages by the Initiating Logical Processor (ILP).

The ILP checks an internal CPU register for the existence of the Intel TXT chipset. The CPU reset process sets the register. The check occurs on each reset and cold boot. The CPU interrogates the chipset, and if the chipset responds appropriately, the CPU indicates the presence of a Intel TXT capable chipset.

Intel TXT chipset support requires the chipset to accept the various Intel TXT special cycles, include the Intel TXT public and private spaces, and fully support a version 1.2 TPM.

Memory Folding

The CPU gains access to system memory through the Graphics/Memory Controller Hub (G/MCH). The physical memory attaches to the G/MCH. The actual memory package allows configuration options that can be set by software.

One of the largest security concerns is memory *folding*. When two bus addresses point to the same physical location, folding occurs. Figure 16.1 illustrates the concept of folding, two addresses pointing to the same physical location.

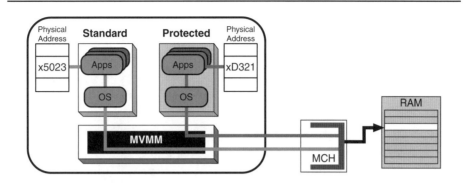

Figure 16.1 Memory Folding

Having two memory locations point at the same physical location leads to an easy attack in which one address is in the protected partition and the other address is not in the protected partition. It is possible to determine the presence of the folded memory configuration. The protected partition launch mechanism must test for and ensure that the folding is not occurring.

Trusting Memory

First, you have to deal with the possibility that folding can occur in system memory and there is no way to use a single byte of the system memory to execute any programs. The system needs some area where code can execute. The solution here is the use of *authenticated code* (AC) modules. An AC module runs without the use of any system memory. One major reason for the design of AC modules is to specifically mitigate memory aliasing threats.

SINIT is the AC module that performs the configuration checks. By using the AC module, not one byte of system memory requires protection prior to the protected partition launch.[1]

---

1   What a happy day that was when the Intel TXT development team came to the realization that AC mode was the mitigation for memory aliasing.

Loading Chipset-specific Code

The mechanisms to configure the physical memory packages are chipset specific. The checks necessary to determine that aliasing is occurring are also chipset specific. Adding chipset-specific code to the CPU is not a good idea, so the SINIT design also provides a way to load and execute chipset-specific code.

The first security idea was to place the memory-fold check in the CPU. Having the check in the CPU results in very good security properties; it does not work well in practice. The CPU works with numerous chipsets. The CPU would need to contain lots of extra code that would never be in use. Using the SINIT places the code execution in the CPU and allows for chipset-specific code. The SINIT module is from the chipset manufacturer and does not need to contain code for other chipsets.

Locking the Memory Configuration

Prior to any memory authentication, the SINIT code, locks the configuration. The rationale behind locking and then verifying is to avoid any chance that the configuration undergoes some change after verification but before the lock. The chances for changing the configuration are low, but it is possible, so the design attempts to mitigate the possibility.

The lock mechanism is a combination of actions. The SINIT code issues the `TXT.CMD.LOCK-MEMCONFIG` command to the chipset. The chipset, upon receipt of the command, locks the memory configuration. The lock remains in place until the execution of the `GETSEC[SEXIT]` operand.

Testing the Configuration

The code necessary to perform the actual test for memory folding is chipset-specific. Those needing to write the code need to understand the nitty-gritty details of the chipset in question. Any failures in the configuration result in the SINIT code issuing a `TXT-shutdown`.

GART/Graphics Aliasing

The SINIT code went to a lot of trouble to verify that two logical addresses do not point to the same physical page. The Graphics Address Relocation Table (GART) provides a mechanism to change the address of a request. The GART allows the page frames for a graphics device to be in a different location then the graphics buffer. The result is a translation that occurs when moving information from one location to the other. Attempts to manipulate an address have a translation that directs the request to the correct physical page.

Figure 16.2 illustrates the translations that the GART performs. Addresses in the graphics aperture undergo a translation to a physical address.

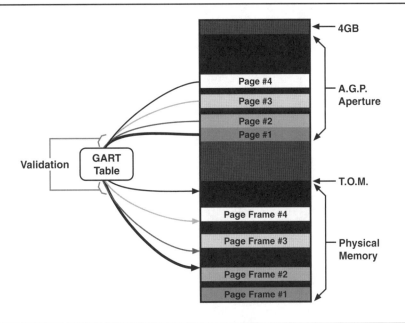

Figure 16.2 Graphics Address Relocation Table (GART) Aliasing

After working so hard to locate and avoid the memory folding, automatically adding it back again is difficult to do.

Intel TXT cannot remove the GART translation; too much code and design already take advantage of the GART. The trick is to ensure that no secrets leak when using the GART.

Ensure GART Properties

Leaving the GART in the design requires a modification to the actual translation. The Intel TXT GART processing allows the translation but ensures no change in protection mode.

If the first address requires protection, the translated address must require protection after GART processing. If the first address has no protection, the translated address also requires no protection. The chipset enforces the validation on each GART translation when protections are in place.

System Memory Overlap

Another potential problem arises when GART addresses overlap the system aperture. The overlap represents a serious vulnerability and one that must not occur. The SINIT code must validate that the aperture does not overlap with GART addresses. If the SINIT discovers such an overlap, the SINIT issues a `TXT-shutdown`.

Power and Frequency

A few years ago, the only consideration for a processor was how fast the processor could execute. Then laptops became popular and speed was not the only consideration; heat and battery life became important.

Heat

A slight detour here for a discussion of the author's background: looking at my biography on the back cover, you will see lots of software experience and little hardware experience. When I started at Intel®, some of the hardware concepts went right over my head. One of the concepts, while blindingly obvious to everyone else, was that a lot of heat builds up inside a PC platform, and platform designers need to spend lots of effort working on airflow, heat sinks, and the like. A corollary to all of the platform heat equations is that the speed you want to go relates directly to the heat in the platform. I thought that all one had to do was put another fan on the platform and all of the problems went away. Boy is that wrong! Proper heat sinks and moving the air from the inside to the outside and around the heat sinks is a difficult job. My group taught me that with modern platforms one gets better cooling with the cover on, as the platform design assumes the cover is present and uses the cover to properly move air and provide cooling. The purpose of the detour is to drive home the fact that correct operation of the platform requires proper configuration of the cooling system. In addition to cooling there are other platform configuration options that require oversight and proper setup.

Overclocking

The question one may be asking right now is what does heat and cooling and frequencies have to do with security? The answer is surprising, lots. Platforms, and especially CPUs, have specific design points for power, frequency, and heat. Run the CPU too hot, or too fast and the CPU might not execute correctly.

A thriving industry takes CPUs and attempts to overclock, or run the CPU faster than recommended by the manufacturer. Overclocking involves adding additional power to the CPU, causing it to run faster and also to run much hotter. Overclockers understand very well that when overclocking, additional cooling is necessary, and this issue is critical, that at some speed the CPU will not function correctly. What does "not function correctly" mean? It means that the CPU will attempt to add 1 + 1 and not get 2. As the overclocking goes even higher, other operations cease to work properly, finally ending in the CPU becoming so confused that the CPU refuses to execute any more instructions.

Many of the overclocking configurations are available through software commands, and if software can manipulate a configuration to cause errors, it represents a security concern. Imagine a configuration that caused the CPU to improperly use the page table. If the attacker can reliably cause the improper page table to be used, the attacker might be able to read supposedly protected pages. One very important item to remember is that getting the same error to occur each time when overclocking is most likely not going to happen. However, the possibility does remain that overclocking represents a configuration that may not provide adequate protections.

While overclocking is an attempt to push the CPU to perform more tasks through faster execution, underclocking is merely an attempt to force bad things to happen. Underclocking involves not sending enough power to meet the listed operating frequency and can result in the same operational issues. Heat is not an issue with underclocking.

SINIT needs to ensure that, on startup, all CPU threads are operating inside of the normal range of power and frequency. SINIT performs the checks by ensuring that the CPU is either at the low end or the high end of the allowable frequency scale. The frequency scale is processor specific and SINIT will know the valid ranges. After SINIT validates the frequency and power, SINIT locks the frequency setting. Once the MLE has control of the platform, the MLE can unlock the frequency settings and more finely tune the use of power and frequency.

SCHECK

Here's a minor piece of additional information—well, hopefully you feel it is minor. The actual implementation of SINIT could split some of the functionality into two modules. The rationale behind the split is timing. Performing all of the checks during the GETSEC [SENTER] process could result in a launch time that is too long. Some of the checks that SINIT performs can be one-time checks. To ensure these one-time checks occur only once, instead of each GETSEC [SENTER], Intel TXT allows for the SCHECK AC module.

The SCHECK module performs the same functions as SINIT but the execution of the SCHECK occurs during platform startup. SCHECK only runs once per platform boot. When SCHECK executes, the module performs the configuration checks and locks the configuration. In addition to locking the configuration, upon successful completion of the SCHECK review, SCHECK sets a flag in the chipset indicating that the configuration is valid. SINIT, in the very first check after digital signature validation, checks that the chipset flag is set and then SINIT knows that the configuration is valid.

SCHECK is an Authenticated Code Module (ACM) and as such has all of the normal ACM protections. The module runs in Cache as RAM (CRAM) mode, has a digital signature, and runs without interruption due to the CRAM features.

Additional Platform Configurations

The areas listed so far do not represent the entirety of the platform configuration items that a MLE must manage. Many of the additional areas are processor specific, and SINIT checks those configuration settings. For those areas that are not processor specific, the MLE must understand the platform, understand the controls necessary to control the platform, and properly manage those controls.

New Issues

It is a very real possibility that a configuration option on a platform will be found, long after the writing of the SINIT code, to represent a security concern. A big advantage of having the SINIT module is that new concerns can be met by issuing a new SINIT module that validates that the configuration option is properly set.

Device Support

Up to this point, this chapter only needed some minor editing[2] from the previous version. From here on out the author has gutted the chapter. The reason for these changes is actually very illuminating as to the some of the elements previously defined.

The first change has to do with that nebulous architectural performance element. The idea that Intel TXT could identify all of the potential devices and channels on the platform and then specify how manufacturers would implement and users would use the channel represents a view of the world that is not reality. In some use cases, a specific device and a specific channel would be appropriate. Some use cases do not equate to all use cases and the cost of supporting some is too high when dealing with generic solutions.

The second change deals with looking at what the platform already provides. The feature that is the most important for trusted channels is VT-d. One can use VT-d to assign a specific device to a specific address and then, by assigning that address to a specific VM, enable a trusted channel.

Configuration issues rear their very ugly heads when attempting to determine how and what the trusted devices are. Intel TXT changes from attempting to deal with specific devices to making use of Intel® Virtualization Technology for Directed I/O (VT-d).

> **VT-d Details**
>
> An excellent article on VT-d is at the Intel site at http://softwarecommunity.intel.com/articles/eng/1416.htm

---

2 Thank goodness for search and replace, how did authors write books before word processors? Did they really go back and type new pages?

Switch to VT-d

The first edition listed the following devices as requiring modifications to support trusted channels:

- *Display adapter.*
- *USB peripheral.*
- *Keyboard and mouse on a mobile platform.*

This edition removes any reference to special devices. All trusted channels use VT-d to assign the device to a specific memory address and then control which partitions can access the memory address.

Figure 16.3 shows the basic idea of why VT-d provides the building block for a trusted channel.

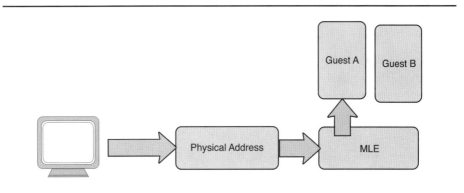

Figure 16.3 VT-d

The illustration in Figure 16.3 shows a display adapter, represented by a monitor, assigned, through the MLE, to just Guest A. Guest B has no knowledge of the display adapter. With the physical address never available to Guest B, the functional result is that only Guest A can use the display. This provides the same functionality as a specialized device that physically assigned some portion of the display to Guest A.

This change to using VT-d places more responsibility on the software using the device to correctly create both the channel, through VT-d, and the trusted path through the other trusted platform building blocks.

Human Interface Design

Discrete graphics adapters and integrated graphics adapters can provide the mechanisms to create trusted channels. These mechanisms do not address the issue of the creation of the trusted path. The entities using the trusted channels must create the trusted paths. Just as SSL creates the channel and then the browser puts the "lock" icon in the window, those entities using the trusted channels must create the "icon" that indicates the presence of the trusted channel. The human must then recognize the "icon" as the trusted channel indication.

Hardware solutions to the trusted path icon are possible, but the solutions have some very severe consequences. It is possible to include an additional LED that lights upon establishment of a trusted channel. However, you would need an LED for each trusted channel and a wire from the display adapter to the LED. Nevertheless, even the LED does not address the problem of indicating to the user which window in a multiple window environment is the trusted window. An additional problem is that putting a wire, an LED, and a hole in the case to display the LED is very expensive and does not solve all of the issues.

Better solutions exist when the entities using the trusted channel include the "icon" in the trusted display. Examples would include special borders, sequences of icons, and other types of information. The issue with special borders or sequences is that some secure storage of the path indicator has to be included. Intel TXT provides the secure storage through sealed storage. In fact, sealed storage is perfect for the protection of the path indicator, as sealing protects the value for the specific MLE. A change in the MLE results in the inability to recover the path indicator.

Trusted Input

What goes out must come back again to paraphrase a famous quote. Just as there are multiple ways of creating the trusted output channel, there are multiple ways of creating the trusted input channels.

One reason that there are multiple input channels is that there are multiple input devices. A keyboard, a mouse, or other device can be a Human Input Device (HID). An HID can connect to the platform through a variety of busses. If the bus and device allow control through VT-d then the device can participate in a trusted channel.

Through the use of VT-d any HID is supportable with a trusted channel. Instead of having to have special keyboards or mice, the trusted platform can have trusted keyboards and mice using standard components and can extend the HID support to joysticks and other devices.

Peripheral or Bus

The previous edition had a long discussion on channel properties and decisions that the designers must make. The whole discussion is now moot. The only decision to worry about is, is the bus controllable with VT-d? If the bus is controllable via VT-d, then a trusted channel is possible. The device does not matter as the control comes from the connection of the channel to a specific memory address and control of which software elements can access the physical address.

Bus Confidentiality

One change that use of VT-d brings up is that while no software entities can intercept the communication between device and driver, there is no confidentiality if any entity can "sniff" the channel.

To provide confidentiality the driver and device must agree on an encryption algorithm, establish some keys, and then perform the encryption. Note that all of this requires agreement between the driver and the device. The idea again is that those devices and use models that require the additional work for confidentiality can provide the services when they need to and not make everyone do things that they do not require.

Trusted USB Peripheral

For this type of protection the HID creates the trusted input channel between the peripheral itself and the driver. The HID information has protection using a cryptographic trusted channel. The plus side to this design is that it protects against hardware attacks; the minus side is that the peripheral requires cryptographic processing and appropriate key setup.

Another advantage of the secure peripheral method is that it places no hardware requirements on the platform to support the peripheral. Consider a protected keyboard and the support necessary to establish the trusted input channel. The two endpoints of the trusted input channel are the peripheral itself and the driver. The driver requires no special hardware support, just an execution environment that allows the driver to run without interference, the exact environment that Intel TXT provides. No requirements are on the USB controller or other USB devices, so the trusted input channel is independent of platform hardware support. The design allows the user to add a trusted input device at any time.

The main features of the Trusted USB Peripheral are:

■ Data to or from a trusted USB peripheral is encrypted when its "trusted" mode is enabled. Encryption/decryption logic is added to the USB peripheral. To hinder replay attacks, where an attacker captures a series of keystrokes or commands, then inserts them at a later time, and to hinder attacks based on deletion of keystrokes, the encrypted data stream contains sequence numbers.

■ You need not trust the primary USB stack. As the HID information is encrypted, and the driver knows how to decrypt the information, the USB stack is a pass-through device. The stack receives the encrypted packet and dispatches the packet to the trusted input driver without any need to decrypt the packet. Using the primary stack allows the system to process a wide variety of USB packets without the need to move the stack code into the MLE or trusted input channel driver.

■ A trusted driver—part of the MLE or a service in a trusted VM— handles the encryption/decryption of the trusted USB data on behalf of the trusted applications making use of the device.

■ The securable USB device is, by default, in an un-trusted state. Specific initialization of the device is required, including the generation and installation of the encryption key. New keys are generated each time the USB peripheral is reset, and they also could be generated at more frequent intervals.

The crucial aspect of this model is the requirement that the trusted driver have an a priori method of sending commands and data, including the encryption key, to the securable USB device without snooping, spoofing, or tampering. These configuration sequences cannot be done using the standard USB software stack, which is not trusted.

If the peripheral contains a unique public/private key and the appropriate cryptographic engines, the problem is solved—an authenticated key exchange can be performed. Both sides, driver and device, prove their identity and establish a common session key, all done safely even in the presence of hostile software or hardware snoopers between them. However, this solution adds significant cost to these devices, both in silicon and in manufacturing overhead.

Expecting a USB mouse to have sufficient processing power to create the cryptographic trusted channel is not really viable. In addition, setting up the trusted input channel key on the mouse is going to be very difficult.

Keyboards make excellent choices for devices that are trusted USB peripherals; a mouse is not a good choice for a trusted USB peripheral.

Verification of Session Key Creation

When initializing a trusted USB peripheral, it is important to verify that the peripheral is in receipt of the correct session key. The trusted input channel driver is responsible for exchanging the session key and validating the peripheral receipt of the key. The mechanism to pass the key can use cryptography, randomness, or user input. The choice is a peripheral manufacturer option. The details of any peripheral initialization mechanisms would be part of the specifications for the actual device.

The main attack to worry about here is a man-in-the-middle attack where the attacker takes the session key and creates two session keys one for the communication between the peripheral and the attacker and one key for the communication between the driver and the attacker. Ensuring that the peripheral has the key is possible on a keyboard and extremely tricky with a mouse.

Trusted USB Controller

The previous edition discussed a trusted USB Controller, Trusted USB Operation, and a Trusted Mobile Keyboard Controller. Just as with the input devices, these special devices are no longer a requirement. VT-d handles these devices and use models quite well.

Trusted I/O and Intel TXT

With the inclusion of the trusted display adapter and a trusted input channel, the Intel TXT platform provides the support necessary to secure communication between the user and a protected application. While the hardware mechanisms are in place to create the channels, the applications still have lots of work to do in creating the trusted paths. The mechanisms provided by Intel TXT enable applications to successfully create trusted paths and protect the trusted path components.

Chapter 17

Hardware Attacks

I always cheer up immensely if an attack is particularly wounding because I think, well, if they attack one personally, it means they have not a single political argument left.

—Margaret Thatcher

If the Intel® TXT system is protecting against software attacks, the attackers have no choice but to mount hardware attacks. The protection and attack matrix from Chapter 10 comes into play here. If the Intel TXT design has successfully pushed the attackers from using software attacks to attempting hardware attacks, can Intel TXT provide some protection from classes of hardware attacks?

When considering hardware attacks, a critical piece of information to remember is that the attacker needs to have physical possession of the machine. If the attacker is launching an attack from a remote location, the only way to execute the attack is with software. While it might be possible to have remote robots launch attacks in the future, this is a very remote possibility today. The hardware attacker must have physical contact, which means that the attacker can only attack one platform at a time.[1]

---

1   Do not lose sight of the BORE attack potential. If the attacker can use a hardware attack on one platform, obtain the software secret, and then launch the remote software attacks, the system is not that robust. The design point is to ensure that all attacks using the same mechanism must be hardware attacks.

Who Is Attacking What?

It is critical to make the distinction between what Intel TXT directly protects and what the MLE needs to be aware of very clear.

To make this explicit now, hardware attacks against Intel TXT directly are those attacks that attempt to cause an inaccurate measurement of the MLE. Hardware attacks that attempt to bypass or manipulate the MLE are indirect Intel TXT attacks. The Intel TXT architecture can help the MLE defend itself, but ultimately the MLE is responsible for maintaining control of the platform.

Topologies

In the first edition of this book, this chapter uses examples and mechanisms from the Front-side Bus (FSB) platform topology. With Intel® QuickPath architecture being the new topology, this chapter needs some additional discussions. Figure 17.1 illustrates the FSB topology and Figure 17.2 illustrates the Intel QuickPath architecture topology. While the layouts look very different, the underlying security principles are the same, make sure all of the hardware devices respond to the GETSEC [SENTER] messages.

After a description of the issues of the differences between FSB and Intel Intel QuickPath architecture, unless there is total disconnect of operations, the chapter uses the FSB mechanisms to describe how to deal with the potential hardware attacks.

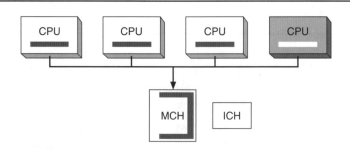

Figure 17.1   Front Side Bus Topology

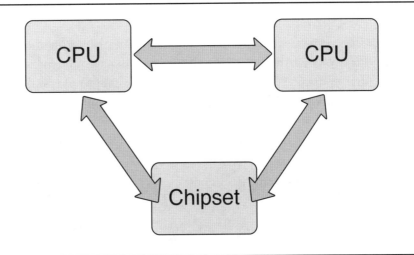

Figure17.2 Intel QuickPath topology

As you can see in Figure 17.1 the FSB topology uses a single bus where all of the CPUs share a single bus and all communicate with the chipset using the same bus. In Figure 17.2 each CPU uses a dedicated path to connect to the chipset and there is a dedicated connector between the CPUs.

In both figures the term CPU in the diagram should really reference CPU package as the package could contain any number of CPU cores.

Identification

To identify a CPU, and internally the CPU core inside of the package, the FSB topology assigns a bus-agent ID to each CPU core. The assignment occurs during the boot process and does not change between reboots.

With the dedicated connectors of Intel QuickPath architecture, the need for a bus-agent ID disappears. However when dealing with very complex topologies messages still need to be sent that are "distant" in that the recipient of the message is not directly attached to the sender; the recipient is many hops away. In this case there is an identifier that is the moral equivalent of the bus-agent ID. For our purposes in this chapter the term "bus-agent ID" means the identifier of the CPU.

Rogue CPU

In a system with multiple CPUs, can an attacker manipulate a single CPU to avoid participation[2] in the protected environment? If the attacker can manipulate a CPU in this manner, the attacker would be able to access memory bypassing the MLE protections. Figure 17.1 illustrates the potential problem, the shaded CPU on the right. If the attacker can manipulate just that single CPU are there concerns?

> ### CPU Cores and Packages
>
> When reviewing these hardware attacks be aware that there is no security difference between a package that has multiple cores (dual core, quad core, and so on) and a platform that has multiple packages (each with multiple cores).
>
> There is most definitely a difference in how the systems operationally handle the differences between multiple cores and multiple packages, but from the outside security view of these operations the same security properties are in place. All CPU threads, cores, and packages participate in the launch and measurement of the MLE.

Not Joining the Protected Environment

The attacker could attempt to hold an RLP[3] in some suspended state, and then after the establishment of the protected environment, take the RLP out of the suspended state. The GETSEC [SENTER] process detects this attack directly by ensuring that all bus-agent IDs respond to the SENTER-ACK message. If the CPU ever sends a message on the FSB, the chipset assigns a bus-agent ID and requires a response from the CPU to indicate the receipt of the SENTER-ACK.

The attacker could attempt to suspend the CPU from the time of reset of the platform. The suspension of the CPU results in no traffic on the FSB and hence no assigned bus-agent ID. Without the bus-agent ID, the chipset would not fail the GETSEC [SENTER] process waiting for the CPU. To handle this

---

2   Participation is any operation that uses a resource external to the CPU package.

3   To reinforce the point the RLP could be a different core inside the same package as the ILP or on a different package.

type of attack, the chipset issues a `TXT-shutdown`, if a CPU without a known bus-agent ID attempts to issue a message on the FSB while the protected environment is executing. The addition of any CPU in the system, while the protected environment is executing, results in a `TXT-shutdown`.

Not Joining in Intel QuickPath architecure

The FSB version uses the assigned bus-agent ID to identify a specific CPU and ensure that the identified CPU responds to the Intel TXT messages. Intel QuickPath architecture uses the same functional mechanism on ensuring that all CPU do issue the `SENTER-ACK` message.

The Intel QuickPath architecture topology has the same response if there is a identification of a new CPU identifier after invocation of `GETSEC` `[SENTER]`, that is the system invokes a `TXT-shutdown`.

Not Exiting the Protected Environment

So you might ask: "with the join covered, can the attacker attempt to keep a CPU in the protected environment while all other CPU's exit the environment?" The answer is that the `GETSEC [SEXIT]` process ensures that all CPUs exit the environment. The ILP sends the `SEXIT-ACK` message, and all bus-agent IDs must respond. If the attacker attempts to keep the MLE executing on an RLP, the chipset times out awaiting the response and causes a `TXT-shutdown`.

The attack of holding the RLP from reset does not matter here. With the attacker waiting until the MLE environment goes away, no protected memory is available. The attacker gains no advantage waiting until the system has no secure environment because the chipset always registers the new bus-agent ID. When the platform attempts to launch another protected environment, the new RLP must respond.

Results of Suspending the CPU

The chipset detects attempts to suspend a CPU through the `GETSEC [SENTER]` process and to add a CPU after the `GETSEC [SENTER]` launch. The chipset detects attempts to hold a CPU in the protected environment through `GETSEC` `[SEXIT]`. The Intel TXT architecture therefore provides protection from a rogue CPU.

■ RESET Protection

The protections on memory require the graceful shutdown of GETSEC [SEXIT]. What happens if the graceful shutdown does not occur and the platform performs a reset? Would that expose protected memory?

Reset Definition

The first order of business is to define a reset. The system programming guide states:

> Following power-up or an assertion of the RESET# pin, each processor on the system bus performs a hardware initialization of the processor (known as hardware reset) and an optional built-in self-test (BIST). A hardware reset sets each processor's registers to a known state and places the processor in real-address mode. It also invalidates the internal caches, translation look-aside buffers (TLBs) and the branch target buffer (BTB). (Intel 2003)

Either by powering the system or by asserting the RESET# pin, initialization of the CPU internal state occurs. For our purposes, we make no distinction between the RESET# pin and power-up when looking at reset attacks. For the rest of this chapter "reset" means RESET# pin or power-up cycling.

System Memory Properties

The rationale behind treating power-up and RESET the same comes from the properties of system memory. Everyone knows that system memory loses the values inside of the memory when power is lost to the physical device. However, the real question is about how fast the physical memory information degrades. The Intel TXT architects at first thought that a way to handle RESET was to require the power to remain off for a few milliseconds and the physical memory would lose information. While this solution is tempting, it turns out that memory can retain information for longer than milliseconds. In fact, it may remain intact for several seconds or longer. Having the memory retain information for seconds could allow an attack. The bottom line is that Intel TXT must handle a power-up exactly as it does a RESET.

Cold Boot

It is very nice to get things right at times. You should notice that the Intel TXT designers are very concerned about not relying on memory decay to protect against a potential attack. The genesis of this protection stems from the early design work around the year 2000.

Fast forward to the early months of 2008, an Internet search on "cold boot attack" should give one a good idea of how attackers are learning about the memory latency issues. The attackers make it even easier by freezing the components to make the latency time even longer.

The SCLEAN mechanism partially mitigates these cold boot attacks.

What to Protect?

The reset clears out the state maintained by the CPU and chipset. System memory could retain information, so Intel TXT needs to protect that system memory until the system can determine that system memory contains no "secrets." It is impossible for Intel TXT to determine what was or was not a secret. The Intel TXT designers adopted this definition of secret: any memory page that is assigned to a protected partition. The content of the page makes no difference. Once assigned to a protected partition, Intel TXT treats the page as one containing a secret.

Who Determines Prior State?

Here's the question the Intel TXT system needs to answer after a reset: were any secrets in the system memory prior to the reset? The platform needs to provide some area for the various components to ask the question and receive a reliable answer upon reset.

First, we can eliminate two places for the question-answer activity:

■ *The CPU has no persistence areas,* and upon reset, it loses all internal state. Trying to add this capability to the CPU would greatly add to the cost of a CPU. As an aside, this persistence question is one place where the author was severely beaten about the head and shoulders by the internal CPU architects for suggesting the addition of some sort of flag that could be maintained across the reset.

■ *The MCH has no persistence areas,* and upon reset, it too loses all internal state. Cost issues are the same as those for the CPU. And after the CPU architects' beating on me, I didn't try to add the persistence here.

So what component determines prior state? The ICH does have persistence. The ICH is where the platform keeps track of the date and time and other such values. The ICH maintains this information in the "power well," which maintains values even when the platform is not plugged into the wall or the mobile battery is flat. The power comes from the small motherboard battery.[4]

Protection Sequence

When the platform starts after a reset, the immediate task is to determine whether or not secrets were in memory. While the platform makes the determination about the previous state, it is possible for some memory access to occur. The easiest way to prevent this vulnerability is to block all access to all system memory. The enforcement of the block occurs in the MCH. Immediately after a reset, the MCH automatically blocks all access to system memory.

Once the system determines that memory contains no secrets, the BSP unlocks the MCH and allows access to memory. In a normal situation, a read of the ICH determines no secrets were in memory, and a message is sent to the MCH to unlock memory and allow the rest of the reset processing to occur.

The flow chart of the sequence is in Figure 17.3.

---

4   The power well also goes by the name of RTC well or VCC well.

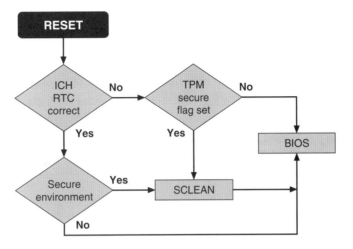

Figure 17.3 Reset Protection

The platform keeps the evidence of a previously running, protected environment in two locations: the ICH and the TPM.

Setting the ICH Flag

The ICH maintains the TXT.HADSECRETS flag. The MLE sets the TXT. HADSECRETS to TRUE using the TXT.CMD.SECRETS command. The flag remains TRUE until the MLE executes the TXT.CMD.NOSECRETS command.

The MCH checks the ICH and the status of the TXT.HADSECRETS flag. If the flag is TRUE then the MCH continues to block memory until after execution of the SCLEAN module. The SCLEAN module has the ability to set the TXT.HADSECRETS flag to FALSE.

The TXT.HADSECRETS flag is held by the ICH in the power well. The power well provides the ability for the ICH to maintain information when no platform power is present. Platform power comes from the wall via a power cord or from the main battery on a mobile system. Platform power is likely go away if the plug is pulled from the wall or if the main battery goes flat. The ICH power well does not rely on these sources of power. Instead, the power well has a dedicated battery. If you have ever opened a PC and looked at the motherboard, you probably have noticed a small dime-sized battery. This battery supplies the power well.

You have no guarantee that the ICH power well battery would maintain power forever. In fact, nothing prevents someone from removing the battery. If the battery goes away, what happens to the power well? On a loss of power, the ICH losses all information held in the power well, such as the current date and time. The ICH has an indicator that is set when power is not sufficient to maintain the information in the power well. Once the low power bit is set, the ICH requires a re-initialization of the ICH information, like resetting the clock.

The obvious attack is for the attacker to remove power from the wall and then pull the battery. The ICH no longer has valid information and the chipset does not know whether blocking should or should not occur after a reset. If the attacker performs this attack fast enough, secrets could be in memory where they are vulnerable.

Adding the TPM

You cannot defend the battery from this type of attack so a location on the platform must keep safe the information regarding the existence of secrets in memory across such loss of power events. The TPM provides that type of area. The issue here is that normal nonvolatile storage has a write limit on it, and the designers would not want to limit the platform to only a certain number of protected environment launches.

The solution is for the TPM to keep track only of the TXT.HADSECRETS flag if there ever was a secured environment, not was the environment present immediately before the reset. The chipset only needs to check the TPM when the power well is invalid, and that event should be a very rare occurrence.

The TPM sets the SECRETS.ESTABLISHED flag to TRUE upon receipt of the TPM_HASHSTART command. If the bit is already TRUE, the TPM does not perform any action on the flag. The TPM maintains the SECRETS.ESTABLISHED flag across all power cycles and system events. The SCLEAN module has the ability to reset the flag.

State Table

Table 17.1 shows the state of the RTC and TPM flags, and the resulting action upon reset.

Table 17.1 Normal Flag Settings

Event	RTC Secrets	RTC BatteryFail	TPM Secrets	Result if Reset occurs
First boot	FALSE	FALSE	FALSE	Normal processing
TPM_HASHSTART	FALSE	FALSE	TRUE[1]	Normal processing
TXT.CMD.SECRETS	TRUE	FALSE	TRUE[2]	SCLEAN required
TXT.CMD.NOSECRETS	FALSE	FALSE	TRUE	Normal processing
RTC battery fail[3]	?	TRUE	TRUE	SCLEAN required
SCLEAN[4]	FALSE	FALSE	FALSE	Normal processing

1 It is possible to execute GETSEC [SENTER] without having the MLE use the TXT.CMD.SECRETS command. If this event occurs then the RTC SECRETS flag is not set.

2 The TXT.CMD.SECRETS command is only available to MLE code, hence the TPM_HASH_START command must execute prior to TXT.CMD.SECRETS command.

3 The battery failure could occur at any time but the RTC BatteryFail flag is only checked during the reset.

4 The assumption is that a new RTC battery is available. If not, the system sets RTC BatteryFail to TRUE again.

SCLEAN AC Module

When secrets appear to be in memory, the SCLEAN module provides a way to remove the secrets. After a reset, the chipset can request the startup code to locate, load, and cause the execution of the SCLEAN module. The module is an authenticated code (AC) module that is specific to each chipset.

Being an AC Module allows SCLEAN to operate in the authenticated code space where it has no reliance on any area of system memory. SCLEAN is attempting to clean up memory and cannot rely on system memory for execution. The only space meeting these requirements is the AC Module execution area.

Running SCLEAN

When the chipset makes the determination that secrets *were* in memory, the chipset blocks access to all of system memory. The block is absolute and extends from address 0 to the top of physical memory.

SCLEAN Location

The BIOS must be able to locate the SCLEAN module in the BIOS flash.[5] Having the SCLEAN module in flash memory allows access to the code without any reliance on system memory.

SCLEAN Loading

After locating the module, the BIOS executes the GETSEC [ENTERACCS] command. The command takes as input the location of the SCLEAN module. The ENTERACCS command then performs the normal AC module digital signature validation of the code using the public key from the chipset.

SCLEAN Execution

As an AC module, SCLEAN has access to all of memory. An AC module can bypass the system memory block that was set by the chipset. The bypass is only available to AC modules, and only signed code is eligible to be an AC module. This restriction prevents an attacker from loading an incorrect SCLEAN module and gaining access to system memory.

SCLEAN configures the memory controller with a default configuration that permits read and write access to all possible memory locations. This configuration does not take advantage of any memory controller enhancements for speed or efficiency.

SCLEAN then writes a data pattern to each byte of memory. SCLEAN reads each byte to ensure that the write functioned as expected. The pattern may be any value from 0x00 to 0xFF.

---

5   While it is possible to put SCLEAN in something other than the flash memory, the other area must be addressable and available without reliance on any memory accesses. While an area with these requirements might be found, it is much more likely that the platform will use the flash memory.

Setting the Flags

After writing to all memory locations, the SCLEAN module needs to reset the flags so that the chipset unblocks system memory access. The first flag to clear is the RTC `HADSECRETS` flag. Setting this flag to FALSE allows the chipset to unlock memory and continue normal reset processing.

The SCLEAN does not manipulate the RTC `BatteryFail` flag. The flag has specific rules as to when and how the flag is set, and SCLEAN does not affect those rules.

The SCLEAN module can reset the TPM `SECRETS.ESTABLISHED` flag. The assumption is that the RTC `BatteryFail` flag is now FALSE and the chipset has no need to communicate with the TPM. That assumption could incorrect, and having SCLEAN reset the `SECRETS.ESTABLISHED` flag removes the loop where the platform performs a scrub on every reset. While modern platforms do not operate very well with a dead RTC battery, having SCLEAN reset the TPM flag does avoid the possibility of unnecessary scrubs.

Continuing Execution

The BIOS can continue execution in two ways. First, it can execute the next instruction in the boot process. This action is tempting, since the user has been sitting watching the machine do nothing for some time. I recommend that you avoid this temptation. Causing a reset at this time ensures that the BIOS understands completely the current state of the platform.[6] During AC module execution, interrupts are off and various events could occur. For example, suppose that devices other than the chipset and CPU were performing initialization and attempts to communicate with the chipset and CPU resulted in no response. The safest path would be to cause a reset and start the process all over again. All devices, including the CPU and chipset, receive the request to reset and restart their initialization process. The CPU and chipset then respond normally to events during the reset process, and the BIOS handles them without a special delay.

---

6   Understanding the platform state allows the BIOS to properly setup the platform. After the termination of SCLEAN, the platform does not guarantee any specific platform state.

Speeding SCLEAN Up

To speed SCLEAN processing up, the chipset can include the ability to lock the memory configuration registers and maintain the contents of the registers across an INIT operation. The information is lost when power is lost. In this context, power means main system power, not the power to the RTC. If this information is available, the SCLEAN operation can use information relative to the chipset to perform faster verification of the memory configuration and use better methods to access memory.

Registering SCLEAN

SCLEAN is an AC module that is embedded in the BIOS. It performs a vital function, ensuring that secrets held in the protected environment do not leak when errors cause an immediate shutdown of that protected environment. The MLE must understand which SCLEAN version is in use. The MLE might require special processing or a special version of the SCLEAN. A registration process for the SCLEAN operation should make it possible for the MLE to validate the SCLEAN module that performs the scrub.

A really unique attack would be to launch a protected environment, load in a bad SCLEAN, force the reset—just unplug the power cord!—and then take advantage of the bad SCLEAN. The definition of bad is an SCLEAN that does not scrub all of memory. Clearly, this version would be unacceptable.

The only way to measure SCLEAN acceptability is to use the hash from the digital signature. Other than loading SCLEAN, you have no way to be sure that the measurement is occurring on the actual SCLEAN module. Loading the SCLEAN and having the SCLEAN register itself on each GETSEC [SENTER] would add too much overhead to the launch. Loading SCLEAN after each reset also adds way too much overhead to the reset processing.

TPM Registration

What the SCLEAN registration needs is a value, set by the SCLEAN, readable by the MLE, and not changeable by any other entity. The TPM provides nonvolatile storage with access control. The location must allow for reads by any entity but for writes, only by locality three or an AC module. The system defines a location, naming it SCLEAN, and the system sets the access to be writeable by locality three and readable by any locality.

SCLEAN Flow

The SCLEAN execution flow has two main branches, a scrub flow and a registration flow. The pseudocode in Figure 17.4 shows the basic code flow.

SCLEAN Module Flow

```
1   registeredDigest := read (TPM "SCLEAN" buffer)
2
3   IF (NOT memory-blocked) THEN
4   // This branch is taken if memory is not blocked
5   // It registers the SCLEAN version if necessary
6   IF (myDigest == registeredDigest)
7   exit with status code (already registered)
8   ENDIF
9   write (TPM "SCLEAN" buffer, myDigest)
10  exit with status code (registered)
11  ENDIF
12  // This branch when memory blocked, and must be scrubbed
13  IF (myDigest != registeredDigest) THEN
14  exit with error (Wrong version, memory remains blocked)
15  ENDIF
16  scrub memory
17  IF (scrub NOT successful) THEN
18  exit with error code (scrub failed)
19  ENDIF
20  remove memory-block
21  exit with status code (memory scrubbed)[7]
```

Figure 17.4   SCLEAN Execution Flow

The self-check in line 13 is critical to the success of SCLEAN. If the attacker ran GETSEC [SENTER], changed the SCLEAN code, and then pulled the plug, the SCLEAN registered value would not match the value calculated on execution. The check prevents the attack and ensures that the MLE knows the identity of the SCLEAN to execute in case of any shutdowns or resets. Since the SCLEAN code is an AC module that comes from the chipset manufacturer, it is reasonable to require inclusion of line 13 in every SCLEAN module.

---

7   Please, no comments from the "peanut gallery" regarding the quality of this code snippet. I was a good coder when I wrote code. Mind you, the last section of code that I wrote was on punch tape—not really, but it sure sounds good.

The TPM SCLEAN buffer definition requires that only locality three has access to the area. The only entities able to assert locality three are AC modules. All AC modules are under control of the chipset manufacturer and again, it is reasonable to assert that only the SCLEAN module can manipulate the TPM SCLEAN buffer.

The BIOS runs SCLEAN whenever the chipset blocks memory. The BIOS also runs SCLEAN whenever the SCLEAN module changes. This requirement allows the SCLEAN to run the registration flow and properly store the SCLEAN identity in the TPM.

Validating the SCLEAN Identity

The TPM contains the SCLEAN identity. Two obvious control points ensure that the SCLEAN is correct before allowing secrets into memory.

The first control point is for the SINIT to validate the SCLEAN identity. Either the SINIT can have an internal list of known good SCLEAN modules or it could have access to a signed list of good SCLEAN modules. Either way, the SINIT would generate an error if the SCLEAN module was unknown. Having the SINIT perform this validation is difficult because the maintenance of the good list is difficult to manage.

For the second control point, the SINIT could merely place the SCLEAN identity into a PCR register. The identity of a module comes from a measurement of the module; all AC modules are digitally signed and the hash value in use for the digital signature also functions as the module identity. When any entity launches the AC module, the launching process can use the module identity as the value to extend into a TPM PCR register. With the module identity in a PCR register, the user and any other entity can use the TPM SEAL process to identify any changes in the SCLEAN module.

As a third alternative control point, the SINIT could ignore the SCLEAN and allow the MLE to perform the same types of validation. The MLE is easier code to modify, and passing in signed lists is much easier. So, the SCLEAN validation may be a job for the MLE. The decision as to what component makes these decisions lies with the system because the Intel TXT architecture supports a wide range of solutions.[8]

---

8 I certainly feel that SCLEAN validation by the MLE is very natural. The other methods are valid, but I think MLE validation is the most flexible.

INIT Protection

The `INIT#` pin requires that the device receiving the signal reset itself. Originally, the Intel TXT architects were under the impression that broadcasting `INIT#` enabled all logical processors to receive the signal at the same time. We were wrong. A single logical processor is capable of being the target of an `INIT#` message. Having one CPU drop out of the protected environment is just as bad as having a logical processor not join in.

The system handles the `INIT#` by requiring the MLE to block all `INIT#` messages. The MLE can determine that the appropriate response is to broadcast an `INIT#` message, but the MLE should have a high assurance that all logical processors would receive the message. Figure 17.5 shows the problem.

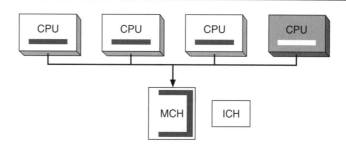

Figure 17.5 INIT Protection

S2/S3/S4 Sleep Protection

The platform has four sleep states: off, on, sleep, and hibernate. The specification for these sleep states is the *Advanced Configuration and Power Interface Specification* (ACPI 2004). The ACPI specification explains how to enter and exit the states, what the CPU and platform do in each state, and what devices should get power.

The specification makes for very fun reading. One of the most interesting points is that various components may respond to the ACPI event by performing a reset. Other devices might not perform a reset in response to the same event. From the standpoint of a protected partition, it is very bad to have one device reset and another device not do so. The S3 state removes power from the CPU but keeps power supplied to memory. The state then causes the CPU to loose track of the details of the protected partition while leaving the protected memory available, which is especially bad for trustworthiness.

The whole point of the ACPI states is to save power and battery life. Ignoring the ACPI events could reduce the platform's available use time drastically. Accepting the ACPI events could expose protected information. These two options cannot coexist.

When notified that an ACPI transition is pending, the MLE makes a decision regarding how to respond. The MLE can encrypt the protected partition information and execute a GETSEC [SEXIT] command, which removes the protected partition. The MLE could ignore the ACPI event and not allow the CPU and other devices to operate on the ACPI event.

The generic response to an ACPI event from the MLE standpoint is:

1. Encrypt the protected partition.

2. Exit from the protected partition using the GETSEC [SEXIT] operation.

3. Change the ACPI state so the system goes to sleep or hibernates.

4. Return to normal operations.

5. Execute GETSEC [SENTER] operation.

6. Decrypt the protected partition.

The most interesting event scenario is: an ACPI sleep event occurs when the protected partition is active. When it receives the ACPI sleep event, the chipset treats the event as an attack. Since this event should not occur, the existence of the event must be an attempt to reset the processors and read memory. The chipset responds with a TXT-shutdown, which in turn causes a complete platform reset. With the TXT.HADSECRETS flag set to TRUE, the platform performs an SCLEAN to remove any secrets in memory. The interesting aspect of this scenario is the reliance on the MLE to ensure that the chipset never receives a sleep request while the MLE is active. As soon as the chipset receives the request with the MLE active, the TXT-shutdown sequence will start.

SMI Handling

System Management Mode (SMM) and the System Management Interrupt (SMI) are really interesting in conjunction with security. SMM handles platform events without notifying or using the operating system. A simple example of an SMI is when the user pushes the volume button on a mobile PC. Usually, this action causes picture of the current volume level to pop up on the bottom of the screen. The button press does the following:

- First, it generates an SMI event.

- The SMM handler wakes upon receipt of the SMI event. Waking up the handler causes other processes to wait.

- The SMM code changes the volume. The change requires intimate knowledge of the platform and is platform specific. Normal SMM-handling code is OEM specific.

- The volume level is displayed and the display requires knowledge of the frame buffer and other display characteristics.

- Control is returned to the normal executing code.

The SMM code runs in Big Real mode, in which no paging is allowed. No paging means that the page tables are inactive. No page table means that all of physical memory is available to the SMM code. Having all of physical memory available to the SMM code means that the handler must have the same trust level as the MLE. Since SMM code tends to be both old and new, it is quite likely that the writers of some SMM code did not consider protection of secrets when they were writing that code.

Removing SMM from the platform is impossible. Numerous entities use SMM to handle device faults, special features, and incompatibilities. If SMM went away, some new mode would have to replace SMM. Instead of eliminating SMM, one needs to find a way to protect SMM by making it unable to access protected resources. The way to accomplish that is to run the SMM code in a protected partition dedicated to SMM.

SMM Transfer Module

The SMM Transfer Module (STM) provides a mechanism to accept the SMI, invoke the SMM, and ensure no leakage of information to the SMM. Figure 17.6 shows the potential for attack during SMI handling activities.

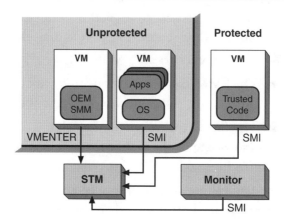

Figure 17.6 SMI Handling

The STM runs as a peer to the MLE. The interaction between the MLE and STM is open to negotiation. Both the STM and MLE can decline the policies set by the other, but the result of a failed negotiation is that the protected environment does not launch.

The STM is part of the trust chain for the platform. It must be possible for an entity requesting the current platform configuration to be able to evaluate the current STM, just as can evaluate the MLE. Therefore, the STM must have the following characteristics:

■ An accurate measurement

■ Reliable storage of the measurement

■ Verifiable reporting of the measurement

The solution to this problem on a Intel TXT platform is to find a way to measure the code and then report the measurement to the TPM.

SMM Loading

The BIOS holds the SMM code, which is normally placed within the Firmware Hub and loaded during the initialization of the platform. As part of the SMM, the STM needs to load at the same time, but loading the STM at this time divorces the STM load from the GETSEC [SENTER] process. Therefore, the measurement technique in use for the SINIT and MLE will not work with the STM.

The current SMM code loads using three addresses: the HSEG, TSEG, and CSEG. The HSEG and CSEG do not affect the STM. The current TSEG splits to include a new MSEG area. The STM resides in the MSEG area. When the BIOS loads the SMM code, it also loads the STM into the MSEG area. The BIOS also sets the TXT.MSEG.BASE, TXT.MSEG.SIZE, and MSEG_MSR.BASE registers. The remainder of the SMM code loads into the TSEG area. Figure 17.7 shows that the HSEG and CSEG are in different areas and that the MSEG and TSEG are in a contiguous area.

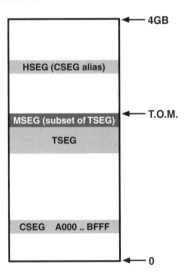

Figure 17.7 STM SMRAM

SMI ACPI Extensions

The BIOS manipulates the registers using ACPI extensions to the `SMI_CMD` port. The new commands to use are as follows:

- `GetMsegStatusCmd` provides information if the MSEG area is set.
- `UpdateMsegSizeCmd` allows the BIOS to change the size of the MSEG area.
- `LoadStmCmd` loads the STM code into the MSEG area.
- `UnloadStmCmd` unloads the STM and clears the MSEG area.
- `GetVendorSmiGuidCmd` returns the identifier of the SMM developer.

STM Loading

The STM can load at two separate points of time. The first takes place during POST, the second upon request of the OS.

When loading during the POST processing, the BIOS locates the STM, which is most likely part of the SMM, and loads the SMM and STM. The BIOS uses the `LoadStmCmd` to perform the actual load. The command ensures that if the load is successful, the `MSR_MSEG.VALID` flag is set to TRUE. The BIOS must have access to the STM image to load the STM. The typical platform implementation would be to put the STM in the flash.

The first implementation of TXT allowed the loading of the STM at any time. The current implementations require the BIOS to load the STM. The BIOS loads the STM through the use of the `LoadStmCmd`.

The STM must be present in the MSEG prior to execution of the GETSEC [SENTER] command. Failure to set the MSEG results in the GETSEC [SENTER] processing failing. GETSEC [SENTER] checks the status of `MSR_MSEG.VALID`, and if FALSE, aborts the GETSEC [SENTER] process. The `MSR_MSEG.VALID` flag is only writable by SMM code, so the loading process ensures that the SMM code sets the flag to TRUE.

STM Measurement

The SINIT code must measure the STM. The SINIT code has access to the MSEG region. SINIT measures the area specified by the `TXT.MSEG.BASE` and `TXT.MSEG.SIZE` parameters. To maintain an accurate identity, the STM must not modify any of the data that resides in the area specified by the base and size registers. If the STM does modify these areas, the measurement would result in two different values and cause problems with SEALed data and attestation evaluations.

After `GETSEC[SENTER]`, the MLE has the opportunity to evaluate the identity of the STM and determine whether the STM provides adequate services that do not conflict with the goals of the MLE. If the MLE does not approve of the STM, the MLE can cause an immediate SEXIT and stop the launch of the protected environment.

STM MLE Negotiation

With the STM and MLE loaded, the two entities need to negotiate what the STM can and cannot do. The MLE requires protection from SMM code that touches registers or other internal CPU state. The STM ensures that the SMM code does not access protected pages or devices that could access protected pages.

After approving of the STM identity, the MLE needs to inform the STM of the policy that the MLE needs the STM to enforce. The policy would include what MSRs to protect, where the MLE page table is, and other information that the STM needs to ensure the enforcement of the proper protection boundary. The STM is free to reject the requests of the MLE, but the likely result of a failure to agree on a policy would be the aborted launch of the protected environment.

Bus Attacks

When the attacker has physical access to the machine, he or she can remove the cover and attach probes to the various busses on the platform. The information gathered by the attacker may allow the attacker access to information under protection of Intel TXT.

The type of bus directly affects the ability and expertise necessary for attacker to read the information. Fast busses require special equipment and special software. Slower busses are readable using equipment found in a college or high school computer lab.

The Intel TXT design point is to provide protection from software attack, so the fact that attackers can succeed using hardware is not a surprise. Future versions might address these busses in different ways.

Front Side Bus

The FSB provides the connection between the CPU and the MCH. The FSB is a fast bus with speeds of 1,066 MHz, in 2005. Watching the bus is possible, and if the attacker has the expertise and equipment, the information is readable.

The information passing on the FSB includes reads and writes to system memory through the MCH. The information includes keys, code, and data. An attacker who is able to read this information can obtain all information under Intel TXT protection. The attack exposes information sent from the TPM to the protected environment, but the attack does not break the TPM protections. The difference is that the TPM still provides the correct protections, but the protected environment does not.

Hublink

The hublink provides the connection between the MCH and ICH. The hublink is a fast bus. Watching the bus is possible, and if the attacker has the expertise and equipment, the information is readable.

The security information passing on the hublink is only information in transit from the TPM to the CPU. The normal reads and writes of system memory do not travel down the hublink.

An attacker is certainly capable of watching this bus, but the work is not worth the effort given the difference between the hublink and the LPC bus.

Low Pin Count Bus

The LPC bus provides the connection between the ICH and the TPM. The LPC bus is slow and very simple, due to the low number of pins required for the bus. The LPC bus is very easy to watch and interpret.

With the LPC bus being so easy to watch, the system must add some protection to the data. Version 1.2 TPMs have the ability to create transport sessions. TPM transport sessions provide confidentiality of the information traveling between the Intel TPM and the CPU by encrypting the data.

The most crucial informational items traveling on the LPC bus are keys that were UNSEALed on the TPM and the resulting plain text sent to the CPU. Encrypting the transaction removes the ability of attackers to watch the LPC bus to obtain the data. The transport sessions only provide protection for the data as it travels between the TPM and the CPU. When the CPU stores information in system memory, the data travels over the FSB to the physical memory and the TPM transport sessions provide no protection for data in system memory. The attacker could still watch the FSB and obtain the data. The difference lies in the resources and expertise needed by the attacker. The LPC bus requires low-cost equipment and little expertise; the FSB requires expensive equipment and high expertise.

Chapter 18

Launch Control Policy

The one who adapts his policy to the times prospers, and likewise that the one whose policy clashes with the demands of the times does not.

—Niccolo Machiavelli

Niccolo is talking about political control; in this book we are talking about security control. In the grand nature of things though, the issues that Niccolo discuss with setting policy for the political arena do match the policy setting issues for the trusted platform. Setting inflexible policies creates a trusted platform that does not meet the needs of the owners and users of the platform. There is a huge need for flexible policies that meet the needs of the times in the trusted platform.

Policy Engine and Policies

In Chapter 6, we describe the policy engine as a trusted platform element. We now want to look at specific policies and how the trusted platform deals with those policies.

If the trusted platform only supported a single policy, what you really have is a single purpose machine. Policies actually come in a wide variety of flavors and the trusted platform must be able to deal with all sorts of policy variations. The goal is for the trusted platform hardware to provide an accurate representation of the policy in force for the platform without forcing the platform designer to create and enforce a single policy.

Age Example

To help with the discussion of policy and the policy engine an example is in order. The data in question is going to be an individual's birth data. There are three components for the date; day, month, and year. The trusted platform policy is to protect the date and only release the information to appropriate parties. Prior to releasing the information, the policy requires a transformation of the date. When reviewing these examples, do not look at them as absolutes or as perfect examples—counter examples are available and possible. The point is to illustrate how the policy decisions that the trusted platform needs to make. Now for the examples.

Bank Request for Birth Date

One's bank typically uses a birth date to help identify an individual. The bank already has lots of personal information regarding the individual and in some locales; the bank needs to have the birth date to meet laws and regulations. The policy then allows the trusted platform to send the entire date to the bank.

Doctor Request for Birth Date

The doctor, unless a personal friend, is most likely going to use the date to determine age. In this case, the doctor only needs a year so the trusted platform would send only an age or the year of birth.[1]

---

1   This was a good example until I went to the doctor on my birthday. I was in a huge amount of pain due to a bad back. My doctor had a student helping and the student took my "history." After asking me lots of questions, he went out to discuss with the doctor and was immediately back in to say happy birthday. It was obvious that my regular doctor told the student to read the chart and truly understand what it told him about me. Mainly that I was going to be extra cranky due to visiting the doctor on my birthday. So maybe doctors do need the entire date. Oh well, what one needs to do is set a policy if the doctor gets the whole date or not. And for those reading the footnotes, that was very tongue in cheek as it illustrates the entire point of the chapter: one needs policies that are flexible according to the situation.

Attempt to Purchase Alcohol

When attempting to purchase alcohol the seller wants assurances that the buyer is over the legal age to purchase these products. The request from the seller would be "Is the buyer over 21[2]?" and the trusted platform would return yes/no. Notice here that the transformation is from a date to a binary yes/no.

Adding to a Birth Date Club

There are clubs that send you birthday greetings on your birth date. For the club to work the database needs a month and day but not the year. The trusted platform sends the month and day but strips the year.

Aggregation

It is possible to aggregate information from different sources to obtain the complete data. For our date example, it would involve noticing the month and day that the birthday club sends greetings and determining how the doctor treats the patient to determine the complete birthday. When the trusted platform transforms data and sends it to some other entity, how the entity uses the data is a factor in how much transformation is necessary. If the birthday club lets anyone join, maybe the user will not participate, or a parent can determine that for their minor child that information is not released.

Policy Engine and Policy

Just to reiterate, from our discussions on engines and policies, the policy is how to handle the date, for example the full date or just the day. This information represents the policy. Note the full platform policy of how to handle the date is a combination of individual decisions.

The engine is the transformation mechanism that returns the portion of the date that the caller needs and or requests. Again note that the engine does not care who gets the full date or just the day, the engine receives a rule and the engine enforces the rule. There is no real intelligence in the engine; rather the policy is what allows the engine to work appropriately.

---

2   The age 21 is the age necessary to purchase alcohol in many areas of the United States.

Measurability and Reporting

There must be some sort of evidence of the engine and policy so that observers can rely on the policy enforcement. If you remember from our earlier discussion of the evidence element, the platform provides either a static piece of evidence or some dynamic piece of evidence. When dealing with policy engines and the enforced policies the choice of the type of evidence is a critical decision that the platform designer must make.

Policy Engine Evidence

Depending on how the platform is put together, the evidence for an engine could be static or dynamic. If one considers Intel® TXT a policy engine, and it most certainly is, then the evidence for the engine would be some sort of static credential for the platform. Considering our date example from above, most likely the transformation agent is a piece of software and the most common way to provide the evidence would be to measure the software at the time of invocation.

Policy Evidence

In contrast to the engine, the evidence for the policy makes a huge difference. We have made the point that we want flexible policies that the platform users can set as they need. Consider what a static or fixed piece of evidence provides. It says that each time one uses the platform this property is present and the property *does not change*. How can you be flexible and allow different policies if the policy never changes? The answer is that you cannot. A static piece of evidence represents a fixed policy.

If the desire is to have flexible policies then the platform design must allow for and implement the ability to measure the policies. The mechanism must ensure that all measured policies have the measurement values stored in a device like the TPM. One would assume that most implementations would normally use the TPM for policy measurement storage as the TPM is a measurement storage device.

Policy Evaluation

Our goal with policies is to have multiple policies on the platform. If there is a chance to have multiple policies, it is extremely likely that others will want to know which policy the platform is enforcing. That is "easy" in the sense that the platform reports, after some measurement, the policy being enforced.

What is not "easy," and in fact is very hard, is to attempt to determine the equivalence of two mostly the same but slightly different policies. Using our date example from above, assume that policy A rejects passing out any information for an individual under the age of 12. Policy B rejects passing out any information for an individual under the age of 14. These policies are very close. The user of policy B may be satisfied with A but more than likely the user of A is not satisfied with B. How does one present the differences in the two policies in a manner that both sides can determine the differences and in a manner that allows outside observers to distinguish the policy differences?

Policy evaluation is difficult, if not impossible, if the policy language does not provide for standardized expressions. There is a need for a standard, or a small number of standards, of policy expressions. With the standard one enclave has the potential to obtain the other policy and appropriately evaluate the policy. There are efforts underway to create these policy expressions but the creators of platform policies must make use of the expression languages.

Exceptions

All policy engines must allow for exceptions. There must be a bypass mechanism around the transformation agent. Consider the following scenario:

> You are in a fox-hole and the bad guys are shooting at you. You need data from a particular database so that you can direct an air strike. The conversation goes like this:

> "I'm sorry, Dave, but you can't have that data; you're not authorized."

> "You don't understand! I'm being shot at and I really, really, really want that data!

> "Okay, but we'll check what you did with that data later on! Have a nice day!"

The data comes, without transformation, but the transaction causes an audit function to kick in and a review is performed by other entities of the transaction and the use of the data. Stated another way, if there is an override of the transformation policy, there is an automatic enforcement of an auditing policy. In this case the move phase and the transformation agent are going to require assurances of delivery and acknowledgement that the data did get to the new platform. The audit mechanism will take all of the evidences of the move and use of the data and create a record that others will review at a later time.

Launch Control Policy

The policy discussion up to this point has been about potential policies. It is now time to switch gears and talk about a specific policy that platforms with Intel Intel TXT can use. The Launch Control Policy (LCP) is available on platforms that implement Intel Intel TXT.

When discussing the launch process of Intel Intel TXT, there is a distinction made between the controls on the ACM and the controls for the MLE. The ACM must be a valid ACM and the hardware enforces a digital signature verification to enable the enforcement. The MLE has no such signature. Why does the architecture not require a digital signature on the MLE?

The answer is easiest to show by way of example. Suppose that there was a signature on the MLE and the signature used the same key as the ACM. Now the MLE has to undergo the same signature process as the ACM. That means that those who create the ACM control which MLE are valid. But that creates a contradiction. The ACM creator is bound to the chipset manufacturer, but there is no need to bind the MLE to the chipset manufacturer. MLE creators are just software developers and they have no desire to communicate with chipset manufacturers. In addition, how does the ACM creator deal with MLE development? Does the ACM creator sign all development MLE? I know when I was doing development that might mean a new version every few minutes. One is led to the conclusion that instead of a fixed policy, the ACM creator performing a digital signature, one needs a dynamic policy that allows for a wide range of MLE.

Why Control

If the MLE is so hard to sign, then why not simply forget about any policy and let any MLE run? While that seems like a fairly good idea, it really is not. Remember that the MLE is software that is going to have complete control of the platform. Is letting *any* software control your platform and protect your information something you feel comfortable with? Most likely the answer is no but let us look even closer at some rational reasons to control the MLE.

Strict Control

A policy that controls which MLE can launch creates a binary situation, in other words either the MLE is known and executing or unknown and not executing. This binary situation creates a strict control policy. The strictness is important in that if an MLE is present and executing, everyone relying on the platform knows that the MLE was authorized to execute. There is no middle ground, the MLE is in the policy or it is not. It does not matter, from the platform viewpoint, what the MLE does or does not do, the platform merely enforces the information in the policy. Notice how the policy decision is moving from the platform designers and implementers, in the case of the ACM, to those who can set and manage the LCP. Who controls the LCP is a really good question and we will cover that later in this chapter.

Enforcement

Having a LCP fundamentally changes when enforcement of a policy occurs. Attestation allows outside entities to query the platform and determine the current configuration, the outside entity then makes a trust decision to allow the requested action, reject, or ask the platform to mitigate, by installing a new configuration, potential problems. The previous sentence is the standard use of attestation with a trusted platform. Chapter 13, when discussing attestation, brought up the "freshness" issue, which is there is a time gap between taking the measurement and the use of the measurement value.

LCP is one mechanism that mitigates the time gap. The timing of policy enforcement occurs not upon request but as part of the measurement process. Immediately, or more accurately as part of the measurement process, the policy wishes of the entity which maintains the LCP are enforced. This immediate enforcement enables trust in the platform that the platform always starts from a good state.

Malware

With the immediate enforcement provided by LCP, malware attacks on platform software have mitigation. Note that this protection does not extend to executing software, rather just the software identified in the launch process.

The result with LCP is that malware is unable to modify software and maintain an infection across invocations of the software; the malware must infect each time the software starts and the infection must occur after the measurement. While these restrictions are still possible for the malware to overcome, it means that the malware must be more complex and hence potentially easier to detect.

Control

With our new LCP, we essentially move control from some remote entity, distant in time, to a local and immediate mechanism. This fundamental change enables our next section.

Proactive Control

The fight against malware requires diligence and perseverance. The fight is not getting any easier. Figure 18.1 shows the number of new malware instances per year. The graph is not pretty.

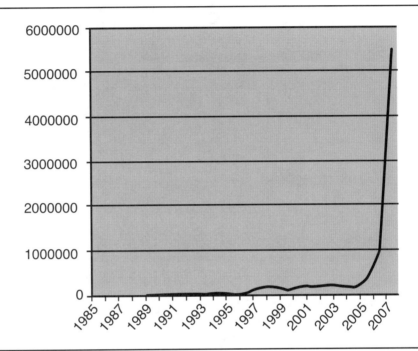

Figure 18.1 Malware by year

What is scary about the graph is that when an anti-malware program has to look for a specific malware image, it must look at the cumulative number of malware programs. The cumulative numbers are in Figure 18.2.

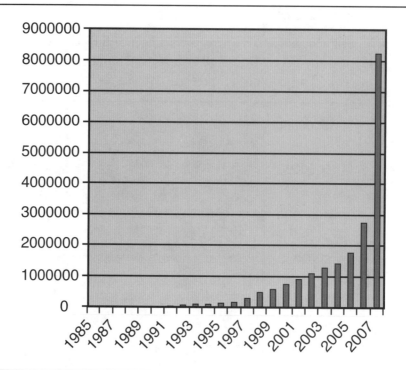

Figure 18.2 Cumulative Malware

If the current pace maintains itself this means that an anti-malware program looking for malware will start with over 14 million entries by the end of 2008. While certainly the anti-malware program can be intelligent in how it maintains the list, the trend is not a kind one in keeping track of what is a potential threat to a platform.

Reactive Anti-Malware

The current anti-malware programs work on a reactive basis, which is they respond, or react, to new malware definitions. Each individual invocation needs to have the current list of malware, those 14 million entries, present when executing the anti-malware program.

As there were approximately 6 million new malware entries in 2007, this means that, on average, there are 11 new malware entries per minute. If one downloads the latest malware list and it takes 10 minutes before you start your malware scan, then there are potentially over 100 new entries in the list that the scan you start is not looking for. Clearly a reactive mechanism, in our current environment, is capable of being overwhelmed.

The anti-malware writers do attempt to mitigate some of these issues by using heuristics and other mechanisms, but even with those advances they are loosing the overall battle.

Help in the Fight Against Malware

LCP is one way to help in the fight against malware. LCP does this by changing the focus from trying to find a "bad" item, to only allowing "good" items. Note very carefully the quotes around good and bad. That is very intentional. What is bad for one may be good for another. Think of our anti-malware writers, they may very well want to execute a piece of malware to determine how it works and exactly what it does. In this case, while most of us would never want to execute the malware the anti-virus researcher most certainly does. So the researcher, while doing the research, would consider the malware "good." When the researcher stopped doing research they would then want to again list the malware as bad.

LCP creates a list, in other words a policy, which contains the known "good" MLE. The system, at the time of measurement, checks the identified MLE against the LCP and if found allows execution to continue, or if not found blocks execution. On a typical system the list of known "good" MLE should be very short, certainly it will contain only a tiny fraction of the 14 million known malware identities. And with this change the trusted platform moves from a reactive platform (look for and react to malware) to a proactive one (only run listed software). If the trusted platform truly maintains a small and accurate MLE list, the trusted platform is very proactive in enforcing which MLE is executing.

No Panacea

LCP is not a panacea in the war against malware. First LCP only helps with attacks against the MLE. While the LCP list is great and limits the number of MLE, it does not help against threats against a specific application, unless the application is the MLE. Additionally the LCP requires knowledge of the MLE identity prior to launching the MLE; this requires an infrastructure to disseminate the MLE identity.

Even with these limitations the move from reactive to proactive provides a huge benefit to trusted platforms. If the MLE represents an entity that does provide good control, the end result of LCP is a controlled platform with protections for both the platform user and outside entities who wish to rely on the platform.

Who Wants Control

Great, so the LCP allows "someone" to control the platform. A later discussion will cover who gets to control but for now we want to discuss who would like to see the control. We will break these into three groups, but the grouping is really arbitrary; it just provides a mechanism to talk about the needs and wishes of the group. Real life will have these arbitrary groups merge into one group or split into ten different groups, but all will be using these basic concepts of why they want the control provided by LCP.

Platform Users

Platform users are the first entities that want control. Most users want to avoid problems and have their platforms work day in and day out. LCP allows a platform user to indicate the set of valid MLE and be assured that only the MLE in the set are executing. The value for the platform user is twofold; first the user has protection from malware and second the user has a lower workload to obtain the protection.

The protection from malware is an inherent part of LCP; only MLE known to the user can execute. It is probable that services will be available to the user, either from IT or commercially, that provide a list of known "good" MLE. These services further reduce the workload of the user to maintain a platform protected from malware.

The workload reduction comes from only have to update the LCP when installing or updating the MLE. The assumption is that changes to the MLE occur on a frequency much slower than anti-malware software which has to update to include the 11 new malware products that appeared in the time it took to read this sentence.

IT Departments

While the user wants control for many of the same reasons the corporate IT department wants to control the software executing on a platform. IT has special builds, special applications, and special protocols to allow a corporation to get their work done. Having control of the platforms that provide these services makes the job of the IT department easier.

One example would be an IT department that had a special MLE designed to provide protections and services for a corporate division. If the MLE is not present, the protected services will not work correctly. What the IT department would do is make sure that each employee of the division had the LCP in place that ensures the launch of the correct MLE. Note here the use of the LCP advantage that enforcement occurs when launching the MLE. The employee doesn't need to be connected to any special server, or for that matter even have any connection at all. The IT department knows that if an MLE is in use it is an MLE on the LCP list.

Regulated industries

Our last group of LCP users is those industries that have requirements on data handling placed on the company from laws or regulations. These groups need to be able to indicate to regulators or auditors they are complying with a law or regulation. The addition of LCP allows the corporation to state, with assurance, that those accessing the data are using the software designed to manipulate the data. This assurance helps the corporation meet their regulatory requirements.

List Requirements

If the LCP does exist, then what are the requirements to use and manage the list? It turns out we have three requirements:

- Accurate identity
- Single control point
- List integrity and management

Accurate Identity

The idea of LCP is to limit the MLE that can execute. If version 1.0 of an MLE has a bug and version 1.1 fixes the bug, having the LCP specify version 1 provides insufficient information to make a real choice. The list has to disambiguate between version 1.0 and version 1.1. The ability to differentiate between the two versions is going to require an accurate identity of the MLE.

One way to obtain an accurate identity is to measure the MLE. If there is an accurate measurement of the MLE the LCP processing can use the result of the measurement process as the LCP identifier. Asking a rhetorical question, is there any process on the trusted platform that takes a measurement of the MLE? The obvious answer is that Intel TXT takes a measurement of the MLE; in fact the hardware goes through numerous steps to help ensure a highly accurate measurement of the MLE. With the Intel TXT measurement of the MLE, the first requirement, the accurate measurement of the controlled entity, for LCP is met.

Control Point

The second requirement is a single control point: a defined entity at a specific point in time that makes the decision if the measured MLE is a member of the LCP. The reason for a single control point is that if you have multiple control points, how entities are measured may be very different. If you measure differently you get different values for the same entity. Going back to our version 1.0 and 1.1 example, if there are two control points, one at load time and one after load, the LCP has to include at least two entries for each version, it is possible that extra entry points may require more than one entry based on the measurement process in use.

Obviously having multiple control points and potentially multiple measurements per control point makes the promise of a simple LCP go away. Therefore the idea is a single control point with a single measurement value. Again Intel TXT provides a mechanism that meets the requirement. The SINIT ACM is the entity that performs the measurement of the MLE. It performs the measurement using a single algorithm so the MLE always gets the same measurement from the MLE. The SINIT creates a single measurement of the MLE for each invocation of SINIT. This single measurement avoids the problem of multiple measurements for the same entity.

The second advantage of SINIT is that SINIT is in sole control of the platform when SINIT executes. SINIT, as an Authenticated Code Module, has all the advantages of execution in the Authenticated Code Execution Area (ACEA). If the reader remembers the properties of the ACEA it provides a protected execution area that makes it difficult to interfere with the ACM execution. With SINIT in sole control of the platform the requirement for a single control point is met.

SINIT provides the mechanism that enables a single control point and a single measurement value.

List integrity and management

Those with a devious security mind are already making the leap to the next requirement, if LCP limits what can run, then as an attacker I will just put my malicious MLE into the LCP list and LCP will ensure that the malicious code can run. It should be obvious then that there is a requirement to carefully protect how the LCP list changes. LCP requires an authentication mechanism to ensure only proper entities make changes to the list and a mechanism to ensure the integrity of the list when SINIT reads and operates on the list.

Editors – The LCP needs at least one editor. The current [2008] mechanism allows for two editors; platform default and platform owner. The use of the term "platform default" is intentional as it implies any of the entities who could set a default. These entities include the platform manufacturer, a value added reseller, or even an IT department. All are potential editors of the platform default policy.

The platform owner is the second editor. As the platform owner they have control over what the platform does and will have a say in the LCP for their platform.

Duplicate editors – Whenever one has multiple editors, and for LCP we have two, platform default and platform owner, a conflict resolution must be decided. Many protocols solve this issue, and the selection of which protocol to use is dependent on platform use, so the policy in use for a specific platform will be platform specific. The policy in use during the writing of this book (late spring 2008) is going to be that the platform owner overrides the platform default. This means that if the platform default specifies some policy options, the platform owner can override those choices.

LCP integrity – With the editors specified, there now has to be a mechanism that allows SINIT to know that the LCP SINIT loads is the same LCP that the editor created. This mechanism makes use of the nonvolatile (NV) storage feature of the TPM. LCP requires that the TPM hold two pieces of information, the identity of the platform default LCP and the platform owner LCP. The identity in this case is the SHA-1 hash of the LCP list.

For the platform default the TPM allows changes to the NV area until the platform manufacturer locks the TPM. One of the TPM features is the ability for the manufacturer to insert values into the TPM that do not change when the TPM is out of the manufacturing process. The platform default LCP is one of those instances. The assumption is that the platform manufacturer would insert into the platform default LCP, the list of MLE shipped with the platform. If the platform was shipping with MLE Version 1.5.2, then the LCP would indicate MLE version 1.5.2 was a valid MLE. Setting the default allows the platform manufacturer to create backup partitions[3] and other such consumer helps in the factory.

The platform owner NV location requires updating in the field as obviously the manufacturer does not know who the owner will be. For the purpose of LCP, the platform owner is the same entity that knows the owner authorization for the TPM. This merging of the LCP platform and the TPM owner allows for efficient use of the TPM authorization mechanisms to prove that a platform owner is manipulating the LCP platform owner list.

Use of integrity value – SINIT reads the TPM NV storage area and obtains the hash of the LCP. SINIT then hashes the LCP passed to SINIT at SINIT invocation. SINIT compares the computed hash with the hash value in the TPM. If they match, SINIT has the correct LCP and can continue, if the hashes do not match, SINIT fails the launch of the MLE and forces `TXT-Shutdown`.

---

3   I really mean this but at the very moment I am writing this chapter I am also providing tech support for my wife's laptop and using the recovery partition provided by the platform manufacturer. Thank you, manufacturers, for putting these features on your platforms.

LCP Recap

We have defined a set of requirements and indicated the mechanisms that meet those requirements. Table 18.1 enumerates out requirements and the mechanisms that meet those requirements.

Table 18.1 LCP List Requirements

Requirement	Mechanism	Comments
Accurate Identity	MLE measurement computed by SINIT	Normal SINIT processing to compute the identify
Single Control Point	SINIT enforces LCP entries	SINIT in a protected environment, ACEA, and only entity that uses LCP
Integrity and Management	TPM NV storage locations	Dual owners, TPM enforces access control to NV storage locations

LCP Additions

LCP provides the control point to restrict the MLE to just the platform owner identified MLE. That use in and of itself makes LCP valuable. In an extremely happy coincidence, LCP enables other platform controls. The requirements for LCP control of the MLE turn out to also to be the requirements for other control issues of the platform.

Launch Environment

It is entirely reasonable that a platform owner may only want to launch a MLE from a specific environment. While the LCP prevents an unknown MLE from executing, the platform owner may want additional control of when the MLE launches. An easy example of this would be a MLE developer who is building new MLEs and where the developer launches the development, or debug, version of the MLE from a specific startup environment. By allowing this type of control the developer can have the debug version only execute when the platform is properly setup to use the development MLE. One very probable restriction would be that the development MLE can only run when the Internet is not enabled as the development MLE does not properly protect itself and the platform from modification.

The LCP includes the ability to identify, through TPM PCR values, the launching environment. The SINIT ACM, when using the LCP, then compares the current environment to the LCP listed environment and if not correct aborts the launch of the MLE.

Additional Policies

Controlling the MLE is major reason for LCP. However, the properties of LCP allow the basic list to expand to cover additional policies. Each platform implementation can add new features to the LCP. Future versions of LCP will contain a richer set of controls that revolve around the launch of the MLE.

Chapter 19

Services

Your mom does not need to buy a strong password generator, she raised one.

—David Wooten, TPM workgroup phone conference

Services are components of the trusted platform that must be present, but are combinations of the platform elements. A good example is auditing, a critical service for many use cases, where auditing is a combination of isolation, persistent storage, and sequencing. The quote from Mr Wooten, a valuable member of the TPM WG, shows how one combines basic elements into a valuable service. The mom in question is elderly and uses a computer for basic services. Her son, a member of the TPM WG, supplies all tech support for hardware and applications on the computer. The comment came from the discussion that the mom needed strong passwords to mitigate certain attacks but that she would have to have a strong password generator program available to create the strong passwords. Mr Wooten then issued his quoted line. The point Mr Wooten makes is that mom does not need a password generator program as she is going to use a service already present, her son, to actually generate the password. The trusted platform works in the same way, to get a specific job done; the service will combine the platform elements present to expose the service to the platform users.

Typical Services

There is no way we are going to attempt to list all of the services it is possible for a trusted platform to provide to the users of the platform. That would defeat a major design goal of allowing for choice and innovation. We can list a few of the obvious services that might be available and then describe how the service uses the platform elements. Our list of services is:

- Auditing
- Trusted Path
- Out of Band

Auditing

One of the hallmarks of security systems is the ability to determine what happened after some event. The security literature is rife with papers that describe when and how the security system is required to produce an audit trail. As the trusted platform is not a new type of entity the previous papers point to the need for an auditing capability on the platform.

An auditing system needs to be able to produce an audit entry when requested to by the system and ensure that the audit records are not tampered with after the generation of the audit event. Rereading the previous sentence leads one to see that the audit system needs isolation, protected execution, persistent storage, and sequencing. Those are the features the trusted platform already provides. Auditing is a service that a trusted platform must provide.

For the remainder of this section we will be using the following terms:

- **Audited operation** – This is the operation that the trusted platform is suppose to keep track of. Think of this as the operation that the user requests. A good example would be the user requests to change a password. Many audit systems keep track of the date of the last password change.

- **Audit event** – The audit event is the record of the audited operation. For our password change operation the event would likely contain the event type, password change, and the date, and potentially even the time.

■ **Audit log** – The audit log is the combination of all of the audit events. The log normally allows for multiple event types, like password change, log on and log off, and illegal operation requests.

Auditing Isolation

Auditing needs isolation to ensure that the audited operation cannot modify the generation of the audit event. If the audited operation can modify the audit event, the operation can masquerade as some other event or change the time and sequence of the event. Any of these modifications to the audit entry invalidates the audit log.

The trusted platform provides an isolated execution area for the audit generation service. No generic requirement exists that specifies how the isolation must be provided. If the operation that generates an auditable event is in a Virtual Machine (VM), it is very likely that the isolation mechanism would be the use of a separate VM to generate the audit event. Attempting to generate audit events inside of a Virtual Machine Monitor (VMM) would require a different mechanism because a VM is not isolated from the VMM.

Auditing Protected Execution

Just as audit generation needs isolation, audit generation also needs protected execution. It is imperative that the generation of the audit event work correctly. If the attackers can prevent the generation of the audit event or modify the event, then to those reviewing the log at a later date it appears as if the event never occurred. If the log is not reliable, it is useless, especially as a forensic witness.

Auditing Persistent Storage

It is critical that the log at least be able to identify potential gaps in the log. The log must be able to identify when the log starts and when it ends and protect the integrity of the log. If the attack on the log is simply to delete it and then there is no evidence whatsoever that the log ever existed, the attacker merely does his operation that creates the audit event and then deletes the log.

The storage requirement is one that the audit log uses to ensure that there are no gaps and attempts to delete the log are detectable. It may not be possible to prevent the log tampering, but detection of a tampered log is mandatory.

One way to provide this is to keep a hash of the log in persistent storage. If the hash in persistent storage matches the current hash of the log, then there is evidence that the log is accurate. A mismatch indicates some error or attack. Just the presence of an inaccurate log could be enough to start additional checks and reviews of the affected platform.

Auditing Sequencing

The log must be able to put the events into a sequence. In fact it is imperative that the log show the correct sequence. It may, or may not be, important to show the time delta between events. Logs may include a monotonic counter to sequence events or they may include time stamps to sequence events. Some logs may even use both mechanisms.

Time stamping is critical when the audit log combines multiple platforms and events on different platforms are important to the sequence the log is tracking. If an IT department is tracking the source of a malware infection, and the "smoking gun" is a specific operation, then the first platform to perform that specific operation is the potential source of the infection. Being able to collect all of the logs from all of the infected machines and then know, by way of the log, which platform first had the infection, can go a long way in determining how the infection got into the enterprise.

All Together

Many people assert that auditing is a basic platform element. Certainly the use model of keeping track of what the platform is doing is a base feature of the trusted platform. But does one really need a special form of isolation, protection, storage, and sequencing? Most likely not. The basic platform elements combine nicely to enable the auditing service. One could argue that some of the other elements are also capable of being decomposed, and that might be true, but at this time the consensus is that auditing is a service and not a basic element.

Trusted Path

Any platform that interacts with a human user and requires that the human user trust the platform needs to provide the building blocks such that the user can be assured of the following:

■ User input delivery. The user must have the assurance that input, defined here as keyboard, mouse, or other such device, is delivered solely to a trusted process. The delivery assurance can come from the creation of a trusted channel between the trusted process and the input device.

■ Process identification. The user must have the assurance that the trusted process that is going to receive the input is the correct process. Identifying the process requires some effort by the human. A typical mechanism for process identification is to include a trusted display on the platform and have the trusted process use the trusted display to uniquely identify the trusted process. The critical point here is that the human *must* participate and make some conscious choices.

The Trusted Path therefore provides the platform with the ability to securely direct input to a specific process and for that process to provide unequivocal feedback that it has received it. Some trusted paths may even include a second feedback path from the user to the machine in order for the machine to confirm that the user acknowledges that the path exists. An example here is the obfuscation techniques, as shown in Figure 19.1, for confirming passwords common to many e-commerce Web sites.

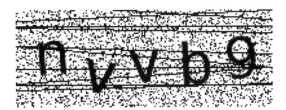

Figure 19.1 Trusted Path Verification

Trusted Path as a Platform Requirement

With so many assurances arising from the trusted path it would seem to be a basic element of the trusted platform. And from so many angles that is correct. However there is one important point that moves the trusted path out of the basic platform elements. The issue is what constitutes a valid process identification mechanism.

Process identification requires action by the human user. Actions by humans are not universally the same. In fact, regional, cultural, ethnic, gender, and other issues all combine to require mechanisms that are very flexible when indicating to the user the existence of the trusted process. This flexibility requires some sort of policy that the trusted platform needs to enforce. The policy is some sort of combination of the other trusted platform elements like trusted channels, isolation, and other elements. As soon as one mentions the word policy, the item relying on the policy should not be a base building block for the trusted platform. Attempting to pick one policy that fits all situations is not possible. Therefore, the trusted path, while extremely useful, is not a basic trusted platform element.

It is entirely possible that the architects of the trusted platform can require that the trusted platform, as delivered to the user, include a trusted path policy appropriate for the circumstances the human user will operate the platform. This requirement is not adding the trusted path to the base elements but requiring that the platform manufacturer appropriately combine the platform elements and expose the trusted path as a service.

Out of Band

The trusted platform needs to have external connections as previously discussed. The external connections in the previous chapter were ones active when the system is operational. There is a growing need to communicate and apply management issues when the system itself is not active. The communication mechanism is known as Out Of Band (OOB) as the mechanism is "out of band" of the normal operational cycle.

OOB provides management of the platform when the platform is having difficulties. If a virus has corrupted the system, management can shut down the platform and send the remediation to the platform using the OOB mechanism. The availability of an OOB mechanism can greatly reduce the management actions on a platform.

OOB also represents a huge security concern. Consider the previous paragraph, the OOB mechanism is allowing changes to the system outside of the control of the normal control points. If the changes from the OOB mechanism are malicious, they totally bypass the control points. The OOB mechanism and the normal control mechanism must coordinate and work together to provide the appropriate protections for all platform features and services. Trusted platforms should avoid OOB systems that do not cooperate with the main control mechanisms.

Enclave and Platform

One service that the trusted platform enables, and it is so exciting it is getting its own little section, is the creation of an enclave. We will work hard here to define enclave and hopefully at the end of this section you will understand why enclaves are such a great idea with trusted platforms.

One definition of an enclave is a group of computing areas that share the same operational policy. What you want the trusted platform to do is provide the policy enforcement mechanisms and mechanisms that allow the aggregation of the various platforms.

Figure 19.2 shows three enclaves; the first two reside on the same platform, while the third is a combination of four separate platforms.

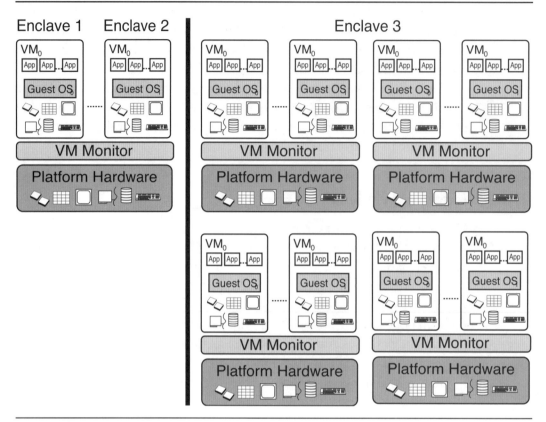

Figure 19.2   Enclaves

An enclave uses the trusted platform to enforce a trust policy. Stated in the reverse, the enforcement of a specific policy by a trusted policy engine creates an enclave. When two areas, either Virtual Machine (VM) guests or separate devices, enforce the same policy, they, logically, merge to form a single enclave. When two areas, either VM guests or separate devices, enforce different policies, they form separate enclaves.

Combining Enclaves and Platforms

Referring to Figure 19.2 again illustrates the wealth of enclave opportunities that a trusted platform supporting virtualization provides. The left side shows two enclaves on the same platform. The implication is that the policy differs between Enclave 1 and Enclave 2. The platform would support a virtually unlimited number of enclaves as the platform supports a virtually unlimited number of guests. When the guests each enforced the same trust policy, the two guests would be part of the same enclave. The platform could be supporting a number of guests that were part of the same enclave.

The real flexibility comes when looking at the right side of Figure 19.2; there one sees many platforms all part of the same enclave. Remember that being in the same enclave means that the system is enforcing the same trust policy. Consider now Figure 19.3, which shows a group of platforms all supporting a mix of trust enclaves.

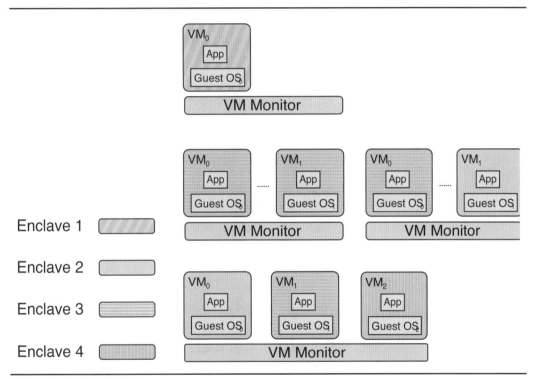

Figure 19.3   Mixed Enclaves

The details of the four enclaves are:

■ *Enclave 1.* This enclave is only on a single platform and on a single guest. No information is shared between any other platform or enclave and Enclave 1.

■ *Enclave 2.* This enclave exists on two different platforms. It can share a platform with any other enclave. The enclave has the ability to express itself when on multiple platforms. Enclave 2 requires a move mechanism to allow data to flow from one platform to the other. To an outside observer, Enclave 2 appears to be a single entity with the two pieces combining to form a coherent whole.

■ *Enclave 3.* This enclave exists on three different platforms. On one platform the enclave takes up all executing guests and on the other platforms Enclave 3 shares the guests. Enclave 3 illustrates the ability of an enclave to either provide total control of the platform or share the platform.

■ *Enclave 4.* This enclave only resides on a single platform but unlike Enclave 1, Enclave 4 shares the platform resources with other enclaves.

The end result of all of these enclaves is a large flexible platform that can support lots of different trust enclaves according to the desires of the platform owners.

Enclave Organization

Enclaves can now be organized to form a number of security policies, which are used by many organizations. These are normally either hierarchical or compartmentalized or a combination of both, as shown in Figure 19.4. In our hierarchical arrangement Enclave 4 is at the bottom of the lattice and is not allowed access to data in Enclave 1, 2, or 3. However, Enclave 3 is allowed access to data in Enclave 4 also, and Enclave 2 is also allowed access to protected by Enclave 3 and 4, and finally Enclave 1 is allowed access to data within Enclaves 2, 3, and 4.

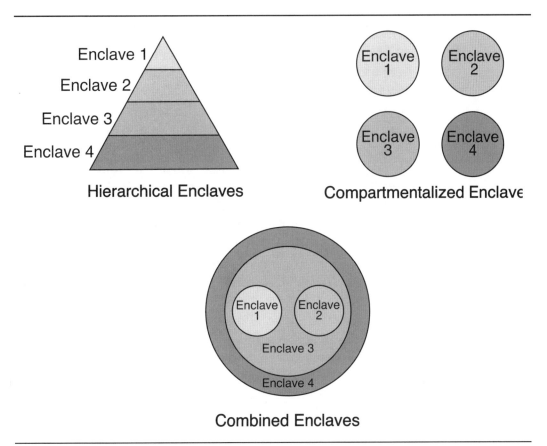

Figure 19.4   Enclave Types

When the enclaves are arranged in a manner that compartmentalizes, the data in the enclaves are kept separate. More realistically organizations normally exhibit both types of enclave arrangements together, in our example Enclaves 3 and 4 are organized as a hierarchy, and top of the hierarchy contains two compartmentalized enclaves.

The way these enclaves are logically ordered can affect the manner in which trusted platform is configured in order to support this configuration.

How many apps in a partition

Platforms of today, and more critically operating systems, combine all of the applications that a user has into one big pot. The OS then attempts to provide isolation between the running applications while allowing for third-party drivers to also execute in the same operational space as the security kernel. The end result is lots of attacks that bypass the OS security system and cause problems for applications.

A very interesting question to ask is: Why execute my online game in the same partition as my online banking application? Certainly part of the answer has been that the ability to isolate one application from another has not been easy and the sharing of various OS components, like the network connection, force the sharing. With a trusted platform should the same rules apply?

What happens if one enclave manages the network connection and another enclave manages the disk drive? Could one then have two other enclaves where one executes the online game and the other the online banking application? The answer should be yes and the trusted platform should be attempting to enhance and promote separate enclaves for single purposes.

Elements for an Enclave

Depending on the enclave requirements, it is entirely possible that all of the trusted platform elements are in use to create an enclave. The necessity for storage, isolation, attestation, sequencing, and any other element can be a requirement for an enclave. Enclaves bring a rich user and execution experience to the trusted platform and the enclave use of the trusted platform elements is what allows the enclave to expose the rich set of services.

Services

Back to our mom who needs a password generator: the idea is to combine the already existing elements into services that provide value to the platform user. The list of services in this chapter only scratches the surface of what is possible. I could write books on subjects like network access control, management of trusted platforms, enclaves in an enterprise data center, and a few others I really do not want in print yet. The bottom line here is that with the elements of a trusted platform there are lots of places where innovation will create entire new industries.

Chapter 20

Defending the Platform Against Attacks

So in war, the way is to avoid what is strong and to strike at what is weak.
—Sun Tzu, *The Art of War*

This same Sun Tzu quote applied to Chapter 4, too. In that chapter, the discussion centered on successful software attacks on platform designs available in the 2004 timeframe. Chapter 20 shows how the design and architecture of Intel® Trusted Execution Technology (Intel® TXT) mitigates these attacks. If the design is successful, attackers need to move from software attacks to hardware attacks. To allow only hardware attacks is a large step forward because the hardware attacks require physical access to the platform.

> **Second Edition Remarks**
>
> Little changes in this chapter from the first edition. Sure, LT changes to Intel TXT, but the basics of what Intel TXT does are still present. Pay particular attention to the trusted channel discussion, but the mitigations that Intel TXT provides changes little.

Vulnerabilities

The goal in Chapter 4 was to examine how the attack finds and exploits a vulnerability. The goal in this chapter is to show how the Intel TXT design mitigates those same vulnerabilities.

The BORE attack revolved around having the same information on every platform. Discovery of the information on one platform allowed the attacker to use the information on all other platforms. The design of Intel TXT does not use keys or other information that is the same on each platform. If it requires an encryption key, the MLE can generate a random number, SEAL the random number to the SINIT and SENTER identities, and only allow use of the key in the correct configuration. A MLE of this design has a unique key on every platform so that any exposure of the key only affects an individual platform and not all Intel TXT platforms.

While an MLE could use the same value on every platform, this design of the MLE would be incorrect. A review of the MLE by an independent reviewer would see this problem, and entities wanting to rely on the platform would not trust the platform that has an incorrect MLE executing.

From a design standpoint, Intel TXT does not provide the repeatable value necessary for a BORE attack. Applications using Intel TXT could use repeatable values but that is an application decision and not part of the Intel TXT design.

The Example Application

The application program from Chapter 5 performs some operations on a special number. The operations are:

- Display the special number
- Update the special number
- Encrypt the special number
- Enter and process the users password

The Chapter 20 version of the application makes use of Intel TXT and performs all of the operations of the application in the protected partition. To distinguish between the versions of the application, "V4" refers to the Chapter 4 version and "V20" identifies the Chapter 20 version.

The Attacker's Goal

The goal of the attacker does not change: discover the special number or find a way to alter the special number. The same restriction is in place. To accomplish the goal, the attacker can use software attacks but not hardware attacks.

Application Functionality

The application functions that were present in V4 remain in V20. The following list provides a breakdown of the functionality into components:

- Display window that requests password
- Mechanism to read the keystrokes that provide the password
- Mechanism to process the password[1]
- Decision to display the special number
- Display window that shows the special number
- Process to update the number

Application Design

While the functionality of V20 mimics V4 and parts of the program remain exactly the same, other parts of the program require modifications. The application developer can make numerous tradeoffs between ease of development and deployment, and complete use of the Intel TXT protection capabilities.

A design characteristic that the V20 architect[2] was following, was an attempt to keep as much of the V4 code in use as possible. Other designs are possible and sometimes desirable, but for V20 code, reuse has the highest priority.

---

1   Our application is severely limited in functionality; there is no way to change the password. Real applications would provide mechanisms to change the password. The change mechanism requires the same protections as the special number change mechanism.

2   The architect is the author and the purpose of V20 is only to illustrate some points, not to be a perfect application. Real life applications will make very different choices depending on the needs of the application.

Figure 20.1 illustrates the basic V20 architecture. The code runs in a separate partition from any other application. The V20 code makes use of trusted input and trusted output channels. Long-term secret protection comes from the SEAL property of the TPM.

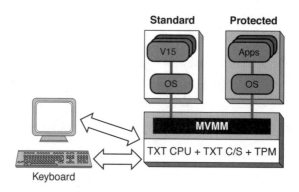

Figure 20.1 Preferred V20 Architecture

V20 Unchanged Program Components

The functionality that does not change in the V20 version includes:

■ *Mechanism to process the password.* The code in V4 takes the input, processes the input (normally a cryptographic hash), and then makes the resulting processed password available to other sections of the application. V20 needs to make no modifications to this section of code. While protections are in place on how to obtain the password, the actual processing can be the same code.

■ *Decision to display the special number.* The code in V4 makes a programming decision, based on various inputs, to display the special number. The same decisions are available in V20 without modification.

■ *Process to update the special number.* The code in V4 obtains the new special number and then processes the input and creates the new special number. V20 uses the same process.

V20 Changed Program Components

The V20 code has the following additions to take advantage of the Intel TXT protections:

- ■ *Trusted output channel.* Both the display window for the user-id and password and the display window that shows the special number require a trusted channel. The V20 code creates the channel to the display adapter, discrete or integrated, and the channel ensures that what the application creates is what the display actually shows.

- ■ *Trusted input channel.* The V4 code accepts keystrokes directly from the keyboard driver. The V20 code accepts keystrokes from the trusted input channel.

- ■ *Trusted path indicator.* To ensure for the user that the trusted output channel is present and operational, the V20 code places a "border" around the display windows. The border is a tartan pattern that appears only when the trusted display is active. The V20 code keeps the tartan pattern secure by encrypting the data. The V20 code provides long-term protection of the tartan pattern by using the TPM SEAL property to ensure that the tartan border is only available when the correct MLE environment is present.

The mechanism to create and manage the trusted channels is Intel© VT-d.

Vulnerabilities

The V4 code has specific vulnerabilities that Chapter 4 enumerated. The V20 code mitigates those vulnerabilities.

Display Window That Requests Password

In the V4 program, the display window had two major vulnerabilities: access to the frame buffer and the ability of an attacker to mimic the window. In the V20 program, the frame buffer obtains protection using the trusted channel between the protected partition and the display adapter. As a result, the attacker does not have access to the buffer and cannot see the buffer or change any data in the buffer, mitigating the V4 vulnerability.

The Intel TXT design, using the trusted display and the SEAL[3] operation, can create a mechanism that allows the user to know that the display is present. The attacker's ability to mimic the window is gone and the vulnerabilities present in V4 are not present in V20. The application designer has mechanisms in place that allows the designer to mitigate the vulnerabilities on the platform.

Mechanism to Read the Keystrokes That Provide the Password

In the V4 code, the attacker accessed system memory to read the keystrokes or install a password sniffer. In V20, access to system memory is not available to the attacker. The MLE protects the physical memory where the MLE itself resides. The MLE also ensures that partitions are properly isolated. The measurement of the MLE allows those wishing to rely on the platform the assurance that the proper components are present and are active.

The V20 version of the application uses the trusted input channel to send the information from the keyboard to the protected partition in a secure way. The protections block the attempts by a keyboard sniffer to obtain the information from the sending of keystrokes from the keyboard to the protected partition. V20 does not prevent the introduction of a sniffer onto the platform, but V20 does prevent the sniffer from obtaining information under protection of the protected partition. V20 has mitigations for both of the vulnerabilities in V4, memory and sniffers. The attackers need to look elsewhere to succeed.

Mechanism to Process the Password

The V4 vulnerability to password processing lay in the ability for attack code to run in ring 0. In V20, with the application running in the protected partition, the attacker cannot install code in ring 0. If the MLE did allow new code to execute in ring 0, the application can still protect itself by using the SEAL operation's properties and ensuring that the application runs only in environments that provide protection.

---

3   Remember that SEAL uses the measurement values of the SINIT and MLE; hence, the system can provide long-term protection for the trusted display trusted path indicator.

Decision to Display the Value

In V4, the decision to display the value was vulnerable to ring 0 code, and in V20, the same protections on password processing apply to the display decision.

Display Window that Shows the Value

In V4, the display window was vulnerable to the same frame buffer attacks as the password window. The V20 program's use of the trusted display mitigates these attacks.

Process to Update the Value

In V4, the value update process was susceptible to a ring 0 attack, and V20 mitigates ring 0 attacks.

Underlying V4 Vulnerabilities

The exploits in V4 revolved around the following vulnerabilities:

- Memory access
- Driver manipulation
- Uncontrolled program access

The Intel TXT design mitigates these underlying vulnerabilities by restricting memory access, preventing driver manipulation, and denying uncontrolled program access.

Memory Access

The protected partition provides excellent memory access protection. Any process outside of the protected partition cannot access memory pages protected by the MLE.

All of the physical memory associated with the MLE is kept separate from operating systems at ring 0 and applications at ring 3. Applications running in ring 3 of a protected partition have complete separation from any other ring 3 process. The separations protect information by making deliberate or unintentional access to the memory impossible. The V4 code attacker had a goal of obtaining access to a ring 0 process. The attacker who gains access to ring 0 in any partition has no access rights to any memory in ring 3 protected partitions. The basic mechanism of obtaining information in V4 is mitigated by the protected partition. The combination of the ring structure and the protected partition removes the attacker's ability to access memory.

DMA Access

In the V4 code, the attacker could also access memory through DMA devices. The V20 code allowed no DMA access to protected pages, preventing it with the Intel VT-d, which blocks all access attempts using DMA. The attacker again has to look for another vulnerability to exploit.

Driver Manipulation

In the V4 code, the attacker could change a driver on the system. Driver manipulation is a mechanism to gain access to ring 0, but as in the case of keyboard sniffers, the new driver could be malicious in and of itself. In V20 code, the location of the driver determines whether manipulation is possible.

If the driver executes in the standard partition, the protections and vulnerabilities present in V4 are still present. Intel TXT does not provide protection for code running in the standard partition. The attacker can manipulate the driver and gain access to ring 0. However, the attacker does not gain an advantage, as ring 0 in the standard partition provides no access to any memory in the protected environment.

If the attacker attempts to change a portion of the code in use for the protected environment—it could change either the MLE or SINIT—the measurement of these entities registers any changes. If the attacker changes SINIT, the ACM digital signature validation fails and the secure launch is terminated. If the attacker changes the MLE code, the measurement changes and no data that was SEALed to the previous environment is available to the new environment. The MLE itself should provide the same type of protections on the code that the MLE uses to launch code in a ring 0 of the protected partition.

Uncontrolled Program Access

In V4 code, once the attacker obtained knowledge of the encryption key, no available mechanism would prevent access to the data. In V20 code, in addition to encryption, the application can SEAL the data to a specific environment. With this change, even knowledge of the encryption key prevents the attacker from manipulating the value.

What Remains

Reading the above mitigations one could get the opinion that all work is done, all attacks have mitigations, and the attackers will all give up and stop attempting to attack applications. Nothing could be further from the truth. Lots of work remains to be done, there are numerous attacks that still require mitigation, and the attackers will still attempt to gain access to information.

Isolation

The V20 design makes a critical and vital assumption: the code runs in a separate partition. Compare Figure 20.1 and Figure 20.2. Notice that while V20 is present in both, only in Figure 20.1 is V20 isolated from the other application. Critically notice that in Figure 20.2, V20 and the other application share the same OS. The sharing violates the separation necessary to obtain the full benefit of Intel TXT. When applications share the same OS, they are sharing the same ring 0 code, and sharing the same ring 0 code allows for all of the current attacks.

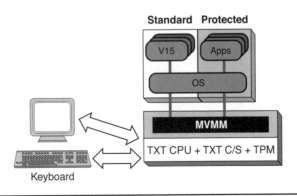

Figure 20.2 Incorrect V20 Architecture

When creating the trusted channels for V20 the OS may provide the basic connection ports for the trusted channels. If the architecture shares the same OS, as Figure 20.2 does, then there is the possibility that the other application can be corrupted and expose V20 information.

Getting to Figure 20.1 requires more effort that Figure 20.2 but the result is a much more robust and trustable architecture.

Hardware Attacks

The V20 architecture is a design that is resistant to software attacks. V20, like Intel TXT, is not resistant to hardware attacks. Attackers wishing to attack V20 using hardware mechanisms may succeed. All of the hardware attacks previously discussed may be successful against the V20 design.

The goal of Intel TXT is to force attackers to use hardware mechanisms to attack the platform. The Intel TXT design protects from attacks accessing memory, changing drivers, or changing the application. The attacker needs to use hardware to gain access to the protected memory.

A critical point is the discussion about the use of the partition isolation. Without partition isolation the full effect of Intel TXT is not available.

Matching Requirements

In Chapter 2, Table 2.1 identified six requirements for a trusted computing platform. Here, near the end of the book, a review of the requirements and the components that provide the features that meet the requirements is in order. To just sum things up, let us look at Table 20.1.

Table 20.1 Requirements and Support

Requirement	Hardware Support	Comments
Isolation of programs	Virtualization Technology Paging and segmentation	Multiple partitions provide isolation and the partition can enforce the ring 0/ring 3 separation
Separation of user from supervisor	MLE Ring 0 and Ring 3 separation	The MLE is a supervisor, and virtualization provides automatic separation of user from supervisor and the ability to maintain multiple partitions provides user supervisor separation in individual partitions
Identification of current configuration	The `GETSEC [SENTER]` measurement of the MLE	Providing the measurement of the MLE identifies the MLE and enables both long-term storage and reporting
Long-term protected storage	MLE measurement and TPM	By ensuring that the MLE measurement is properly stored in the TPM, the MLE can use the TPM SEAL capability to have long-term protection of secrets
Verifiable report of current configuration	TPM	With the MLE measurement in the PCR registers, any observer can use the defined TPM properties to obtain a verifiable report of the PCR register contents
Hardware basis for protections	Intel® Virtualization Technology LaGrande Technology TPM	The combination of VT, Intel TXT, and TPM provides a hardware base of the features

Chapter **21**

The Future

Neither a wise man nor a brave man lies down on the tracks of history to wait for the train of the future to run over him.

—Dwight D. Eisenhower

Security requirements do not stand still. What is an appropriate protection today may be inadequate tomorrow. The first version of Intel® Trusted Execution Technology (Intel® TXT) sets a protection boundary and attempts to mitigate vulnerabilities within that boundary. It is unreasonable to assume that Intel TXT never has to respond to additional threats or to a change in the boundary. Future versions will change the protection boundary.

How Did We Do?

It is dangerous, as President Eisenhower states, to wait for history to catch up with you. In the first edition of this book, we made some predictions as to where attacks would come from.

The idea that an unknown virtualization kernel represents potential platform vulnerability is one that is gaining ground in the security world. There have been papers published that explain some of these attacks. The design of Intel TXT is such that an unknown Virtual Machine Monitor (VMM) will not execute on the platform.

363

Maybe in the third edition (and no I make no promises about that edition right now) we will have more attacks to consider but for now we will just perform some crystal ball reading as we did in the first edition.

New Attacks

As in the first edition, there is one section of the crystal ball that is not hazy. That section shows those persons wishing to break into our computers and networks still at work attacking vulnerable systems. The ball is hazy on the exact mechanisms the attackers are using, but the attacking is clearly visible. Given the haziness on the exact attack mechanisms, the nature of responses and mitigations are obviously hazy at this time also.

The truth is that this will never change, there will always be attackers looking for vulnerable systems and attempting to disrupt or steal information from those platforms. The trusted platform mitigates some of the threats, but the trusted platform does not instantly mitigate all threats. With no complete mitigation of all threats, attackers will continue to probe and be successful in subverting platform protections.

Changing the Protection Boundary

One area of change that will occur over time is the inclusion of mitigations to current threats. The current boundary specifically mitigates some threats and places other threats outside of the protection boundary. Future versions of the trusted platform will change the boundary and add mitigations to threats outside the current boundary. Many of these mitigations will be responses to specific hardware attacks.

Devious Attackers

It is imperative to understand that attackers will not only use current mechanisms to launch software and hardware attacks. Attackers can be extremely devious; they thrive on looking at systems and finding new ways to access information.

Attempting to create a protection boundary ensures that attackers will attempt to cross the boundary. Some of the attempts will succeed. The possibility of success will continue to depend on the skill, motivation, resources, and desire of the attacker. Future versions of the trusted platform will respond to these attacks by providing new forms of mitigations.

Being Perfect

Providing security is not about providing absolutes. Those who say a product is 100-percent secure are 100-percent wrong! Security is always risk mitigation. Some risks have mitigations, some do not. New threats appear and old threats migrate to access and manipulate new areas. The crystal ball is hazy as to which threats will require mitigation, so attempting to predict what hardware and software changes will occur in the next versions of Intel TXT is impossible.

What is certain is that future versions of the trusted platform will respond to new attacks. I just have no way to predict the roadmap,[1] the when, and the how of these future responses.

New Features

Just as I see a guarantee of new attacks, I also expect the desire of system developers to extend the protection boundary to other areas of the platform. Providing protections to hard drives or printers or the new finger implants[2] could become a requirement for future versions of the trusted platform.

When evaluating what new devices need protection, many choices must be made. The architecture, planning, and marketing teams will meet and evaluate the necessity of protecting one device over another, or for providing some generic protections. As with attacks, the only certainty is that changes are in the future.

Chipset Topologies

The current Intel TXT system topology uses a single chipset to control any and all of the CPUs that might be on the system. Future topologies, like the one shown in Figure 21.1, are possible and desirable in many usage models. The Intel TXT mechanism and messages will work in the Figure 21.1 layout, but there are some architectural issues to solve.

---

1 I am an architect and not a planner. The meetings I've had with my planning counterpart are always fun meetings that attempt to balance architectural needs and business decisions.

2 The finger implants are just a joke.

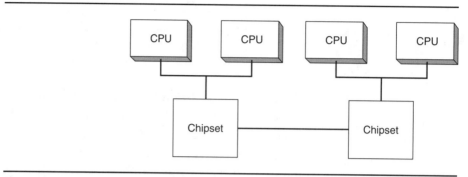

Figure 21.1 Future Topology

TPM Location

One issue that the Trusted Computing Group (TCG) is working on is where does the TPM reside in Figure 21.1? Numerous designs are possible and the simplest is a single TPM attached to one of the chipsets. All communication to the TPM would then route through the chipset connected to the TPM.

While a single TPM is a simple response, there are many reasons why system designers would desire multiple TPMs. Figure 21.1 is normally a server topology and on servers the addition of multiple components to assist with throughput and reliability is a very common occurrence. Multiple TPMs would increase the reliability, but what about the uniqueness that each TPM carries? How does the system designer use the uniqueness appropriately? The answers to these questions are the tasks currently in front of the TCG Server workgroup.[3]

SEXIT ACM

SINIT is the ACM in use during GETSEC [SENTER] but no corresponding ACM for use during GETSEC [SEXIT] exists. The rationale behind the lack of a GETSEC [SEXIT] ACM is that the GETSEC [SENTER] ACM provides a secure execution area and during GETSEC [SEXIT] there is already a secure

---

3   One request I always make is to indicate that membership in the TCG allows one to help solve the questions in front of the TCG. Having spent many years working on these issues, the introduction of new points of views and new individuals can certainly be the catalyst for innovative solutions.

execution area, the MLE itself. Certainly the rationale feels right at this time but are there circumstances where an exiting ACM would solve some architectural problems? The answer is yes. The infrastructure to invoke an exiting ACM is present, but not currently in use. Future versions could invoke an ACM during GETSEC [SEXIT].

Additional Hardware Protections

The main protection feature of Intel TXT is to provide protection from software attacks. Future versions of Intel TXT could change that attack model and include some hardware attack protections.

Following the Principles

While you could expect new features to respond to new attacks or provide protections to new features, the basic design principles are also guaranteed to drive the future versions of the trusted platform. The list in Chapter 11 of the basic security principles will hold true in the future, and the author lists them here again:

- Least privilege
- Economy of mechanism
- Complete mediation
- Open design
- Separation of privilege
- Least common mechanism
- Psychological acceptability

These security principles do not change with attempts to mitigate new threats or to provide protections to new entities; in fact, the principles become even more of a driving factor. With the protection boundary set by the first version of Intel TXT, subsequent versions should not roll back the boundary. The security principles drive many of the internal architectural decisions. Trying to remove one of the principles or making a fundamental change in the support for the principle undermines all previous versions of Intel TXT.

Parting Words

Woot, the end of the book. I would like to thank you for getting this far. I hope that you have learned something about the trusted platform and Intel TXT. I also hope that you will take this information and use the trusted platform to solve the security issues you face.

After doing all this writing it is time to put down the pen and get back to real work. May you always have tight lines[4].

---

4   This is a fishing reference. A tight line means you have a fish on and the fish is pulling hard on your line. A little side note, during the period while writing this book I was able to take my Intel sabbatical. Eight weeks of no work and lots of fishing. I had a wonderful time.

Glossary

Application Code written to perform an operation that the user wants

Attack An entity taking advantage of some vulnerability. The vulnerability could be either a hardware or software.

Authenticated Code Module (ACM)

BIOS Basic Input/Output System The built-in software that discovers and configures the hardware available on the platform

BIOS Boot Block The built-in software that discovers and configures the BIOS such that the BIOS can perform its job

Boot Strap Processor (BSP) The CPU that is designated to receive control after the platform reboots

Break Once Run Everywhere (BORE) An attack mounted by a single attacker that, when successful, allows duplication by all other attackers merely with information supplied by the first attacker

CPU Central Processing Unit

Bus Agent ID Chipset-assigned identifier for each CPU on the platform

Capability A capability combines one or more technologies to enable a specific use model. An example would be a key generation application that uses the TPM to generate keys.

CRX[1] or Control register X The five control registers (CR0 through CR4) determine the operating mode of the processor and the characteristics of the currently executing task. See the "Control Registers" section in Chapter 2 of the IA-32 Intel® Architecture Software Developer's Manual, Volume 3.

Digital Signature A guarantee that the information vouched for has not changed. The digital nature of the signature comes from the use of cryptography to create the signature and the ability of the system to validate the signature using software processes.

Direct Memory Access (DMA) is a mechanism to allow faster memory access to hardware peripherals. Typically, this mechanism would be something done by a hard drive to allow faster transfer of information from the drive to the platform memory.

Domain manager The application that controls the standard and protected partitions

Denial of Service (DoS) An attack where the attack consumes all of the resources and denies the user the facilities of the platform

Element An element is the base functional unit of the trusted platform. An example element is randomness: all trusted platforms have one, or more, devices that provide a source of entropy

Endorsement key A Trusted Computing Group term that refers to the cryptographic uniqueness inside of a Trusted Platform Module

Entropy A measure of the randomness in a system. Cryptographic key generation requires high entropy

Field Replaceable Unit (FRU) A physical component that can be quickly and easily removed from the platform and replaced by the user or technician without having to send the platform back to the manufacturer

FirmWare Hub (FWH) Flash device that holds BIOS code

Front Side Bus (FSB) The link between the CPU and MCH. The FSB allows for multiple CPU to connect to a single MCH

Graphics Aperture Relocation Table (GART) The mechanism to allow the graphics system to translate buffer addresses to physical page addresses

---

1   This is not the postal code prefix for Cryodon, UK

Global Descriptor Table Register (GDTR) The control register that provides the base pointer for the paging mechanism

Graphics Translation Table The mechanism that allows a logical address, in use for displaying graphics, to point to a physical memory page.

Grid Computing Many separate platforms are connected into a coherent whole platform and the larger platform then attempts to solve a problem that requires vast computing resources.

Hash the execution of a cryptographic hash algorithm such as SHA-1. The hash algorithm converts a string of arbitrary length into a fixed-size output. The properties of the resulting output are: given a hash value it is computationally infeasible to construct the input. A second property of the hash algorithm is that the resulting value is order dependent. That is, hashing A then B results in a different value when one hashes B then A.

Human Input Device (HID) A device that transmits information from the user to the computer. Typical HIDs include keyboards, mice, and microphones.

HW Shorthand for hardware, where hardware is the physical mechanisms of a computer

Hyperthreading (HT) is the mechanism that allows a single CPU to act as two operational threads.

Input/Output Controller Hub (ICH) the device that provides connections to various peripherals including USB devices

Initiating Logical Processor (ILP) The processor that initiates the MVMM measurement process. The GETSEC [SENTER] instruction is only valid on the ILP.

Interprocess Communication (IPC) A protocol to send information from one execution unit to another execution unit

I/O Acronym for input and output

LaGrande Technology often called LT for short, this technology provides for measurement of a virtual machine monitor and the ability to create protected virtual guest partitions.

Late launch The invocation of the protected environment at a time other than platform reset

Load Descriptor Table (LDTR) Control register for segmentation support.

Low Pin Count (LPC) A bus available on the PC platform that has a limited number of pins and works at a slow bus speed. Typical devices on the LPC bus include the Firm Ware Hub (FWH) and the Super I/O. The LPC bus connects to the ICH.

LT see LaGrande Technology

Malware Code that written to perform some operation that harms the information on the platform. This could be a virus, Trojan, worm or other type of code.

Memory Controller Hub (MCH) Device that provides a connection between the CPU and physical memory. The MCH also provides connections to display adapters and the ICH.

Measure to take a hash value of some information

Multiplexer (MUX) Combines several different signals onto a single communication channel for transmission. While the multiplexing could be done for video, audio, or other communications, the MUX in LaGrande Technology combines the video channels for normal and trusted displays.

NoDMA protection mechanism in the first version of TXT Deprecated and no longer in the TXT hardware.

Nonce A number used once, nonces provide protection in cryptographic protocols from reuse of messages

Non-Volatile (NV) Storage is a type of memory that preserves the value even when no power is available to the memory device. See also volatile storage.

Option ROM software on hardware devices that helps the BIOS and the device to properly configure the platform and the device

Opt-in is the process whereby the user decides to turn a feature on as the feature ships initially turned off.

Pass phrase Related to a password but hopefully longer and harder to guess. A password would look like "password1" or "hne76$3". While a pass phrase would look like "this is a t3st phrase!" The idea behind a pass phrase is that it is longer but easier to remember.

PCR Platform Configuration Register

Personal Identifying Information (PII) is any piece of information that allows an entity to potentially uniquely identify, contact, or locate a single person

Physical presence a Trusted Computing Group term to indicate that a human is directly using, i.e. has their hands on, the platform

Prime number A number that is only divisible by itself and 1. (2, 3, 5, 7 …)

Property Fixed capability of the platform

Protected partition A VT guest that has physical pages that have NoDMA protection

PS2 Connector that allows connection of keyboard and mouse to platform

Random Number Generator (RNG) The RNG provides a source of numbers that are not related to any previous or subsequent numbers.

Ring 0 through Ring 3 the protection mechanism that isolates user applications from OS components

Responding Logical Processor (RLP) Any processor that responds to the SENTER message

Remeasurement Determining the integrity of a running process

Remote procedure call (RPC) a protocol to send information from one platform to another

Root of Trust for Measurement (RTM) a Trusted Computing Group term to describe the entity that is implicitly trusted to measure platform components

Root of Trust for Reporting (RTR) a Trusted Computing Group term to describe the entity that has uniqueness capable of validating attestation requests. Normally the RTR is a cryptographic key.

Root of Trust for Storage (RTS) a Trusted Computing Group term to describe the entity that provides the basis for long-term non-volatile protection of data. Normally the RTS is a cryptographic key

Security Architecture Specification (SAS) The name of the underlying LT security specification and the name of the team and meetings that defined the specification

Sealed Storage the use of the TPM to encrypt data such that the data is will only successfully decrypt when the platform measurements are in a defined state

SENTER the process to start and measure the MLE

SHA-1 Secure Hash Algorithm A cryptographic hash algorithm defined in FIPS 180-1 http://csrc.nist.gov/cryptval/shs.html

SINIT the authenticated code module that validates the platform is in a valid configuration during the launch of the MVMM

System Management Interrupt (SMI) an event on the platform that invokes a special event manager

SMI Transfer Module (STM) software that receives an SMI event when the MVMM is executing and sends the event on to a SMI handler

Standard partition refers to a VT guest that has no pages requiring NoDMA protection

Storage Root Key is a Trusted Computing Group term that defines the cryptographic key that forms part of the Root of Trust for Storage.

SW Acronym for software

Safer Mode Extensions (SMX) The CPU instructions necessary to run LT

Technology A technology is a specific implementation that provides one or more elements. An example of a technology is the Intel® Trusted Platform Module (Intel® TPM) that provides randomness amongst other elements.

Timing Attack An attack that uses small tidbits of performance information to deduce a cryptographic key

Trusted Channel A secure, with integrity and potentially confidentiality, communication between two computing entities

Trusted Platform Module (Intel® **TPM)** The Intel® TPM is the root of trust for both storage and reporting. The Intel® TPM uses the version-1.2 definition from the Trusted Computing Group (TCG).

Trusted Graphics Translation Table (TGTT) The mechanism that allows a logical address, in use for displaying trusted graphics, to point to a physical memory page.

Trusted Path An indication from a computing entity to a human regarding the presence of a trusted channel

Virtual Machine Extensions (VMX) The CPU instructions that enable virtualization, through Vanderpool Technology (VT)

Volatile storage is a type of memory that does not preserve the value when power is lost to the memory device. See also Non-volatile storage

Wild Attacks that can arrive on an individual platform

Index

Continuing Education is Essential

It's a challenge we all face – keeping pace with constant change in information technology. Whether our formal training was recent or long ago, we must all find time to keep ourselves educated and up to date in spite of the daily time pressures of our profession.

Intel produces technical books to help the industry learn about the latest technologies. The focus of these publications spans the basic motivation and origin for a technology through its practical application.

Right books, right time, from the experts

These technical books are planned to synchronize with roadmaps for technology and platforms, in order to give the industry a head-start. They provide new insights, in an engineer-to-engineer voice, from named experts. Sharing proven insights and design methods is intended to make it more practical for you to embrace the latest technology with greater design freedom and reduced risks.

I encourage you to take full advantage of Intel Press books as a way to dive deeper into the latest technologies, as you plan and develop your next generation products. They are an essential tool for every practicing engineer or programmer. I hope you will make them a part of your continuing education tool box.

Sincerely,

Justin Rattner
Senior Fellow and Chief Technology Officer
Intel Corporation

Turn the page to learn about titles
from Intel Press for system developers

Service Oriented Architecture Demystified
A pragmatic approach to SOA for the IT executives

By Girish Juneja, Blake Dournaee, Joe Natoli, and Steve Birkel

ISBN 1-934053-02-3

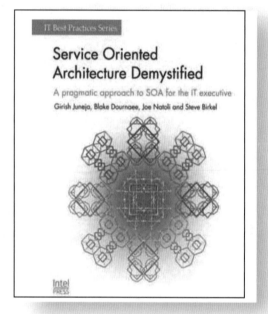

The authors of this definitive book on SOA debunk the myths and demonstrate through examples from different vertical industries how a "crawl, walk, run" approach to deployment of SOA in an IT environment can lead to a successful return on investment.

One popular argument states that SOA is not a technology per se, but that it stands alone and can be implemented using a wide range of technologies. The authors believe that this definition, while attractive and elegant, doesn't necessarily pass pragmatic muster.

Service Oriented Architecture Demystified describes both the technical and organizational impacts of adopting SOA and the pursuant challenges. The authors demonstrate through real life deployments why and how different industry sectors are adopting SOA, the challenges they face, the advantages they have realized, and how they have (or have not) addressed the issues emerging from their adoption of SOA. This book strikes a careful balance between describing SOA as an enabler of business processes and presenting SOA as a blueprint for the design of software systems in general. Throughout the book, the authors attempt to cater to both technical and organizational viewpoints, and show how both are very different in terms of why SOA is useful. The IT software architect sees SOA as a business process enabler and the CTO sees SOA as a technology trend with powerful paradigms for software development and software integration.

SOA can be characterized in terms of different vertical markets. For each such market, achieving SOA means something different and involves different transformational shifts. The vertical markets covered include healthcare, government, manufacturing, finance, and telecommunications. SOA considerations are quite different across these vertical markets, and in some cases, the required organizational shifts and technology shifts are highly divergent and context dependent.

Whether you are a CTO, CIO, IT manager, or IT architect, this book provides you with the means to analyze the readiness of your internal IT organization and with technologies to adopt a service oriented approach to IT.

Managing IT Innovation for Business Value

Practical Strategies for IT and Business Managers

By *Esther Baldwin and Martin Curley*

ISBN 1-934053-04-X

Successful companies actively cultivate new ideas, put those ideas to work quickly and efficiently, and harvest the business value benefits of successful innovations. Discussions of innovation often focus on what a company offers, that is, its products and services. In *Managing Information Technology Innovation for Business Value*, Esther Baldwin and Martin Curley show how successful IT innovations pay back handsomely as well. Innovation is not just about what a company offers, innovation is also about how a company conducts business and how IT innovation can transform an organization into a significantly more efficient company.

Drawing on their experience with innovation in Intel's engineering operations, Baldwin and Curley emphasize that IT innovation does not require whole-scale invention. An innovative IT solution reapplied in a new context can provide even greater business value because the initial investment in developing the solution has already been made.

Managing Information Technology Innovation for Business Value includes examples and case studies from IT organizations as well as from Intel Corporation. It also includes assessment techniques, skill set descriptions, and a capability maturity framework to help IT organizations understand where they stand as innovators and what steps they can take to strengthen their competencies.

> ❝ Innovation is not just about new products and services. It's also about how an innovative organization conducts business practices and the invaluable role of IT in those processes. For innovation to 'stick' it must become a systemic mindset like quality and safety. *Managing Information Technology Innovation for Business Value* offers invaluable and fresh stories that can be applied to any size IT organization. ❞ -
> Charles Chic Thompson, Batten Fellow at the UVA Darden Business School

> ❝ What can a small-medium business (SMB) learn from the IT experts at Intel? Some common-sense lessons on IT innovation management. Innovation can be incremental, for example, and a proven innovation can be re-applied over and over in new and different settings. That's a key message for those of us who serve the SMB market. ❞ — Mathew Dickerson, AXXIS Technology, Australia.

The Business Value of Virtual Service Oriented Grids
Strategic Insights for Enterprise Decision Makers

By Enrique Castro-leon, Jackson He, Mark Chang, Parviz Peiravi
ISBN 978-1-934053-10-2

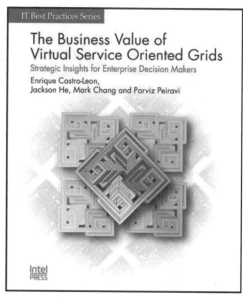

"In this book the authors track the trends, create new rules based on new realities, and establish new market models. With virtual service-oriented grids, the sky is the limit," writesWei-jen Lee, a University of Texas – Arlington professor, about *The Business Value of Virtual Service Oriented Grids*, a new book published by Intel. The application of service-oriented architecture (SOA) for business will interest application developers looking for the latest advances in technology and ideas on how to utilize those advances to keep up in a global economy. *The Business Value of Virtual Service Oriented Grids* provides a framework that describes how the convergence of three well-known technologies are defining a new information technology model that will fundamentally change the way we do business. The first step, say the authors, is the development of new applications for the consumer market. However, even bigger is the development of new applications in a federated fashion using services modules called *servicelets*. These federated or composite applications can be built in a fraction of the time it takes to develop traditional applications. This new environment will lower the bar for applications development, opening opportunities for thousands of smaller players worldwide.

"We live in exponential times. . . . The economy is now thoroughly global. The Internet has replaced many of the middle layers of business, has enabled many to work from home or from a small company, and is revolutionizing the retail industries." writes Portland State University professor Gerald Sheble. "The advent of SOA is going to impact information processing and computer services on a scale not previously envisioned." The speed-up in application development and integration will accelerate the deployment of IT capabilities, which in turn will have a consequential effect on the organization's business agility. Corporate decision makers will enjoy the ability to pick and choose among capital and operations expenses to suit their organization's business goals. The book describes the business trends within which this convergence is taking place and provides insight on how these changes can affect your business. It clearly explains the interplay between technology, architectural considerations, and standards with illustrative examples. Finally, the book tells you how your organization can benefit from *servicelets*, alerts you about integration pitfalls, and describes approaches for putting together your technology adoption strategy for building your virtual SOA environment using *servicelets*.

Applied Virtualization Technology

Usage Models for IT Professionals and Software Developers

By Sean Campbell and Michael Jeronimo
ISBN: 0-9764832-3-8

Server and desktop virtualization is one of the more significant technologies to impact computing in the last few years, promising the benefits of infrastructure consolidation, lower costs, increased security, ease of management, and greater employee productivity.

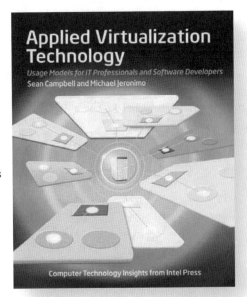

Using virtualization technology, one computer system can operate as multiple "virtual" systems. The convergence of affordable, powerful platforms and robust scalable virtualization solutions is spurring many technologists to examine the broad range of uses for virtualization. In addition, a set of processor and I/O enhancements to Intel server and client platforms, known as Intel® Virtualization Technology (Intel® VT), can further improve the performance and robustness of current software virtualization solutions.

This book takes a user-centered view and describes virtualization usage models for IT professionals, software developers, and software quality assurance staff. The book helps you plan the introduction of virtualization solutions into your environment and thereby reap the benefits of this emerging technology.

Highlights include:
- The challenges of current virtualization solutions
- In-depth examination of three software-based virtualization products
- Usage models that enable greater IT agility and cost savings
- Usage models for enhancing software development and QA environments
- Maximizing utilization and increasing flexibility of computing resources
- Reaping the security benefits of computer virtualization
- Distribution and deployment strategies for virtualization solutions

Multi-Core Programming
Increasing Performance through Software Multi-threading

By Shameem Akhter and Jason Roberts
ISBN 0-9764832-4-6

Software developers can no longer rely on increasing clock speeds alone to speed up single-threaded applications; instead, to gain a competitive advantage, developers must learn how to properly design their applications to run in a threaded environment. This book helps software developers write high-performance multi-threaded code for Intel's multi-core architecture while avoiding the common parallel programming issues associated with multi-threaded programs. This book is a practical, hands-on volume with immediately usable code examples that enable readers to quickly master the necessary programming techniques.

Discover programming techniques for Intel multi-core architecture and Hyper-Threading Technology

The Software Optimization Cookbook, Second Edition
High-Performance Recipes for IA-32 Platforms

By Richard Gerber, Aart J.C. Bik, Kevin B. Smith, and Xinmin Tian
ISBN 0-9764832-1-1

Four Intel experts explain the techniques and tools that you can use to improve the performance of applications for IA-32 processors. Simple explanations and code examples help you to develop software that benefits from Intel® Extended Memory 64 Technology (Intel® EM64T), multi-core processing, Hyper-Threading Technology, OpenMP†, and multimedia extensions. This book guides you through the growing collection of software tools, compiler switches, and coding optimizations, showing you efficient ways to get the best performance from software applications.

❝ *A must-read text for anyone who intends to write perform-ance-critical applica-tions for the Intel processor family.* ❞
—*Robert van Engelen,*
Professor,
Florida State University

Special Deals, Special Prices!

To ensure you have all the latest books and enjoy aggressively priced discounts, please go to this Web site:

www.intel.com/intelpress/bookbundles.htm

Bundles of our books are available, selected especially to address the needs of the developer. The bundles place important complementary topics at your fingertips, and the price for a bundle is substantially less than buying all the books individually.

About Intel Press

Intel Press is the authoritative source of timely, technical books to help software and hardware developers speed up their development process. We collaborate only with leading industry experts to deliver reliable, first-to-market information about the latest technologies, processes, and strategies.

Our products are planned with the help of many people in the developer community and we encourage you to consider becoming a customer advisor. If you would like to help us and gain additional advance insight to the latest technologies, we encourage you to consider the Intel Press Customer Advisor Program. You can register here:

www.intel.com/intelpress/register.htm

For information about bulk orders or corporate sales, please send e-mail to:
bulkbooksales@intel.com

Other Developer Resources from Intel

At these Web sites you can also find valuable technical information and resources for developers:

www.intel.com/technology/rr	Recommended reading list for books of interest to developers
www.intel.com/technology/itj	Intel Technology Journal
developer.intel.com	General information for developers
www.intel.com/software	content, tools, training, and the Intel® Early Access Program for software developers
www.intel.com/software/products	Programming tools to help you develop high-performance applications
www.intel.com/netcomms	Solutions and resources for networking and communications
www.intel.com/idf	Worldwide technical conference, the Intel Developer Forum

If serial number is missing, please send an
e-mail to Intel Press at intelpress@intel.com

IMPORTANT

You can access the companion Web site for this book on
the Internet at:

www.intel.com/intelpress/secc2

Use the serial number located in the upper-right hand
corner of this page to register your book and access
additional material, including the Digital Edition of
the book.
